AF814222

Checkmate

Competency Based Questions (CBQs)

Accountancy

CBSE Class 12

Author
Nitin Gandhi
M.Com, MA Education, B.Ed
(20 Years of Teaching Experience)

arihant
SUCCESS AND NOTHING LESS

Checkmate

arihant
SUCCESS AND NOTHING LESS

ARIHANT PRAKASHAN (SCHOOI DIVISION SERIES), MEERUT

Administrative & Production Offices

Regd. Office
'Ramchhaya' 4577/15, Agarwal Road, Darya Ganj, New Delhi -110002
Tele: 011- 47630600, 43518550

Head Office
Kalindi, TP Nagar, Meerut (UP) - 250002
Tel: 0121-7156203, 7156204

Sales & Support Offices
Agra, Ahmedabad, Bengaluru, Bareilly, Chennai, Delhi, Guwahati, Hyderabad, Jaipur, Jhansi, Kolkata, Lucknow, Nagpur & Pune.

PRICE ₹ 245.00

PO No : TXT-XX-XXXXXXX-X-XX

Published by Arihant Publications (India) Ltd.

For further information about the books published by Arihant, log on to www.arihantbooks.com or e-mail at info@arihantbooks.com

Follow us on

Checkmate CBQs Series

MASTER YOUR COMPETENCY!

01 **All types of Competency-Based Questions (CBQs)**, including Multiple Choice Questions (MCQs), Assertion-Reason, Correct/Incorrect Statements, Case-Based/Source-Based, and Subjective/Open-Ended Questions, providing a well-rounded preparation.

02 Meticulously selected **competency-based questions from past exams** to ensure thorough preparation and familiarity with question formats.

03 **Detailed Solutions** for effective self-study and a deeper understanding of each topic, enabling you to learn at your own pace.

04 **Self Scoring feature** to track your performance and progress on your own, helping you identify strengths and areas for improvement.

05 **Indication of suggested time** with each set of questions to help you learn time management skills to maximize your efficiency and confidence during exams.

केन्द्रीय माध्यमिक शिक्षा बोर्ड

(शिक्षा मंत्रालय, भारत सरकार के अधीन एक स्वायत संगठन)

Central Boards of Secondary Education

(An Autonomous Organisation Under the Ministry of Education, Govt. of India)

CBSE/ACADEMIC/JS (SH)/2024/ 3rd April, 2024 Circulars No. Acad 30/2024

The changes for classes IX-XII year-end Board Examinations (2024-25)

(Classes IX-X)

Particulars	**Academic Session 2023-24**	**Academic Session 2024-25** (No change from previous academic session)
Composition of question paper for year-end examination/ Board Examination (Theory)	• Competency Focused Questions in the form of MCQs/ Case Based Questions, Source-based Integrated Questions or any other type = 50% • Select response type questions (MCQ) = 20% • Constructed response questions (Short Answer/Long Answer Type Questions, as per existing pattern) = 30%	• Competency Focused Questions in the form of MCQs/Case Based Questions, Source-based Integrated Questions or any other type = 50% • Select response type questions (MCQ) = 20% • Constructed response questions (Short Answer/Long Answer Type Questions, as per existing pattern) = 30%

(Classes XI-XII)

Particulars	**Academic Session 2023-24**	**Academic Session 2024-25**
Composition of question paper for year-end examination/ Board Examination (Theory)	• Competency Focused Questions in the form of MCQs/ Case Based Questions, Source-based Integrated Questions or any other type = 40% • Select response type questions (MCQ) = 20% • Constructed response questions (Short Answer Questions/Long Answer type Questions, as per existing pattern) = 40%	• Competency Focused Questions in the form of MCQs/ Case Based Questions, Source-based Integrated Questions or any other type = 50% • Select response type questions (MCQ) = 20% • Constructed response questions (Short Answer Questions/Long Answer type Questions, as per existing pattern) = 30%

Curriculum document released by the Board for the Academic Session 2024-25 and the Sample Question Papers may also be referred to for details of the QP design of individual subjects. Learning frameworks for various subjects for classes IX-XII are available at the link https://cbseacademic.nic.in for reference.

Contents

PART A : Accounting for Partnership Firms and Companies

1. Accounting for Partnership Firm : Fundamentals	**1-18**
Multiple Choice Questions	2-6
Assertion-Reason Questions	7-8
Correct/Incorrect Statements	8-9
Case Based Questions	9-10
Subjective Questions	10-11
• Answers and Explanations	12-18
2. Reconstitution of a Partnership Firm : Change in Profit Sharing Ratio Among the Existing Partners	**19-39**
Multiple Choice Questions	20-25
Assertion-Reason Questions	25-26
Correct/Incorrect Statements	26-27
Case Based Questions	27-28
Subjective Questions	28-31
• Answers and Explanations	31-39
3. Reconstitution of a Partnership Firm : Admission of a Partner	**40-59**
Multiple Choice Questions	41-45
Assertion-Reason Questions	45-46
Correct/Incorrect Statements	47-48
Case Based Questions	48-49
Subjective Questions	49-52
• Answers and Explanations	52-59
4. Reconstitution of a Partnership Firm : Retirement/Death of a Partner	**60-81**
Multiple Choice Questions	61-65
Assertion-Reason Questions	66
Correct/Incorrect Statements	67-68
Case Based Questions	68
Subjective Questions	69-72
• Answers and Explanations	73-81
5. Dissolution of Partnership Firm	**82-101**
Multiple Choice Questions	83-87
Assertion-Reason Questions	88
Correct/Incorrect Statements	89
Case Based Question	90
Subjective Questions	90-94
• Answers and Explanations	94-101

6. Accounting for Share Capital	**102-122**
Multiple Choice Questions	103-107
Assertion-Reason Questions	108-109
Correct/Incorrect Statements	109-110
Case Based Questions	110-111
Subjective Questions	111-113
• Answers and Explanations	113-122
7. Accounting for Debentures	**123-137**
Multiple Choice Questions	124-127
Assertion-Reason Questions	128
Correct/Incorrect Statements	129
Case Based Questions	130
Subjective Questions	131-132
• Answers and Explanations	132-137

PART B Financial Statement Analysis

8. Financial Statements and Their Analysis	**138-152**
Multiple Choice Questions	139-142
Assertion-Reason Questions	142-143
Correct/Incorrect Statements	143-144
Case Based Questions	144-145
Subjective Questions	145-147
• Answers and Explanations	148-152
9. Accounting Ratios	**153-165**
Multiple Choice Questions	154-156
Assertion-Reason Questions	157
Correct/Incorrect Statements	158
Case Based Questions	159
Subjective Questions	160
• Answers and Explanations	161-165
10. Cash Flow Statement	**166-182**
Multiple Choice Questions	167-170
Assertion-Reason Questions	171
Correct/Incorrect Statements	172
Case Based Questions	173
Subjective Questions	174-176
• Answers and Explanations	177-182

Syllabus

PART A : Accounting for Partnership Firms and Companies

150 Periods/60 Marks

UNIT 1 Accounting for Partnership Firms

105 Periods/36 Marks

Units/Topics

- Partnership: features, Partnership Deed
- Provisions of the Indian Partnership Act 1932 in the absence of partnership deed.
- Fixed v/s fluctuating capital accounts. Preparation of Profit & Loss Appropriation account- division of profit among partners, guarantee of profits.
- Past adjustments (relating to interest on capital, interest on drawing, salary and profit sharing ratio).
- Goodwill: Meaning, nature, factors affecting and methods of valuation - average profit, super profit and capitalization.

Note: Interest on partner's loan is to be treated as a charge against profits.

Goodwill to be adjusted through partners capital/current account.

Accounting for Partnership Firms : Reconstitution and Dissolution

- **Change in the Profit Sharing Ratio** among the existing partners - sacrificing ratio, gaining ratio, accounting for revaluation of assets and reassessment of liabilities and treatment of reserves, accumulated profits and losses. Preparation of revaluation account and balance sheet.
- **Admission of a Partner** effect of admission of a partner on change in the profit sharing ratio, treatment of goodwill (as per AS 26), treatment for revaluation of assets and reassessment of liabilities, treatment of reserves, accumulated profits and losses, adjustment of capital accounts and preparation of capital, current account and balance sheet.
- **Retirement and Death of a Partner** effect of retirement/death of a partner on change in profit sharing ratio, treatment of goodwill (as per AS 26),

Learning Outcomes

After going through this unit, the students will be able to:

- State the meaning of partnership, partnership firm and partnership deed.
- Describe the characteristic features of partnership and the contents of partnership deed.
- Discuss the significance of provision of Partnership Act in the absence of partnership deed.
- Differentiate between fixed and fluctuating capital, outline the process and develop the understanding and skill of preparation of Profit and Loss Appropriation Account.
- Develop the understanding and skill of preparation of profit and loss appropriation account involving guarantee of profits.
- Develop the understanding and skill of making past adjustments.
- State the meaning, nature and factors affecting goodwill.
- Develop the understanding and skill of valuation of goodwill using different methods.
- State the meaning of sacrificing ratio, gaining ratio and the change in profit sharing ratio among existing partners.
- Develop the understanding of accounting treatment of revaluation assets and re-assessment of liabilities and treatment of reserves and accumulated profits by preparing revaluation account and balance sheet.
- Explain the effect of change in profit sharing ratio on admission of a new partner.

treatment for revaluation of assets and reassessment of liabilities, adjustment of accumulated profits, losses and reserves, adjustment of capital accounts and preparation of capital, current account and balance sheet. Preparation of loan account of the retiring partner.

- Calculation of deceased partner's share of profit till the date of death. Preparation of deceased partner's capital account and his executor's account.
- **Dissolution of a partnership firm:** Meaning of dissolution of partnership and partnership firm, types of dissolution of a firm. Settlement of accounts - preparation of realization account, and other related accounts: capital accounts of partners and cash/bank a/c (excluding piecemeal distribution, sale to a company and insolvency of partner(s)).

Note

(i) If the realised value of tangible assets is not given, it should be considered as realised at book value itself.

(ii) If the realised value of intangible assets is not given, it should be considered as nil (zero value).

(iii) In case, the realization expenses are borne by a partner, clear indication should be given regarding the payment there of.

- Develop the understanding and skill of treatment of goodwill as per As-26, treatment of revaluation of assets and re-assessment of liabilities, treatment of reserves and accumulated profits, adjustment of capital accounts and preparation of capital, current account and balance sheet of the new firm.
- Explain the effect of retirement/death of a partner on change in profit sharing ratio.
- Develop the understanding of accounting treatment of goodwill, revaluation of assets and re-assessment of liabilities and adjustment of accumulated profits, losses and reserves on retirement/death of a partner and capital adjustment.
- Develop the skill of calculation of deceased partner's share till the time of his death and prepare deceased partner's and executor's account.
- Discuss the preparation of the capital accounts of the remaining partners and the balance sheet of the firm after retirement/death of a partner.
- Understand the situations under which a partnership firm can be dissolved.
- Develop the understanding of preparation of realisation account and other related accounts.

UNIT 2 Accounting for Companies

45 Periods /24 Marks

Units/Topics

Accounting for Share Capital

- Features and types of companies
- Share and share capital: nature and types.
- Accounting for share capital: issue and allotment of equity and preference shares, Public subscription of shares - over subscription and under subscription of shares; issue at par and at premium, calls in advance and arrears (excluding interest), issue of shares for consideration other than cash.
- Concept of Private Placement and Employee Stock Option Plan (ESOP), sweat equity.
- Accounting treatment of forfeiture and re-issue of shares.
- Disclosure of share capital in company's Balance Sheet.

Learning Outcomes

After going through this unit, the students will be able to:

- State the meaning of share and share capital and differentiate between equity shares and preference shares and different types of share capital.
- Understand the meaning of private placement of shares and Employee Stock Option Plan.
- Explain the accounting treatment of share capital transactions regarding issue of shares.
- Develop the understanding of accounting treatment of forfeiture and re-issue of forfeited shares.

Accounting for Debentures

- Debentures: Meaning, types, Issue of debentures at par, at a premium and at a discount. Issue of debentures for consideration other than cash; Issue of debentures with terms of redemption; debentures as collateral security-concept, interest on debentures. Writing off discount/loss on issue of debentures.

Note : Discount or loss on issue of debentures to be written off in the year debentures are allotted from Security Premium Reserve (if it exists) and then from Statement of Profit and Loss as Financial Cost (AS 16).

- Describe the presentation of share capital in the balance sheet of the company as per schedule III part I of the Companies Act 2013.
- Explain the accounting treatment of different categories of transactions related to issue of debentures.
- Develop the understanding and skill of writing of discount/loss on issue of debentures.
- Understanding the concept of collateral security and its presentation in balance sheet.
- Develop the skill of calculating interest on debentures and its accounting treatment.
- State the meaning of redemption of debentures.

PART B : Financial Statement Analysis

50 Periods/20 Marks

UNIT 3 Analysis of Financial Statements

30 Periods/12 Marks

Units/Topics	Learning Outcomes
• **Financial Statements of a Company:** Meaning, nature, uses and importance of financial statement. Statement of Profit and Loss and Balance Sheet in the prescribed form with major headings and sub headings (as per Schedule III to the Companies Act, 2013). **Note:** Exceptional items, extraordinary items and profit (loss) from discontinued operations are excluded. • **Financial Statement Analysis:** Meaning, objectives, importance and limitations. • **Tools for Financial Statement Analysis:** Comparative statements, common size statements, ratio analysis and cash flow analysis. • **Accounting Ratios:** Meaning, objectives, advantages, classification and computation. • **Liquidity Ratios:** Current ratio and Quick ratio. • **Solvency Ratios**: Debt to Equity Ratio, Total Asset to Debt Ratio, Proprietary Ratio and Interest Coverage Ratio. Debt to Capital Employed Ratio. • **Activity Ratios:** Inventory Turnover Ratio, Trade Receivables Turnover Ratio, Trade Payables Turnover Ratio, Fixed Asset Turnover Ratio, Net Asset Turnover Ratio and Working Capital Turnover Ratio. • **Profitability Ratios:** Gross Profit Ratio, Operating Ratio, Operating Profit Ratio, Net Profit Ratio and Return on Investment.	**After going through this unit, the students will be able to:** • Develop the understanding of major headings and sub-headings (as per Schedule III to the Companies Act, 2013) of balance sheet as per the prescribed norms / formats. • State the meaning, objectives and limitations of financial statement analysis. • Discuss the meaning of different tools of 'financial statements analysis'. • State the meaning, objectives and significance of different types of ratios. • Develop the understanding of computation of current ratio and quick ratio. • Develop the skill of computation of debt equity ratio, total asset to debt ratio, proprietary ratio and interest coverage ratio. • Develop the skill of computation of inventory turnover ratio, trade receivables and trade payables ratio and working capital turnover ratio and others. • Develop the skill of computation of gross profit ratio, operating ratio, operating profit ratio, net profit ratio and return on investment.

Note: *Net Profit ratio is to be calculated on the basis of profit before and after tax.*

UNIT 4 Cash Flow Statement

20 Periods/8 Marks

Units/Topics	Learning Outcomes
• Meaning, objectives, benefits, cash and cash equivalents, classification of activities and preparation [as per AS 3 (Revised) (Indirect Method only] **Scope:** (I) Adjustments relating to depreciation and amortization, profit or loss on sale of assets including investments, dividend (both final and interim) and tax. (ii) Bank overdraft and cash credit to be treated as short term borrowings. (iii) Current Investments to be taken as Marketable securities unless otherwise specified.	**After going through this unit, the students will be able to:** • State the meaning and objectives of cash flow statement. • Develop the understanding of preparation of Cash Flow Statement using indirect method as per AS 3 with given adjustments.

Note: *Previous years' proposed dividend to be given effect, as prescribed in AS-4, events occurring after the balance sheet date. Current years' proposed dividend will be accounted for in the next year after it is declared by the shareholders.*

PART C : Project Work

20 Periods/20 Marks

Please refer to the guidelines published by CBSE.

Accountancy -1	Class XII	NCERT Publication	Accountancy -II	Class XII	NCERT Publication

Accounting for Partnership Firm: Fundamentals

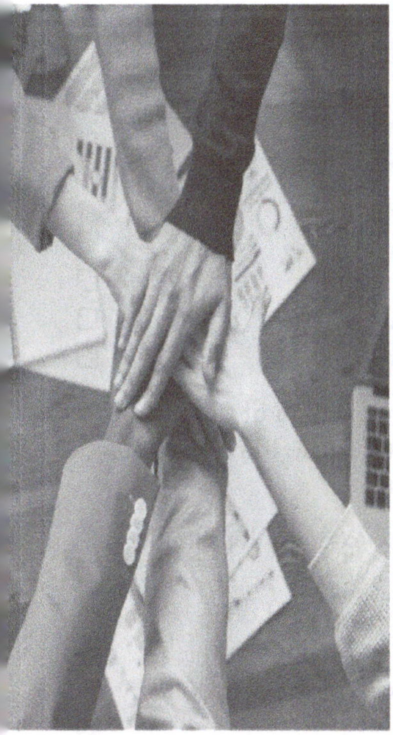

Types & Nos. of Questions

Multiple Choice Questions	– 35
Assertion-Reason Questions	– 9
Correct/Incorrect Statements	– 9
Case Based Questions	– 2 Cases, *each with 2 Questions*
Subjective Questions	– 8

Trend Analysis

On the basis of analysis of last 2 years' papers, it is found that as an average 2 Multiple Choice Questions, 1 Case Study Based Question and 1 Short Answer Type Question are asked from this chapter.

Focus Topics of the Chapter

- Partners' Capital Account
- Profit and Loss Appropriation Account
- Past Adjustments
- Guarantee of Minimum Profits to a Partner

Multiple Choice Questions

No. of Questions : **35** Suggested Time : **55 Minutes**

Direction Each of the question given below is Multiple Choice Question (MCQ) i.e. there are Four Options/Choices for answer, out of which ONLY ONE is correct. You have to select the correct option. A response box is given with each option, mark (✓) in the box of the correct option. For each correct answer you will get 1 mark, while there is no penalty for incorrect answer or missed out questions.

1. The partnership deed should be properly drafted and prepared as per the provisions of the .... and preferably registered with the ....
   (A) Indian Partnership Act, 1932, Registrar of Companies ☐
   (B) Indian Partnership Act, 1932, Registrar of Firms ☐
   (C) Stamp Act, Registrar of Companies ☐
   (D) Stamp Act, Registrar of Firms ☐

2. Which of the following is not a feature of partnership?
   (A) Atleast 2 persons ☐
   (B) Agreement between partners ☐
   (C) Maximum number of partners are 50 as per Indian Partnership Act, 1932 ☐
   (D) Mutual agency ☐

3. A, B and C are in partnership business. A used ₹ 2,00,000 belonging to the firm without informing to other partners and made a profit of ₹ 35,000 by using this amount. Which decision should be taken by the firm to rectify this situation?
   (A) A need to return only ₹ 2,00,000 to the firm ☐
   (B) A is required to return ₹ 35,000 to the firm ☐
   (C) A is required to pay back ₹ 35,000 only equally to B and C ☐
   (D) A need to return ₹ 2,35,000 to the firm ☐

4. In the absence of deed, partners are entitled to ....
   (i) profit share in capital ratio
   (ii) commission for making additional sale
   (iii) interest on loan and advances by them to firm
   (iv) salary for working extra hours
   (v) interest on capital

   Codes
   (A) (i), (iv) and (v) ☐
   (B) (ii) and (iii) ☐
   (C) Only (iii) ☐
   (D) (i) and (iii) ☐

5. Pick the odd one out.
   (A) Rent to partner ☐
   (B) Manager's commission ☐
   (C) Interest on partner's loan ☐
   (D) Salary to partner ☐

6. In a partnership firm, which of the following statements is true in respect of liability of a partner?
   (A) It is limited to the extent of his capital contribution ☐
   (B) It is limited to the extent of debit balance in his capital account, if any ☐
   (C) It is unlimited only for the acts done by her/him as a partner ☐
   (D) It is unlimited jointly and severally for all the acts of the firm done while he is a partner ☐

7. Which of the following is correct?
   (i) Under fixed capital account, interest on capital is not allowed.
   (ii) Under fixed capital account, capitals of partners fluctuate.

(iii) Under fixed capital account, only capital introduce or capital withdrawn affect the capital.

(iv) Under fixed capital account, salary of partners is not shown.

Codes

(A) Only (iii) ☐ (B) (i) and (iv) ☐

(C) (iii) and (iv) ☐ (D) (i), (ii) and (iv) ☐

8. A, B and C are partners in the firm sharing profits in the ratio of ₹ 5 : 3 : 2. If B's share of profit at the end of the year amounted to ₹ 1,50,000, what will be A's share of profit?

(A) ₹ 1,50,000 ☐

(B) ₹ 2,50,000 ☐

(C) ₹ 3,00,000 ☐

(D) ₹ 5,00,000 ☐

9. Anil and Vimal are partners in a firm sharing profits and losses in the ratio of 3 : 2. Sunil, manager of a firm, receives salary of ₹ 20,000 in addition to commission of 10% on net profit after charging such commission. Total remuneration to Sunil is ₹ 70,000. What was the profit for the year before charging salary and commission?

(A) ₹ 5,50,000 ☐ (B) ₹ 4,70,000 ☐

(C) ₹ 6,30,000 ☐ (D) ₹ 5,00,000 ☐

10. X and Y are partners sharing profits and losses in the ratio 3 : 2 with capitals of ₹ 1,50,000 and ₹ 1,00,000 respectively. They are allowed 6% p.a. interest on capital and charged 6% interest on drawings of each partner. Interest on drawings calculated as ₹ 3,000 and ₹ 2,000. Y's share of profit as per profit and loss appropriation account is ₹ 20,000. Net profit earned during the year before any appropriation was

(A) ₹ 65,000 ☐

(B) ₹ 60,000 ☐

(C) ₹ 55,000 ☐

(D) ₹ 50,000 ☐

11. Kanha, Resham and Nisha were partners in a firm. Nisha had given a loan of ₹ 1,00,000 to the firm @ 10% p.a.

The accountant of the firm is emphasising that interest on loan will be paid @ 6% p.a. At what rate the interest on loan will be paid to Nisha? *[CBSE 2024]*

(A) 6% p.a. ☐

(B) 10% p.a. ☐

(C) 8% p.a. ☐

(D) No interest on loan will be paid ☐

12. After doing the adjustments regarding drawings ₹ 40,000, share of profit ₹ 24,000 and the additional capital introduced ₹ 32,000, the capital of Ashok, a partner, as on 31st March, 2022 was ₹ 5,00,000. His capital as on 1st April, 2021 was ....

(A) ₹ 4,84,000 ☐ (B) ₹ 5,16,000 ☐

(C) ₹ 4,46,000 ☐ (D) ₹ 5,96,000 ☐

13. Which of the following is not correct?

(i) Interest on drawings @ 6% p.a. on total drawings of ₹ 10,000 will be ₹ 600.

(ii) Interest on drawings @ 6% p.a on drawings of ₹ 1,000 on beginning of every month will be ₹ 390.

(iii) Interest on drawings @ 6% p.a. on drawings of ₹ 1,000 at the end of every month will be ₹ 330.

(iv) Interest on drawings @ 6% on drawings of ₹ 10,000 will be ₹ 600.

Codes

(A) Only (i) ☐

(B) Only (iv) ☐

(C) (i), (ii) and (iii) ☐

(D) (ii), (iii) and (iv) ☐

14. Vanya and Aanya were partners in a firm sharing profits and losses in the ratio of 3 : 2. Their capitals were ₹ 5,00,000 and ₹ 1,00,000 respectively. Vanya was entitled to interest on capital @ 8% p.a. and Aanya was entitled to salary @ ₹ 5,000 per month. The net profit before any appropriation was ₹ 1,75,000. Vanya's share in divisible profit will be *[CBSE 2024]*

(A) ₹ 45,000 ☐ (B) ₹ 30,000 ☐

(C) ₹ 37,500 ☐ (D) ₹ 40,000 ☐

15. Omkar and Shiva were partners in a firm. Omkar was entitled to a salary of ₹ 20,000 p.a. while Shiva was entitled to a salary of ₹ 50,000 p.a. Net profit for the year ended 31st March, 2023 after charging salary of Omkar and Shiva was ₹5,60,000. The total amount credited to Omkar's capital account will be [CBSE 2024]

(A) ₹ 2,45,000 ☐ (B) ₹ 2,65,000 ☐
(C) ₹ 3,15,000 ☐ (D) ₹ 3,00,000 ☐

16. A and B were partners in a firm. Their capitals at the end of the year were ₹ 3,00,000 and ₹ 1,50,000 respectively. During the year B withdrew ₹ 10,000. Profit for the year was ₹ 32,000. Calculate B's opening capital.

(A) ₹ 1,28,000 ☐
(B) ₹ 1,44,000 ☐
(C) ₹ 1,08,000 ☐
(D) ₹ 1,24,000 ☐

17. X and Y are partners sharing profits and losses in the ratio of 3:2. Their capitals are ₹ 2,00,000 and ₹ 1,00,000 respectively. Interest on capital is allowed @8% p.a. Firm earned a profit of ₹ 15,000 for the year ended 31st March, 2024. Interest on capitals will be

(A) ₹ 16,000, ₹ 8,000 ☐
(B) ₹ 9,000, ₹ 6,000 ☐
(C) ₹ 10,000, ₹ 5,000 ☐
(D) ₹ 7,500, ₹ 7,500 ☐

18. Arun and Varun are partners in a firm and sharing the profits and losses in the ratio of 2 : 3 with a capital of ₹ 1,00,000 and ₹ 80,000 respectively. Calculate the amount of profit and loss to be distributed among the partners if partnership deed provides interest on capital (charge) @ 10% p.a. and loss for the year is ₹ 52,000. Loss distributed among the partners are

(A) X = ₹ 20,800, Y = ₹ 31,200 ☐
(B) X = ₹ 28,000, Y = ₹ 42,000 ☐
(C) X = ₹ 42,000, Y = ₹ 28,000 ☐
(D) X = ₹ 31,200, Y = ₹ 20,800 ☐

19. A drew ₹ 10,000 on 1st day of every quarter for 9 months. Calculate the number of months for which interest will be charged.

(A) 5 months ☐
(B) 6 months ☐
(C) 7.5 months ☐
(D) 4.5 months ☐

20. Calculate rate of interest, if a partner drew ₹ 2,000 at the end of every month and interest on drawings calculated is 660.

(A) 10% p.a. ☐ (B) 6% p.a. ☐
(C) 8% p.a. ☐ (D) 5% p.a. ☐

21. A, B and C are partners, their partnership deed provides for interest on drawings at 8% p.a. B withdrew a fixed amount in the middle of every month and his interest on drawings amounted to ₹ 4,800 at the end of the year. What was the amount of monthly drawings?

(A) ₹ 5,000 ☐ (B) ₹ 10,000 ☐
(C) ₹ 48,000 ☐ (D) ₹ 1,20,000 ☐

22. Ravi, Mohan and Raju are partners sharing profits and losses in the ratio of 5 : 3 : 2. Their capitals were ₹ 5,00,000, ₹ 3,00,000 and ₹ 2,00,000 respectively. Interest on capital was allowed at 6% p.a and salary of each partner is ₹ 10,000 per quarter. Firm earned a profit of ₹ 80,000. Calculate the ratio in which profits were distributed.

(A) 5 : 3 : 2 ☐
(B) 1 : 1 : 1 ☐
(C) 35 : 30 : 15 ☐
(D) 35 : 29 : 26 ☐

23. Manoj and Ravi are partners in a firm sharing profits and losses equally. Their fixed capitals were ₹ 1,00,000 and ₹ 50,000 respectively. The deed provides for interest on capital @ 10% p.a but it was wrongly credited by 8% p.a. In adjustment entry

(A) Manoj's capital account will be debited ☐
(B) Manoj's current account will be debited ☐
(C) Ravi's capital account will be debited ☐
(D) Ravi's current account will be debited ☐

24. A, B and C are partners in the ratio of 4 : 3 : 2. Salary to A ₹ 15,000 and to C ₹ 3,000 omitted to be recorded. For rectification, X will be

(A) credited with ₹ 7,000 ☐
(B) credited with ₹ 15,000 ☐
(C) debited with ₹ 7,000 ☐
(D) debited with ₹ 15,000 ☐

25. Ajay and Vinod are partners in the ratio of 3 : 2. Their fixed capital were ₹ 3,00,000 and ₹ 4,00,000 respectively. After the close of accounts for the year it was observed that the interest on capital which was agreed to be provided at 5% p.a. was erroneously provided at 10% p.a.

By what amount will Ajay's account be affected if partners decide to pass an adjustment entry for the same?

(A) Ajay's current account will be debited by ₹ 15,000 ☐
(B) Ajay's current account will be credited by ₹ 6,000 ☐
(C) Ajay's current account will be credited by ₹ 35,000 ☐
(D) Ajay's current account will be debited by ₹ 20,000 ☐

26. A, B and C are partners, C has been given a guarantee of minimum profit of ₹ 8,000 by the firm. Firm suffered a loss of ₹ 5,000 during the year. Capital of B will be .... by ....

(A) credited, ₹ 6,500 ☐
(B) debited, ₹ 6,500 ☐
(C) credited, ₹ 1,500 ☐
(D) debited, ₹ 1,500 ☐

27. A and B are partners in a firm sharing profits and losses in the ratio 3 : 2. On 1st July, C join the firm for 1/6th share in profit. C is given a guarantee of minimum profit of ₹ 12,000 during the year. Profit for the year ended 31st March, 2024 amounted to ₹ 48,000.

Deficiency met by A and B will be

(A) A– ₹ 2,400, B– ₹ 1,600 ☐
(B) A– ₹ 600, B– ₹ 400 ☐
(C) A– ₹ 7,200, B– ₹ 4,800 ☐
(D) A– ₹ 2,000, B– ₹ 2,000 ☐

28. Choose the correct sequence related to guarantee of partners.

(i) Guarantee by partner to partner
(ii) Guarantee by firm to partner
(iii) Guarantee by partners to firm
(iv) Transfer of net profit to profit and loss appropriation account

Codes

(A) (i), (iii), (iv), (ii) ☐
(B) (iv), (iii), (ii), (i) ☐
(C) (ii), (iii), (iv), (i) ☐
(D) (iii), (i), (ii), (iv) ☐

29. X, Y and Z are partners in a firm sharing profits and losses in the ratio of 6 : 4 : 1. X guaranteed a profit of ₹ 15,000 to Z. The net profit for the year ending 31st March, 2019 was ₹ 99,000. X's share in the profit of the firm will be

(A) ₹ 30,000 ☐
(B) ₹ 15,000 ☐
(C) ₹ 48,000 ☐
(D) ₹ 45,000 ☐

30. E, F and G are partners sharing profits in the ratio of 3 : 3 : 2. According to the partnership agreement, G is to get a minimum amount of ₹ 80,000 as his share of profits every year and any deficiency on this account is to be personally borne by E.

The net profit for the year ended 31st March, 2021 amounted to ₹ 3,12,000. Calculate the amount of deficiency to be borne by E.

(A) ₹ 1,000 ☐
(B) ₹ 4,000 ☐
(C) ₹ 8,000 ☐
(D) ₹ 2,000 ☐

31. Which of the following statements are correct?

(i) The liability of a partner for acts of the firm is unlimited.
(ii) Private assets of a partner can also be used for paying the debts of the firm.
(iii) Each partner is liable jointly with all other partners and also severally to the third parties for all the acts of the firm done, while he is partner.
(iv) The liability of partner is limited to the extent of his capital contribution.

Codes

(A) (i) and (iii) ☐
(B) (i) and (ii) ☐
(C) (i), (ii) and (iii) ☐
(D) (i), (ii), (iii) and (iv) ☐

32. Match the Column I with Column II in the following information

Column I	Column II
A. Manager's commission	(i) Appropriation of profits
B. Interest on capital	(ii) Charge against profits
C. Itnerest on drawings	(iii) Revenue to the firm

Codes

	A	B	C	
(A)	(iii)	(ii)	(i)	☐
(B)	(ii)	(i)	(iii)	☐
(C)	(i)	(ii)	(iii)	☐
(D)	(iii)	(i)	(ii)	☐

33. Match the Column I with Column II in the following information

Column I	Column II
A. Maximum partners prescribed by government	(i) Consent of all partners
B. Partnership deed is also known as	(ii) 50
C. Maximum partners as per Indian Companies Act, 2013	(iii) Articles of partnership
D. Admission of a partner	(iv) 100

Codes

	A	B	C	D	
(A)	(iv)	(iii)	(i)	(ii)	☐
(B)	(ii)	(iii)	(iv)	(i)	☐
(C)	(iv)	(i)	(ii)	(iii)	☐
(D)	(ii)	(i)	(iv)	(iii)	☐

34. Match the following, if interest on drawings is calculated @ 8% p.a.

Column I	Column II
A. A drew ₹ 3,000 at the end of each quarter for 9 months	(i) 600
B. A drew ₹ 3,000 at the beginning of each quarter	(ii) 180
C. A drew ₹ 3,000 at the beginning of each half year	(iii) 360

Codes

	A	B	C	
(A)	(ii)	(i)	(iii)	☐
(B)	(i)	(ii)	(iii)	☐
(C)	(ii)	(iii)	(i)	☐
(D)	(iii)	(i)	(ii)	☐

35. Match the Column I with Column II in the following information

Column I	Column II
A. Interest on capital	(i) Debit side of profit and loss account
B. Interest on drawings	(ii) Debit side of profit and loss appropriation account
C. Interest on partner's loan	(iii) Credit side of profit and loss appropriation account

Codes

	A	B	C	
(A)	(iii)	(ii)	(i)	☐
(B)	(i)	(ii)	(iii)	☐
(C)	(ii)	(i)	(iii)	☐
(D)	(ii)	(iii)	(i)	☐

Assertion-Reason Questions

No. of Questions : **9** Suggested Time : **15 Minutes**

Direction Each of the question given below consist of the two statements; one labelled as **Assertion** (A) and other as **Reason** (R). List of common options applicable for each question is given below.

(A) Both Assertion (A) and Reason (R) are true and Reason (R) is the correct explanation of Assertion (A)

(B) Both Assertion (A) and Reason (R) are true, but Reason (R) is not the correct explanation of Assertion (A)

(C) Assertion (A) is true, but Reason (R) is false

(D) Assertion (A) is false, but Reason (R) is true

You have to select the codes as *A, B, C* or *D* as your answer to the question by marking (✓) in the response box given against each option.

1. **Assertion (A)** Batman, a partner in a firm with four partners, has advanced a loan of ₹ 50,000 to the firm for last six months of the financial year without any agreement. He claims an interest on loan of ₹ 3,000 despite the firm being in loss for the year.

   Reason (R) In the absence of any agreement/ provision in the deed, provision of Indian Partnership Act, 1932 would apply.

   (A) ☐ (B) ☐ (C) ☐ (D) ☐

2. **Assertion (A)** A minor cannot be admitted in a firm as a partner.

   Reason (R) A minor can participate in the profits of a firm.

   (A) ☐ (B) ☐ (C) ☐ (D) ☐

3. **Assertion (A)** A and B are partners without any deed. A had advanced a loan of ₹10,000. At the end of the year, both agreed to allow interest on loan @ 9% p.a.

   Reason (R) In the absence of deed, interest on loan is to be allowed @ 6% p.a.

   (A) ☐ (B) ☐ (C) ☐ (D) ☐

4. **Assertion (A)** A and B are partners in a firm. Interest on drawings to be charged at 6% p.a. A drew ₹ 1,000 per month at the beginning of every month. At the end of year, firm incurred a loss of ₹ 16,000, hence no interest will be charged on drawings.

   Reason (R) Interest on drawings will be charged for 6.5 months.

   (A) ☐ (B) ☐ (C) ☐ (D) ☐

5. **Assertion (A)** Salary is not allowed to partner in case of loss to firm, although he is devoting more time than other partners.

   Reason (R) Salary to partner is an appropriation of profit and not a charge against profit.

   (A) ☐ (B) ☐ (C) ☐ (D) ☐

6. **Assertion (A)** Under the fixed capital method, partners' capital accounts always show a credit balance.

   Reason (R) Under the fixed capital method, all items like share of profit or loss, interest on capital, drawings, interest on drawings are recorded in a separate account called partners' current account. *[CBSE 2024]*

   (A) ☐ (B) ☐ (C) ☐ (D) ☐

7. **Assertion (A)** Commission provided to partner is shown in profit and loss appropriation account.

   Reason (R) Commission provided to partner is charge against profits and is to be provided at fixed rate.

   (A) ☐ (B) ☐ (C) ☐ (D) ☐

8. **Assertion** (A) The fixed capital account balance of a partner may change due to additional capital introduced or capital withdrawn or both, during the year.

Reason (R) Under fixed capital method, the partner's capital accounts balance always remains same.

(A) ☐ (B) ☐ (C) ☐ (D) ☐

9. **Assertion** (A) Transfer to reserves is shown in profit and loss appropriation account.

Reason (R) Reserves are charge against the profits.

(A) ☐ (B) ☐
(C) ☐ (D) ☐

Correct/Incorrect Statements

No. of Questions : **9** Suggested Time : **15 Minutes**

Direction Each of the question given below consist of the two statements. List of common options applicable for each question is given below.

(A) Both statements are correct
(B) Statement I is correct and Statement II is incorrect
(C) Statement II is correct and Statement I is incorrect
(D) Both statements are incorrect

You have to select the codes as *A, B, C* or *D* as your answer to the question by marking (✓) in the response box given against each option.

1. **Statement I** In the absence of deed, the provisions of Partnership Act, 1932 will apply.

Statement II In partnership firm, maximum number of partners will be 50 as per Rule 10 of the Companies Rules, 2014.

(A) ☐ (B) ☐ (C) ☐ (D) ☐

2. **Statement I** Fixed capital account can never show a negative balance.

Statement II Fluctuating capital account always shows a positive balance.

(A) ☐ (B) ☐ (C) ☐ (D) ☐

3. **Statement I** Interest on loan by partner is debited to profit and loss appropriation account.

Statement II Interest on loan to a partner is credited to profit and loss appropriation account.

(A) ☐ (B) ☐ (C) ☐ (D) ☐

4. **Statement I** No interest on capital will be allowed, if deed is silent about interest on capital.

Statement II No interest on capital will be allowed in case of loss.

(A) ☐ (B) ☐
(C) ☐ (D) ☐

5. **Statement I** Drawings against profit means drawings by a partner against his expected share of profit for the year.

Statement II Such drawings are debited to partner's capital account.

(A) ☐ (B) ☐ (C) ☐ (D) ☐

6. **Statement I** In the absence of deed, if a partner is devoting more time than other partners, he is entitled to get a salary.

Statement II Salary to partner is an appropriation of profit.

(A) ☐ (B) ☐ (C) ☐ (D) ☐

7. **Statement I** Profit and Loss Appropriation Account is prepared to distribute the net profit of the firm among its partners.

   Statement II Profit and Loss Appropriation Account does not follow the concept of matching principle.

   (A) ☐ (B) ☐ (C) ☐ (D) ☐

8. **Statement I** The mamixum number of partners as per The Indian Partnership Act, 1932 is 100.

   Statement II Central government has prescribed maximum number of parnters to be 50.

   (A) ☐ (B) ☐
   (C) ☐ (D) ☐

9. **Statement I** To participate in the management of the business is one of the rights of every partner.

   Statement II Each partner is liable individually and collectively with all other partners to the third party for all the acts of the firm, while he is a partner.

   (A) ☐ (B) ☐
   (C) ☐ (D) ☐

Case Based Questions

No. of Questions : **2** Suggested Time : **10 Minutes**

Direction This section contains 2 cases having 2 questions of 1 mark each. You have to write the answer of each question based on the context of the related case.

Case 1 Puneet and Raju are partners in a clay toys making firm. Their capitals were ₹ 5,00,000 and ₹ 10,00,000 respectively. The firm allowed Puneet to get a commission of 10% on the net profit before charging any commission and Raju to get a commission of 10% of net profit after charging all commissions. Following is the profit and loss appropriation account for the year ending 31st March, 2022.

Profit and Loss Appropriation Account
for the year ending 31st March, 2022

Dr Cr

Particulars	Amt (₹)	Particulars	Amt (₹)
To Puneet's Capital A/c (commission) (... × 10/100)	44,000	By Profit & Loss A/c	...
To Raju's Capital A/c (Commission)	...		
To Profit transferred to			
Puneet's Capital A/c	...		
Raju's Capital A/c	...		
	...		...

Questions

(i) Raju's commission will be

(A) ₹ 40,000 ☐ (B) ₹ 44,000 ☐ (C) ₹ 36,000 ☐ (D) ₹ 36,440 ☐

(ii) Puneet's share of profit will be

(A) ₹ 1,80,000 ☐ (B) ₹ 1,44,000 ☐ (C) ₹ 2,16,000 ☐ (D) ₹ 1,60,000 ☐

Case 2 Aditi and Saurabh were partners in a firm sharing profits and losses in the ratio of 2 : 1. On 1st April, 2022, their capitals were ₹ 5,00,000 and ₹ 4,00,000 respectively. Before any appropriation, the firm earned a net profit of ₹ 81,000 for the year ended 31st March, 2023. According to the partnership deed, interest on capital was to be provided @ 10% p.a. *[CBSE 2024]*

Questions

(i) Interest on capital will be provided to Aditi and Saurabh in which of the following ratio?

(A) 5 : 4 ☐ (B) 2 : 1 ☐

(C) 1 : 1 ☐ (D) 8 : 1 ☐

(ii) Interest on Aditi's capital will be

(A) ₹ 50,000 ☐

(B) ₹ 45,000 ☐

(C) ₹ 40,500 ☐

(D) ₹ 54,000 ☐

Subjective Questions

Free Response Questions, Open-ended Questions etc.

No. of Questions : **8** Suggested Time : **60 Minutes**

1. L, M, N and O were partners in a firm sharing profits in 4 : 3 : 2 : 1. They do not have partnership deed and following dispute had arised among them. Suggest proper remedy for the following

(i) L is an active partner and carry on all the business almost alone. So he demanded incentive of ₹ 40,000 annually for the above services. But other partners have objection on it.

(ii) M had advanced ₹ 20,000 as loan to the firm and agreed to take interest @ 5% p.a. to which others have no objection but Chartered Accountant of the firm insist on 6% p.a.

(iii) N bring order of ₹ 10,00,000 to the firm and charged 1% commission from firm for the given order. O opposed it, but other partners not.

(iv) O wants to bring his son P into business as a new partner. L and M agrees on it but N does not agree. O suggest that new partner can be admitted as majority is in his favour.

2. P.Q and R are partners with capital balance of ₹ 1,00,000, ₹ 40,000 and ₹ 20,000 respectively.

They share profits in 2 : 2 : 1 and earned profit of ₹ 50,000 during the year. Partners are entitled to

(i) Interest on capital @ 5% p.a.

(ii) Commission to Q @10% on turnover. (Turnover is ₹ 1,00,000).

(iii) R is entitled to a commission of 5% of net profit after charging interest on capital.

(iv) S gave given a loan of ₹ 50,000 to the firm.

(v) Rent paid to R for running business in his personal property for ₹ 4,000.

Prepare profit and loss appropriation account and partners' capital account.

3. Fill the missing figures.

Particulars		Amt (₹)	Particulars		Amt (₹)
To Interest on Capital			By Profit and Loss A/c		...
A	2,000		By Interest on Drawings		
B	...	4,000	A (Drew ₹ 4,000 during the year @ 5%)	...	
To Salary			B (Drew ₹ 2,000 on 1st July @ 5% p.a.)	...	...
A (400 per month)	...				
B (600 quarterly)	...	...			
To Profit transferred to					
A's Capital (3/5th)	...				
B's Capital (2/5th)	16,000	...			
		...			...

4. A and B are partners in a firm sharing profits in the ratio 3 : 2. Their capital balance were ₹ 5,00,000 and ₹ 2,00,000 respectively after necessary adjustments in respect of drawings and net profit.

The firm earned a profit of ₹ 50,000 during the year and A drew ₹ 4,000 quarterly and B drew ₹ 20,000 annually.

It was subsequently found that interest on capital @ 10% p.a. of A had been omitted. It was decided to pass an adjustment entry to rectify above errors. Pass an adjustment entry.

5. Atul and Gita were partners in a firm sharing profits and losses in the ratio of 3 : 2. Their fixed capitals were ₹ 4,00,000 and ₹ 2,00,000 respectively. After the accounts for the year were prepared, it was noticed that interest on capital @ 6% p.a., as provided in the partnership deed, was not credited to the capital accounts of partners before distribution of profits.

Pass the necessary adjusting journal entry. Show your workings clearly. *[CBSE 2024]*

6. Cheese and Slice are equal partners. Their capitals as on 1st April, 2022 were ₹ 50,000 and ₹ 1,00,000 respectively. After the accounts for the financial year ending 31st March, 2023 have been prepared, it is observed that interest on capital @ 6% per annum and salary to Cheese @ ₹ 5,000 per annum, as provided in the partnership deed has not been credited to the partners' capital accounts before distribution of profits.

You are required to give necessary rectifying entries using profit and loss adjustment account.

7. Tilu and Pilu started business on 1st July, 2023 with capitals of ₹ 30,000 and ₹ 20,000 respectively.

They admit Nilu in business for 1/4th share in the business with minimum guarantee of profit of ₹ 10,000 p.a. The firm earned a profit of ₹ 24,000 during the year.

Prepare profit and loss appropriation account for the year ending 31st March, 2024.

8. Monika, Bhoomika and Kamolika are partners sharing profits in the ratio of 6 : 4 : 1. Kamolika is guaranteed a minimum amount of ₹ 3,00,000 as her share in profits. The firm earned a net profit of ₹ 22,00,000 for the year ended 31st March, 2022.

Prepare profit and loss appropriation account of the firm of the year ended 31st March, 2022. *[CBSE 2023]*

Answers

If your answer matches with the answer given here then put (✓) in the box otherwise put (✗). In case you did not attempt the question leave the box blank.

Multiple Choice Questions

1. D ☐	2. C ☐	3. D ☐
4. C ☐	5. D ☐	6. D ☐
7. C ☐	8. B ☐	9. A ☐
10. B ☐	11. B ☐	12. A ☐
13. A ☐	14. A ☐	15. D ☐
16. B ☐	17. C ☐	18. B ☐
19. B ☐	20. B ☐	21. B ☐
22. D ☐	23. D ☐	24. A ☐
25. B ☐	26. B ☐	27. B ☐
28. B ☐	29. C ☐	30. D ☐
31. C ☐	32. B ☐	33. B ☐
34. A ☐	35. D ☐	

Your Score__________ *(No. of Correct Answers)*

Assertion-Reason Questions

1. D ☐	2. B ☐
3. B ☐	4. D ☐
5. A ☐	6. A ☐
7. C ☐	8. C ☐
9. C ☐	

Your Score__________ *(No. of Correct Answers)*

Correct/Incorrect Statements

1. A ☐	2. B ☐
3. D ☐	4. B ☐
5. A ☐	6. C ☐
7. A ☐	8. C ☐
9. A ☐	

Your Score__________ *(No. of Correct Answers)*

Case Based Questions

1. (i) C ☐
   (ii) A ☐
2. (i) A ☐
   (ii) B ☐

Your Score__________ *(No. of Correct Answers)*

Explanations

Multiple Choice Questions

1. (D) Stamp Act, Registrar of Firms
2. (C) Maximum number of partners are 50 as per Indian Partnership Act, 1932
3. (D) A need to return ₹ 2,35,000 to the firm
4. (C) Only (iii)
5. (D) Option (A), (B) and (C) are charge against profits whereas option (D) is an appropriation of profits.
6. (D) It is unlimited jointly and severally for all the acts of the firm done while he is partner.
7. (C) (iii) and (iv)
8. (B) Total Profit $\times \frac{3}{10} = 1,50,000$

$$\therefore \quad \text{Total Profits} = 1,50,000 \times \frac{10}{3}$$

$$\text{A's share} = 1,50,000 \times \frac{10}{3} \times \frac{5}{10} = ₹\ 2,50,000$$

9. (A) Total Remuneration = Salary + Commission

$$70,000 = 20,000 + \left(\text{Net Profit } \times \frac{10}{110}\right)$$

$$50,000 = \text{Net Profit} \times \frac{10}{110}$$

$$\text{Net Profit} = 50,000 \times \frac{110}{10} = ₹\ 5,50,000$$

10. (B) **Profit and Loss Appropriation Account**

Dr for the year ended... Cr

Particulars		Amt (₹)	Particulars		Amt (₹)
To Interest on Capital			By Profit & Loss A/c		60,000*
X	9,000		By Interest on		
Y	6,000	15,000	Drawings		
To Profit transferred to			X	3,0000	
X	30,000		Y	2,000	5,000
Y	20,000	50,000			
		65,000			65,000

Y's Divisible Profit = Divisible Profit × Y's Share

$$20{,}000 = \text{Divisible Profit} \times \frac{2}{5}$$

$$\therefore \text{ Divisible Profit} = 20{,}000 \times \frac{5}{2} = ₹\ 50{,}000$$

*Net Profit = Divisible Profit + Expenses – Reserves

$$= 50{,}000 + 15{,}000 - 5{,}000 = ₹\ 60{,}000$$

11. (B) 10% p.a.

12. (A) Opening capital

$$= 5{,}00{,}000 + 40{,}000 - 32{,}000 - 24{,}000$$

$$= ₹\ 4{,}84{,}000$$

13. (A) Interest of Drawings $= 10{,}000 \times \frac{6}{100} \times \frac{6}{12}$

$$= ₹\ 300$$

14. (A) **Profit and Loss Appropriation Account**

Dr for the year ended... Cr

Particulars		Amt (₹)	Particulars	Amt (₹)
To Interest on Capital (Vanya5,00,000 × 8%)		40,000	By Net Profit	1,75,000
To Salary (Aanya 5,000 × 12)		60,000		
To Profit transferred to Capital A/cs				
Vanya	45,000			
Aanya	30,000	75,000		
		1,75,000		1,75,000

15. (D) **Amount Credited to Omkar's Capital Account**

Capital Account	**Amt (₹)**
Salary	20,000
Share of Profit (5,60,000 × 1/2)	2,80,000
	3,00,000

16. (B) Opening Capital

$$= 1{,}50{,}000 + 10{,}000 - 16{,}000 \text{ (B's profit)}$$

$$= ₹\ 1{,}44{,}000$$

17. (C) Interest on Capital

X – ₹ 16,000 Y – ₹ 8,000

But profit of 15,000 is insufficient. So, we will divide profits in interest on capital ratio of interest on capital i.e. 2 : 1.

$$\text{X' Interest on Capital} = 15{,}000 \times \frac{2}{3} = ₹\ 10{,}000$$

$$\text{Y's Interest on Capital} = 15{,}000 \times \frac{1}{3} = ₹\ 5{,}000$$

18. (B) Total Loss = 52,000 + 18,000

= ₹ 70,000 (2 : 3)

$$\text{X's Loss} = 70{,}000 \times \frac{2}{5} = ₹\ 28{,}000$$

$$\text{Y's Loss} = 70{,}000 \times \frac{3}{5} = ₹\ 42{,}000$$

19. (B) Time left after 1st Drawing = 9 months

Time left after Last Drawings = 3 months

Average Period

$$= \frac{\text{Time left after 1st Drawing + Time left after Last Drawings}}{2}$$

$$= \frac{9+3}{2} = \frac{12}{2} = 6 \text{ months}$$

20. (B) $660 = (2{,}000 \times 12) \times \frac{R}{100} \times \frac{5.5}{12}$

$$R = \frac{660 \times 12 \times 100}{2{,}000 \times 12 \times 5.5}$$

R = 6% p.a.

21. (B) $4{,}800 = \text{Total Drawings} \times \frac{8}{100} \times \frac{6}{12}$

$$\text{Total Drawings} = 4{,}800 \times \frac{100}{8} \times \frac{12}{6}$$

Total Drawings = ₹ 1,20,000

$$\text{Monthly Drawings} = \frac{1{,}20{,}000}{12} = ₹\ 10{,}000$$

22. (D)

Interest on Capital	30,000	18,000	12,000
Salary	40,000	40,000	40,000
	70,000	58,000	52,000
Ratio	70,000 :	58,000 :	52,000

⇒ 70 : 58 : 52 *or* 35 : 29 : 26

23. (D) Ravi's current account will be debited

24. (A)

Statement	**A**	**B**	**C**
Amount to be Credited	15,000	—	3,000

Amount Credited	8,000	6,000	4,000
	7000	6,000	1,000
	Cr	Dr	Dr

25. (B)

Particulars	Ajay		Vinod		Firm	
	Dr (₹)	Cr (₹)	Dr (₹)	Cr (₹)	Dr (₹)	Cr (₹)
Interest on Capital @ 5 taken back	15,000	—	20,000	—	—	35,000
Correct Profits Distributed (3 : 2)	—	21,000	—	14,000	35,000	—
Total	15,000	21,000	20,000	14,000	35,000	35,000
Net Effect	—	6,000	6,000	—	—	—

26. (B) After giving profit of ₹ 8,000 to C, total loss of firm was ₹ 13,000 to be distributed equally between A and B.

$$\text{B's share} = 13{,}000 \times \frac{1}{2} = ₹\,6{,}500$$

27. (B) $\text{A's Profit} = 48{,}000 \times \frac{3}{6} = 24{,}000 - 600$

$= ₹\,23{,}400$

$\text{B's Profit} = 48{,}000 \times \frac{2}{6} = 16{,}000 - 400$

$= ₹\,15{,}600$

$\text{C's Profit} = 48{,}000 \times \frac{1}{6} = 8{,}000 + 1{,}000$

$= ₹\,9{,}000$ (For 9 months)

28. (B) (iv), (iii), (ii), (i)

29. (C) $X = 99{,}000 \times \frac{6}{11} = 54{,}000$

$Y = 99{,}000 \times \frac{4}{11} = 36{,}000$

$Z = 99{,}000 \times \frac{1}{11} = 9{,}000$

X will sacrifies his share of profit

$= 15{,}000 - 9{,}000 = ₹\,6{,}000$

So, X's share in profit of the firm

$= 54{,}000 - 6{,}000 = ₹\,48{,}000$

30. (D) Profit at the end (31st March, 2021)

$= ₹\,3{,}12{,}000$

Share of Profit	E (₹)	F (₹)	G (₹)
	$3{,}12{,}000 \times \frac{3}{8}$ = 1,17,000	$3{,}12{,}000 \times \frac{3}{8}$ = 1,17,000	$3{,}12{,}000 \times \frac{2}{8}$ = 78,000
Guarantee share of G	—	—	80,000
Deficiency born by E	(2,000)	—	2,000

31. (C) (i), (ii) and (iii)

32. (B) (ii) (i) (iii)

33. (B) (ii) (iii) (iv) (i)

34. (A) A. Interest on Drawings

$$= 9{,}000 \times \frac{8}{100} \times \frac{3^*}{12} = ₹\,180$$

$$\text{*Average period} = \frac{6+0}{2} = 3$$

B. Interest on Drawings

$$= 12{,}000 \times \frac{8}{100} \times \frac{7.5}{12} = ₹\,600$$

C. Interest on Drawings

$$= 6{,}000 \times \frac{8}{100} \times \frac{9}{12} = ₹\,360$$

35. (D) (ii) (iii) (i)

Assertion-Reason Questions

1. (D) Interest on Loan $= 50{,}000 \times \frac{6}{100} \times \frac{6}{12}$

   $= ₹\,1{,}500$
2. (B) Both Assertion (A) and Reason (R) are true, but Reason (R) is not the correct explanation of Assertion (A)
3. (B) Both Assertion (A) and Reason (R) are true, but Reason (R) is not the correct explanation of Assertion (A)
4. (D) Since interest on drawings is a revenue, it will be provided irrespective of profits or losses.
5. (A) Both Assertion (A) and Reason (R) are true and Reason (R) is the correct explanation of Assertion (A)
6. (A) Both Assertion (A) and Reason (R) are true and Reason (R) is the correct explanation of Assertion (A)
7. (C) Commission to partner is an appropriation of profit.
8. (C) Additional capital and withdrawal of capital can change the capital balance.
9. (C) Reserves are appropriation of profits.

Correct/Incorrect Statements

1. (A) Both statements are correct
2. (B) Fluctuating capitals may as may not show a positive balance.
3. (D) Interest on loan is a charge and is debited to profit and loss account.

4. (B) Interest on capital can be provided even in case of losses, if it is a charge against profits.
5. (A) Both statements are correct
6. (C) In the absence of deed, no partner will recieve any salary against work done by him.
7. (A) Both statements are correct
8. (C) The mamixum number of partners are prescribed in The Indian Companies Act, 2013 and not in The Indian Partnership Act, 1932.
9. (A) Both statements are correct

Case Based Questions

1. (i) (C) Net Profit $\times \frac{10}{100} = ₹\ 44{,}000$

Net Profit $= 44{,}000 \times \frac{100}{10} = ₹\ 4{,}40{,}000$

Raju's Commission

$= (4{,}40{,}000 - 44{,}000) \times \frac{10}{110} = ₹\ 36{,}000$

(ii) (A) Divisible Profit

$= 4{,}40{,}000 - 44{,}000 - 36{,}000$

$= ₹\ 3{,}60{,}000$

Puneet's share $= 3{,}60{,}000 \times \frac{1}{2} = ₹\ 1{,}80{,}000$

2. (i) (A) Interest on Capital

	Amt (₹)
Aditi (5,00,000 × 10%)	50,000
Saurabh (4,00,000 × 10%)	40,000
	90,000

which is more than available profit i.e. ₹ 81,000. Thus, available profit will be divided in partners' capital ratio.

(ii) (B) Interest on Aditi's Capital $= 81{,}000 \times \frac{5}{9}$

$= ₹\ 45{,}000$

Subjective Questions

1. In the absence of deed, the provisions of Indian Partnership Act, 1932 will apply.
   (i) In the absence of deed, no remuneration (salary, commission, etc) will be paid to the partner.
   (ii) The Chartered Accountant is correct. In the absence of deed, interest on loan will be provided @ 6% p.a.
   (iii) N cannot charge commission since there is no deed.
   (iv) O is wrong. In the absence of deed, to admit a partner, the consent of all the partners is required.

2. **Profit and Loss Appropriation Account**

Dr — for the year ending .... — Cr

Particulars		Amt (₹)	Particulars		Amt (₹)
To Interest on Capital			By Profit and Loss A/c	50,000	
P	5,000		(−) Interest on Loan	(3,000)	
Q	2,000			47,000	
R	1,000	8,000	(−) Rent	(4,000)	43,000
To Commission to Q		10,000			
To Commission to R		1,750			
To Profit transferred to Capital A/cs					
P	9,300				
Q	9,300				
R	4,650	23,250			
		43,000			43,000

Partners' Capital Account

Dr | Cr

Particulars	P (₹)	Q (₹)	R (₹)	Particulars	P (₹)	Q (₹)	R (₹)
To Balance c/d	1,14,300	61,300	31,400	By Balance b/d	1,00,000	40,000	20,000
				By Interest on Capital	5,000	2,000	1,000
				By Commission	—	10,000	1,750
				By P and L App. A/c (Profit)	9,300	9,300	4,650
				By Rent	—	—	4,000
	1,14,300	61,300	31,400		1,14,300	61,300	31,400

3. **Profit and Loss Appropriation Account**
for the year ending...

Dr | Cr

Particulars		Amt (₹)	Particulars		Amt (₹)
To Interest on Capital			By Profit and Loss A/c		**50,925**
A	2,000		By Interest on Drawings		
B	**2,000**	4,000	A	**200**	
To Salary A/c			B	**75**	**275**
A	**4,800**				
B	**2,400**	**7,200**			
To Profit transferred to					
A's Capital A/c	**24,000**				
B's Capital A/c	16,000	**40,000**			
		51,200			**51,200**

4. Calculation of Opening Capital (It was subsequently found that interest on capital @ 10% p.a.)

	A	B
Closing Capital	5,00,000	2,00,000
(+) Drawings	16,000	20,000
	5,16,000	2,20,000
(–) Net Profit (3 : 2)	(30,000)	(20,000)
Opening Capital	4,86,000	2,00,000

Statement	A	B
Amount to be Credited	48,600	—
Amount Credited	29,160	19,440
	19,440	19,440
	Cr	Dr

B's Capital A/c	Dr	19,440	
To A's Capital A/c			19,440
(Being adjustment entry passed)			

5. **JOURNAL**

Date	Particulars		LF	Amt (Dr)	Amt (Cr)
	Gita's Current A/c	Dr		2,400	
	To Atul's Current A/c				2,400
	(Being the adjustment entry passed)				

Adjustment Table

Particulars	Atul (₹)	Gita (₹)	Total (₹)
I. **Amount to be Credited**			
Interest on Capital @ 6%	24,000	12,000	36,000
II. **Amount to be Debited**			
Share of Profit	21,600	14,400	36,000
Net Effect (I – II)	2,400 (Cr)	2,400 (Dr)	Nil

6. **JOURNAL**

Date	Particulars		LF	Amt (Dr)	Amt (Cr)
	Profit and Loss Adjustment A/c	Dr		9,000	
	To Cheese's Capital A/c				3,000
	To Slice's Capital A/c				6,000
	(Being interest on capital omitted earlier now provided)				
	Profit and Loss Adjustment A/c	Dr		5,000	
	To Cheese's Capital A/c				5,000
	(Being salary omitted earlier now provided)				
	Cheese's Capital A/c	Dr		7,000	
	Slice's Capital A/c	Dr		7,000	
	To Profit and Loss Adjustment A/c				14,000
	(Being loss on adjustment transferred to partners)				

7. **Profit and Loss Appropriation Account**

Dr for the year ending 31st March, 2024 Cr

Particulars		Amt (₹)	Particulars	Amt (₹)
To Profit transferred to Capital A/c			By P& L A/c	24,000
Tilu (9,000 – 750)	8,250			
Pilu (9,000 – 750)	8,250			
Nilu (6,000 + 1,500)	7,500 *	24,000		
		24,000		24,000

*Nilu's Guarantee (For 9 months) = 10,000 × 9/12 = ₹ 7,500

8. **Profit and Loss Appropriation Account**
for the year ended 31st March, 2022

Dr | | | | Cr

Particulars		Amt (₹)	Particulars	Amt (₹)
To Profit transferred to			By Profit and Loss A/c (Net profit)	22,00,000
Monika's Capital A/c	12,00,000			
(–) Transferred to Kamolika	60,000	11,40,000		
Bhoomika's Capital A/c	8,00,000			
(–) Transfer to Komalika	(40,000)	7,60,000		
Komalika's Capital A/c	2,00,000			
(+) Transfer from Monika	60,000			
(+) Transfer from Bhoomika	40,000	3,00,000		
		22,00,000		22,00,000

Working Note

Profit share in ratio of 6 : 4 : 1

Monika $= \frac{6}{11} \times 22{,}00{,}000 =$ ₹ 12,00,000

Bhoomika $= \frac{4}{11} \times 22{,}00{,}000 =$ ₹ 8,00,000

Kamolika $= \frac{1}{11} \times 22{,}00{,}000 =$ ₹ 2,00,000

The deficiency amount of ₹ 1,00,000 in share of Kamolika contributed by Monika and Boomika in there profit sharing ratio 6 : 4

Share contributed by Monika $= 1{,}00{,}000 \times \frac{6}{10} =$ ₹ 60,000

Share contributed by Bhoomika $= 1{,}00{,}000 \times \frac{4}{10} =$ ₹ 40,000

CHAPTER -2

Reconstitution of a Partnership Firm :
Change in Profit Sharing Ratio Among the Existing Partners

Types & Nos. of Questions

Multiple Choice Questions	– 32
Assertion-Reason Questions	– 8
Correct/Incorrect Statements	– 7
Case Based Questions	– 2 Cases, *each with 3 Questions*
Subjective Questions	– 9

Trend Analysis

On the basis of analysis of last 2 years' papers, it is found that on an average 1 Multiple Choice Question and 1 Short Answer Type Question are asked from this chapter.

Focus Topics of the Chapter

- Goodwill and its Valuation
- Revaluation of Asset and Reassessment of Liabilities
- Accounting Treatment of Reserves, Accumulated Profits or Losses
- Adjustment of Capital

Multiple Choice Questions

No. of Questions : **32** Suggested Time : **50 Minutes**

Direction Each of the question given below is Multiple Choice Question (MCQ) i.e. there are Four Options/Choices for answer, out of which ONLY ONE is correct. You have to select the correct option. A response box is given with each option, mark **(✓)** in the box of the correct option. For each correct answer you will get 1 mark, while there is no penalty for incorrect answer or missed out questions.

1. Which of the following is not true about self-generated goodwill?

(A) It is internally generated over long period of time ☐

(B) It is shown in balance sheet as an asset ☐

(C) A true valuation cannot be possible ☐

(D) It is not recorded in books of accounts ☐

2. From the following statements, choose the incorrect option.

(A) Profit on sale of machine must be deducted out of net profit ☐

(B) Loss by fire should be added back to the net profit ☐

(C) Income from investment must be added to net profit ☐

(D) Salary of employee omitted to record must be deducted from profit ☐

3. The profits for the last 4 years were ₹ 1,30,000, ₹ 1,50,000, ₹ 1,90,000 and ₹ 1,80,000 respectively. Profit of 1st year include abnormal loss of ₹ 20,000 and profit of 4th year include abnormal gain of ₹ 30,000.

Average profit for valuation of goodwill will be

(A) ₹ 1,62,500 ☐ (B) ₹ 1,60,000 ☐

(C) ₹ 1,47,500 ☐ (D) ₹ 1,72,500 ☐

4. The net profit for the last 3 years were 2019-20 ₹ 82,000; 2020-21 ₹ 66,400 and 2021-22 ₹ 70,000. On 1st October, 2020, machine costing ₹ 30,000 was purchased and wrongly charged as travelling expense. Depreciation on machine was to be charged @ 20% p.a on written down value method.

Average profit after adjustment will be

(A) ₹ 66,000 ☐ (B) ₹ 71,000 ☐

(C) ₹ 78,000 ☐ (D) ₹ 80,000 ☐

5. Find out profit or loss for the year 2020-21 from the following.

Year	2018-19	2019-20	2020-21	2021-22	2022-23
Profits/ Loss	60,000	80,000	?	50,000	70,000

Goodwill is valued at 3 years purchase of average profit of last 5 years as ₹ 1,50,000.

(A) Profit ₹ 10,000 ☐

(B) Loss ₹ 10,000 ☐

(C) Profit ₹ 20,000 ☐

(D) Loss ₹ 20,000 ☐

6. A firm had assets of ₹ 2,00,000 excluding stock of ₹ 40,000. The current liabilities were ₹ 20,000. If the normal rate of return is 8% and goodwill is valued at ₹ 1,20,000 at 4 years purchase of super profit, average profit of firm will be

(A) ₹ 41,600 ☐

(B) ₹ 43,600 ☐

(C) ₹ 45,600 ☐

(D) ₹ 47,600 ☐

7. If firm had total assets of ₹ 10,00,000 (including goodwill of ₹ 50,000) and goodwill is valued at ₹ 3,50,000 on the basis of capitalisation of average profit, calculate outside liabilities, if rate of return is 10% and average profit is ₹ 60,000.

(A) ₹ 6,50,000 ☐ (B) ₹ 7,50,000 ☐

(C) ₹ 7,00,000 ☐ (D) ₹ 8,00,000 ☐

8. Which of the following does not result into reconstitution of a firm?
(A) Change in profit sharing ratio of existing partners ☐
(B) Dissolution of partnership ☐
(C) Dissolution of partnership firm ☐
(D) Death of a partner ☐

9. Identify the situation where sacrifice/gain ratio is not applicable.
(A) When there is change in profit sharing ratio ☐
(B) When new partner is admitted ☐
(C) At the time of retirement/death of a partner ☐
(D) When purchased goodwill is written-off from the books ☐

10. A, B and C are partners in a firm sharing profits and losses in the ratio of 1 : 1: 1. Now, they decided to share profits and losses in the ratio of 5 :3 : 2. At the time of change in profit sharing ratio, A provided a loan to the firm. This loan will be shown in
(A) balance sheet, asset side ☐
(B) balance sheet, liability side ☐
(C) partners' capital account ☐
(D) partners' current account ☐

11. Gain/Loss on revaluation at the time of change in profit sharing ratio of existing partners is shared by .... whereas in case of admission of a partner it is shared by ....
(A) remaining partners, all partners ☐
(B) all partners, old partners ☐
(C) new partner, all partner ☐
(D) sacrificing partner, incoming partner ☐

12. P, Q and R are partners in a firm sharing profits and losses equally. On 1st April, 2022, they decided to change their profit sharing ratio in a way that P will gain 1/6th share from Q and R, and Q and R will sacrifice 1/12th share each in favour of P. What will be their new profit sharing ratio?
(A) 3:2:1 ☐
(B) 2:2:1 ☐
(C) 2:1:1 ☐
(D) 1:2:2 ☐

13. B, P and O are partners in a firm sharing profits in the ratio of 3:1:1. On 1st April, 2022, they decided to change their profit sharing ratio in a way that B will sacrifice 8/30th share in favour of P and O, and P will gain 2/15th share each from B. What will be the new profit share of O?
(A) 1/3 ☐
(B) 4/15 ☐
(C) 1/2 ☐
(D) 2/15 ☐

14. Niva, Naman and Nityam were partners sharing profits and losses in the ratio of 4 : 3 :2. Niva and Naman each given 1/9 from their share to Nityam on reconstitution of the firm. The new profit sharing ratio among Niva, Naman and Nityam will be *[CBSE 2023]*
(A) 3 : 4: 2 ☐ (B) 2 : 3: 4 ☐
(C) 4: 2: 3 ☐ (D) 3 : 2: 4 ☐

15. A and B are partners with the profit sharing ratio of 3:2. They decided to change this ratio to 2:3 with effect from 1st April, 2021. In adjustment entry, B's account will be .... by .... assuming goodwill of firm is valued at ₹ 15,000.
(A) debited, ₹ 15,000 ☐
(B) credited, ₹ 15,000 ☐
(C) credited, ₹ 3,000 ☐
(D) debited, ₹ 3,000 ☐

16. C, M and O are partners in a firm sharing profits and losses in the ratio of 5:3:2. From 1st April, 2022, they decided to change their profit sharing ratio in such a way that C will sacrifice 1/10th of his share in favour for M.

The goodwill of the firm is valued at ₹ 3,750. What will be the journal entry for distribution of goodwill?

(A) Debit C's Capital A/c and Credit M's Capital A/c by ₹ 3,750 ☐

(B) Debit M's Capital A/c and Credit C's Capital A/c by ₹ 3,750 ☐

(C) Debit C's Capital A/c and Credit M's Capital A/c by ₹ 1,875 ☐

(D) Debit M's Capital A/c and Credit C's Capital A/c by ₹ 375 ☐

17. Aman, Subash and Vishal are partners sharing profits in the ratio of 5 : 3 : 2. They decided to share future profits in the ratio of 2:3:5 with effect from 1st April, 2023. They had the balance of profit and loss account (Debited) ₹ 50,000. Vishal's capital account will be

(A) debited by ₹ 50,000 ☐

(B) debited by ₹ 10,000 ☐

(C) credited by ₹ 50,000 ☐

(D) credited by ₹ 10,000 ☐

18. X, Y and Z are partners sharing profits in the ratio 3:2:1. They decided to share future profits in the ratio of 4:3:2. At the time of change in ratio, firm had investment fluctuation reserve of ₹ 40,000. Investment appears in balance sheet at ₹ 1,00,000. (Market value is ₹ 70,000). X's account will be

(A) debited by ₹ 5,000 ☐

(B) credited by ₹ 5,000 ☐

(C) credited by ₹ 30,000 ☐

(D) debited by ₹ 30,000 ☐

19. Aarti and Bharti are partners with ratio of 2:3. They decided to share profits in 3:2 and at the time of change in ratio general reserve appearing in books at ₹ 40,000. They do not want to distribute it. Bharti's capital account will be

(A) debited with ₹ 24,000 ☐

(B) debited with ₹ 16,000 ☐

(C) credited with ₹ 8,000 ☐

(D) credited with ₹ 40,000 ☐

20. Malika, Meera and Madhu were partners sharing profits and losses in the ratio of 2 : 2 : 1. They decided to share future profits in the ratio of 7 : 5 : 3 with effect from 1st April, 2021. Their balance sheet as on that date showed a balance of ₹ 30,000 in advertisement suspense account. Amount, that will be debited/ credited to the capital accounts of Malika, Meera and Madhu if they decide to carry forward the amount of advertisement suspense account.

(A) ₹ 12,000 (Dr); ₹ 12,000 (Dr) and ₹ 6,000 (Dr) respectively to the capital accounts of Malika, Meera and Madhu ☐

(B) Debit ₹ 10,000 each to all partner's capital accounts ☐

(C) Debit Meera's Capital A/c and Credit Malika's Capital A/c by ₹ 2,000 ☐

(D) Debit Malika's Capital A/c and credit Meera's Capital A/c by ₹ 2,000 each ☐

21. A, B and C who were sharing profits and losses in the ratio of 4 : 3 : 2 decided to share the future profits and losses in the ratio to 2 : 3 : 4 with effect from 1st April, 2023. An extract of their balance sheet as at 31st March, 2023 is

Liabilities	Amt (₹)	Assets	Amt (₹)
Workmen Compensation Reserve	65,000		

At the time of reconstitution, a certain amount of claim on workmen compensation was determined for which B's share of loss amounted to ₹ 5,000.

The claim for workmen compensation would be

(A) ₹ 15,000 ☐ (B) ₹ 70,000 ☐

(C) ₹ 50,000 ☐ (D) ₹ 80,000 ☐

22. Arun, Babita and Charu are partners in a firm sharing profits and losses in the ratio of 3 : 3 : 2. They decided to share future profits and losses in the ratio of 1 : 1 : 1 with effect from 1st April, 2021.

They decided to record the effect of the following without affecting their book values.

(i) Profit and Loss A/c (Cr) ₹ 8,000
(ii) General Reserve ₹ 4,000

The necessary adjusting entry for the same will be

(A) Charu's Capital A/c Dr 1,000
 To Arun's Capital A/c 500
 To Babita's Capital A/c 500 ☐

(B) Arun's Capital A/c Dr 500
 Babita's Capital A/c Dr 500
 To Charu's Capital A/c 1,000 ☐

(C) Charu's Capital A/c Dr 1,000
 To Babita's Capital A/c 1,000 ☐

(D) Charu's Capital A/c Dr 3,000
 To Arun's Capital A/c 1,500
 To Babita's Capital A/c 1,500 ☐

23. Samiksha, Arshiya and Divya were partners in a firm sharing profits and losses in the ratio of 5 : 3 : 2. With effect from 1st April, 2022, they agreed to share future profits and losses in the ratio of 2 : 5 : 3.

Their balance sheet showed a debit balance of ₹ 50,000 in the profit and loss account and a balance of ₹ 40,000 in the investment fluctuation fund.

The market value of an investment is ₹ 30,000 against the book value of ₹ 50,000. Partners have decided, not to show revised valued in the balance sheet and to pass an adjusting entry for it.

Which of the following is the correct treatment of the above?

(A) Samiksha's Capital A/c Dr 9,000
 To Arshiya's Capital A/c 6,000
 To Divya's Capital A/c 3,000 ☐

(B) Arshiya's Capital A/c Dr 5,000
 To Samiksha's Capital A/c 2,000
 To Divya's Capital A/c 3,000 ☐

(C) Arshiya's Capital A/c Dr 2,000
 Divya's Capital A/c Dr 1,000
 To Samiksha's Capital A/c 3,000 ☐

(D) Arshiya's Capital A/c Dr 6,000
 Divya's Capital A/c Dr 3,000
 To Samiksha's Capital A/c 9,000 ☐

24. M, N and O are partners in a firm sharing profits and losses in the ratio of 3:2:1. They decided to change their ratio to 2:1:1 with effect from 1st April, 2024. N decide to take over the firm's furniture of ₹ 30,000 at book value. This transaction will be recorded on the

(A) debit side of revaluation account ☐
(B) credit side of realisation account ☐
(C) credit side of partners' capital account ☐
(D) None of the above ☐

25. A, B and C are partners in a firm sharing profits and losses in the ratio of 4:2:1. They decided to change their ratio to 1:1:1 with effect from 1st April, 2022. C decided to take over the firm's stock of ₹ 30,000 at an agreed value of ₹ 28,000. This transaction will be

(A) debited to revaluation account by ₹ 28,000 ☐
(B) credited to revaluation account by ₹ 28,000 ☐
(C) debited to revaluation account by ₹ 2,000 ☐
(D) credited to revaluation account by ₹ 28,000 ☐

26. P, Q and R are partners in a firm sharing profits and losses in the ratio of 3:2:1. They decided to share profits equally with effect from 1st April, 2022.

The partners decided not to change the values of assets and liabilities in the books of accounts. The values of assets and liabilities are as follows

	Book Value (₹)	Market Value (₹)
Furniture	25,000	30,000
Printers	20,000	16,500
Machinery	18,000	12,000
Stock	10,000	20,000
Creditors	13,500	13,000

Journal entry passed for the above adjustments will be

(A) Debit R's Capital A/c by ₹ 1,000 and Credit P's Capital A/c by ₹ 1,000 ☐

(B) Debit R's Capital A/c by ₹ 6,000 and Credit P's Capital A/c by ₹ 6,000 ☐

(C) Debit Revaluation A/c by ₹ 6,000 and Credit Partners' Capital A/c by ₹ 3,000; 2,000; 1,000 ☐

(D) Debit Revaluation A/c by ₹ 6,000 and Credit Partners' Capital A/c by ₹ 2,000 each ☐

27. On the reconstitution of a firm, the value of land was to be appreciated by ₹ 2,00,000 and plant and machinery was to be reduced to ₹ 7,00,000 from ₹ 10,00,000. Gain or loss on revaluation will be

(A) ₹ 1,00,000 Gain ☐

(B) ₹ 1,00,000 Loss ☐

(C) ₹ 5,00,000 Loss ☐

(D) ₹ 5,00,000 Gain ☐

28. Arun and Vijay are partners in a firm sharing profits and losses in the ratio of 5:1.

Balance Sheet (Extract)

Liabilities	Amt (₹)	Assets	Amt (₹)
		Machinery	40,000

If the value of machinery reflected in the balance sheet is overvalued by $33\frac{1}{3}$ %, find out the value of machinery to be shown in the new balance sheet.

(A) ₹ 44,000 ☐ (B) ₹ 48,000 ☐

(C) ₹ 32,000 ☐ (D) ₹ 30,000 ☐

29. Profit of the firm during the year was ₹ 2,50,000. What will be the effect on profit in the following cases?

Column I	Column II
A. Sale of furniture (book value ₹ 10,000) for ₹ 15,000	(i) ₹ 2,30,000
B. Overvaluation of closing stock by ₹ 10,000	(ii) ₹ 2,40,000
C. Abnormal loss included ₹ 10,000	(iii) ₹ 2,45,000
D. Repair of machine for ₹ 20,000 was wrongly capitalised	(iv) ₹ 2,60,000

Codes

	A	B	C	D	
(A)	(ii)	(iii)	(i)	(iv)	☐
(B)	(iii)	(ii)	(i)	(iv)	☐
(C)	(ii)	(iv)	(i)	(iii)	☐
(D)	(iii)	(ii)	(iv)	(i)	☐

30. Average profit = ₹ 3,00,000, capital employed = ₹ 10,00,000, rate of return = 10%, no. of years purchase = 4.

Calculate goodwill in the following cases and match it.

Column I	Column II
A. Goodwill (by average profit method)	(i) ₹ 8,00,000
B. Goodwill (by capitalisation of average profit)	(ii) ₹ 12,00,000
C. Goodwill (by super profit method)	(iii) ₹ 20,00,000

Codes

	A	B	C	
(A)	(ii)	(iii)	(i)	☐
(B)	(iii)	(ii)	(i)	☐
(C)	(ii)	(i)	(iii)	☐
(D)	(i)	(ii)	(iii)	☐

31. P, Q and R are partners in a firm sharing profits and losses in 3:2:1, they decided to share future profits in the ratio of 4:3:2. Workmen compensation reserve on that date is ₹ 42,000.

Column I	Column II
A. There is no claim against workmen compensation reserve	(i) Nil
B. Claim for workmen compensation is estimated at ₹ 30,000	(ii) A = ₹ 6,000 B = ₹ 4,000 C = ₹ 2,000
C. Claim for workmen compensation is estimated at ₹ 45,000	(iii) A = ₹ 21,000 B = ₹ 14,000 C = ₹ 7,000

Codes

	A	B	C	
(A)	(ii)	(i)	(iii)	☐
(B)	(i)	(ii)	(iii)	☐
(C)	(iii)	(ii)	(i)	☐
(D)	(ii)	(iii)	(i)	☐

32. Match Column I with Column II and select the correct answer

Column I	Column II
A. Increase in liabilities	(i) Credit-revaluation account
B. Bad debts recovered	(ii) Credit-partners' capital account
C. Accumulated losses	(iii) Debit-revaluation account
D. Profit and loss account (credit)	(iv) Debit-partners' capital account

Codes

	A	B	C	D	
(A)	(iii)	(i)	(ii)	(iv)	☐
(B)	(i)	(iii)	(iv)	(ii)	☐
(C)	(i)	(iii)	(ii)	(iv)	☐
(D)	(iii)	(i)	(iv)	(ii)	☐

Assertion-Reason Questions

No. of Questions : **8**

Suggested Time : **15 Minutes**

Direction Each of the question given below consist of the two statements; one labelled as **Assertion** (A) and other as **Reason** (R). List of common options applicable for each question is given below

(A) Both Assertion (A) and Reason (R) are true and Reason (R) is the correct explanation of Assertion (A)

(B) Both Assertion (A) and Reason (R) are true, but Reason (R) is not the correct explanation of Assertion (A)

(C) Assertion (A) is true, but Reason (R) is false

(D) Assertion (A) is false, but Reason (R) is true

You have to select the codes as *A, B, C* or *D* as your answer to the question by marking (✓) in the response box given against each option.

1. **Assertion (A)** It is desirable to value goodwill on the basis of super profits and not the actual profits.

Reason (R) The real profit is the amount which is in excess of normal profits in the business.

(A) ☐ (B) ☐ (C) ☐ (D) ☐

2. **Assertion (A)** Goodwill is an intangible asset.

Reason (R) It is the value of the reputation of a firm in respect of the profits expected in future.

(A) ☐ (B) ☐ (C) ☐ (D) ☐

3. **Assertion (A)** Internally generated goodwill should not be recognised as an asset.

Reason (R) Purchased goodwill may be accounted for in the books and shown as an asset.

(A) ☐ (B) ☐ (C) ☐ (D) ☐

4. **Assertion (A)** Good relations with customer will increase the goodwill of the firm.

Reason (R) Good relations will increase sales and in turn profits of the business.

(A) ☐ (B) ☐ (C) ☐ (D) ☐

5. **Assertion (A)** The existing agreement will change when the partners decides to change their profit sharing ratio.

Reason (R) As a result of this, some partners will lose their profit share while others will gain.

(A) ☐ (B) ☐
(C) ☐ (D) ☐

6. **Assertion (A)** Sacrificing Ratio = Old Ratio – New Ratio.

Reason (R) If the new ratio is more than the old ratio, the partner will lose.

(A) ☐ (B) ☐
(C) ☐ (D) ☐

7. **Asserttion (A)** The gaining partner will compensate the sacrificing partner by way of payment to him as goodwill according to gaining ratio.

Reason (R) At the time of reconstitution of partnership, reserves are distributed among partners in old ratio.

(A) ☐ (B) ☐ (C) ☐ (D) ☐

8. **Assertion (A)** Revaluation account is a nominal account by nature.

Reason (R) The revaluation account is debited in case there is a loss due to revaluation of assets and reassessment of liabilities.

(A) ☐ (B) ☐ (C) ☐ (D) ☐

Correct/Incorrect Statements

No. of Questions : **7** Suggested Time : **15 Minutes**

Direction Each of the questions given below consists of the two statements. List of common options appliacable for each question is given below

(A) Both statements are correct
(B) Statement I is correct and Statement II is incorrect
(C) Statement I is incorrect and Statement II is correct
(D) Both statements are incorrect

You have to select the codes as *A, B, C* or *D* as your answer to the question by marking (✓) in the response box given against each option.

1. **Statement I** The gain or loss on revaluation of each asset and liability is transferred to revaluation account.

Statement II The revaluation account is credited with increase in the value of each asset and decrease in its liabilities because it is a gain.

(A) ☐ (B) ☐
(C) ☐ (D) ☐

2. **Statement I** Goodwill is an intangible asset.

Statement II Goodwill is the future value of a firm's anticipated excess earnings.

(A) ☐ (B) ☐ (C) ☐ (D) ☐

3. **Statement I** Partners changing their profit sharing ratio will lead to dissolution of partnership.

Statement II Change in profit sharing ratio does not affect the relationship of the partners.

(A) ☐ (B) ☐ (C) ☐ (D) ☐

4. **Statement I** A, B and C are partners. If A's share is decreased as a result of change in profit sharing ratio, A will be called sacrificing partner.

   Statement II Accumulated profits are distributed among the partners in their sacrificing/gaining ratio.

   (A) ☐ (B) ☐ (C) ☐ (D) ☐

5. **Statement I** If the liability against workmen compensation exceeds the amount of reserve, the difference amount will be transferred to the debit side of revaluation account.

   Statement II If one partner is sacrificing his share, at least one partner will gain.

   (A) ☐ (B) ☐ (C) ☐ (D) ☐

6. **Statement I** At the time of reconstitution of the partnership, the partners can choose not to distribute the accumulated profits.

   Statement II Employees provident fund is a reserve and will be distributed among the partners.

   (A) ☐ (B) ☐
   (C) ☐ (D) ☐

7. **Statement I** Reconstitution of partnership is not different from dissolution of partnership.

   Statement II Revaluation account is prepared in both the cases.

   (A) ☐ (B) ☐
   (C) ☐ (D) ☐

Case Based Questions

No. of Questions : **2** Suggested Time : **10 Minutes**

Direction This section contains 2 cases having 3 Questions of 1 mark each. You have to write the answer of each question based on the context of the related case.

Case 1 A and B are partners in a firm. They agree to value goodwill at 2 years purchase of average profit of last 4 years which are as follows

Year ending 31st March, 2019 ₹ 4,00,000; Year ending 31st March, 2020 ₹ 5,00,000
Year ending 31st March, 2021 ₹ 6,00,000; Year ending 31st March, 2022 ₹ 7,00,000

Following errors were found out

- Profit of year ending 31st March, 2019 include an abnormal loss of ₹ 50,000.
- Profit of year ending 31st March 2021 include an abnormal gain of ₹ 50,000.
- Closing stock as on 31st March, 2020 was undervalued by ₹ 40,000.
- Repairs to machine amounting to ₹ 40,000 was wrongly debited to machine on 1st January, 2019. Depreciation to be charged on machine @ 10% p.a. on straight line method.
- To cover management cost, an annual charge of ₹ 4,800 should be made for the purpose of goodwill valuation.

Questions

(i) Adjusted profit for the year ended 31st March, 2021 will be

(A) ₹ 6,39,200 ☐ (B) ₹ 5,09,200 ☐
(C) ₹ 5,39,200 ☐ (D) ₹ 6,09,200 ☐

(ii) Adjusted profit for the year ended 31st March, 2020 will be

(A) ₹ 4,06,200 ☐ (B) ₹ 5,09,200 ☐
(C) ₹ 5,39,200 ☐ (D) ₹ 6,99,200 ☐

(iii) Average profit will be

(A) ₹ 5,80,900 ☐ (B) ₹ 5,39,200 ☐ (C) ₹ 5,38,450 ☐ (D) ₹ 5,00,200 ☐

Case 2 Three friends R, S and M started their partnership few years back with profit share of 5:3:2. With effect from 1st April, 2024, they decided to share profits and losses in the ratio of 2:2:1.

On that date, there was a workmen's compensation fund of ₹ 1,35,000 in their books. They all agreed to value the firm's goodwill at ₹ 1,05,000. A workman raised claim against workmen compensation fund of ₹ 60,000. Profit on revaluation of assets and re-assessment of liabilities amounted to ₹ 60,000.

You are required to answer the following questions

Questions

(i) Which of the following partners is not sacrificing or gaining?

(A) R ☐

(B) S ☐

(C) M ☐

(D) Both S and M ☐

(ii) While adjusting for workmen compensation, M's capital account will be

(A) credited by ₹ 60,000 ☐

(B) credited by ₹ 37,500 ☐

(C) credited by ₹ 22,500 ☐

(D) credited by ₹ 15,000 ☐

(iii) While adjusting the revaluation gain, S's capital account will be

(A) credited by ₹ 30,000 ☐

(B) credited by ₹ 18,000 ☐

(c) credited by ₹ 12,000 ☐

(D) credited by ₹ 22,500 ☐

Subjective Questions

Free Response Questions, Open-ended Questions etc.

No. of Questions : **9** Suggested Time : **70 Minutes**

1. The fixed capital of partners A and B are ₹ 5,00,000 and ₹ 3,00,000 respectively. Their current account balance are A ₹ 1,50,000 (Cr) and B ₹ 50,000 (Dr). General reserve stood at ₹ 1,00,000. The market rate of interest is 15%.

Annual salary to the partner is ₹ 60,000 each. The profit for the last 3 years were ₹ 3,00,000, ₹ 3,60,000 and ₹ 4,20,000. Calculate the goodwill of the firm at 2 years purchase of super profits.

2. Sam, Arsh and Dona were partners sharing profits and losses in 5:3:2 raatio. With effect from 1st April, 2023, they agree to share future profits and losses in the ratio 2:3:5.

Their balance sheet showed a debit balance of ₹ 50,000 in profit and loss account and a balance of ₹ 40,000 in the investment fluctuation fund.

(i) Goodwill of the firm is valued at ₹ 70,000

(ii) Investment of book value of ₹ 5,00,000 be valued at 4,80,000.

Pass necessary journal entries to record above transactions.

3. A, B and C are partners sharing profits and losses in the ratio 2:3:4. They decided to share future profits and losses in the ratio 4:3:2. They also decided to record the effect of the following without affecting their book values.

General Reserve ₹ 40,000

Profit and Loss Account ₹ 20,000

Advertisement Suspense Account ₹ 15,000

Pass a single adjustment entry for above.

4. A, B and C are in partnership sharing profits and losses in the ratio of 5:4:3. On 31st March, 2023, their balance sheet was as follows

Liabilities		Amt (₹)	Assets	Amt (₹)
Creditors		25,000	Cash	20,000
Bills Payable		5,000	Debtors	2,00,000
Profit and Loss		50,000	Stock	2,50,000
Capital A/cs			Furniture	50,000
A	1,00,000		Building	1,60,000
B	2,00,000			
C	3,00,000	6,00,000		
		6,80,000		6,80,000

It was decided that from 1st April, 2023, the profit sharing ratio will be 4:3:2. For this purpose the following revaluations were made

(i) Furniture be taken at ₹ 40,000.

(ii) Stock appreciated by 10% and building by ₹ 20,000.

(iii) Bills payable increased by ₹ 3,000.

Partners agreed that altered values are not to be recorded in the books and they also do not want to distribute profit and loss account.

You are required to pass a single journal entry to show the effect and prepare partner's capital account.

5. Mehak, Ayush and Anshu were partners in a firm sharing profits and losses in the ratio of 5 : 3 : 2.

With effect from 1st April, 2023, they agreed to share profits and losses in the ratio of 4 : 3 : 3.

On that date, there was a general reserve of ₹ 80,000 in the books of the firm.
It was agreed that

(i) Goodwill of the firm be valued at ₹ 3,00,000.

(ii) Loss on revaluation of assets and re-assessment of liabilities amounted to ₹ 50,000.

Pass necessary journal entries for the above transactions in the books of the firm. *[CBSE 2024]*

6. Asha, Rina and Chahat were partners in a firm sharing profits and losses in the ratio of 2 : 2 : 1. Their balance sheet as at 31st March, 2019 was as follows

Balance Sheet of Asha, Rina and Chahat
as at 31st March, 2019

Liabilities		Amt (₹)	Assets		Amt (₹)
Creditors		12,00,000	Plant and Machinery		14,80,000
General Reserve		2,00,000	Stock		2,20,000
Capital A/cs			Sundry Debtors	2,60,000	
Asha	3,00,000		(–) Provision for Doubtful Debts	(20,000)	2,40,000
Rina	2,00,000		Bank		60,000
Chahat	1,00,000	6,00,000			
		20,00,000			20,00,000

Asha, Rina and Chahat decided to share future profits equally with effect from 1st April, 2019. For this, it was agreed that

(i) Goodwill of the firm be valued at ₹ 1,50,000.

(ii) Bad debts amounted to ₹ 40,000. A provision for doubtful debts was to be made @ 5% on debtors.

Pass the necessary journal entries to record the above transactions in the books of the firm.

7. Hari, Kunal and Uma are partners in a firm sharing profits and losses in the ratio of 5 : 3 : 2. From 1st April, 2018 they decided to share future profits and losses in the ratio of 2 : 5 : 3.

Their balance sheet showed a balance of ₹ 75,000 in the profit and loss account and a balance of ₹ 15,000 in investment fluctuation fund.

For this purpose, it was agreed that

(i) Goodwill of the firm was valued at ₹ 3,00,000.

(ii) Investments (having a book value of ₹ 50,000) were valued at ₹ 35,000.

(iii) Stock having a book value of ₹ 50,000 be depreciated by 10%.

Pass the necessary journal entries for the above in the books of the firm.

8. R, S and T were partners in a firm sharing profits in 1 : 2 : 3 ratio. Their balance sheet as at 31st March, 2024 was as follows

Balance Sheet
as at 31st March, 2024

Liabilities		Amt (₹)	Assets	Amt (₹)
Creditors		50,000	Land	50,000
Bills Payable		20,000	Building	50,000
General Reserve		30,000	Plant	1,00,000
Capital A/cs			Stock	40,000
R	1,00,000		Debtors	30,000
S	50,000		Bank	5,000
T	25,000	1,75,000		
		2,75,000		2,75,000

From 1st April, 2024, R, S and T decided to share the future profits equally. For this purpose it was decided that

(i) Goodwill of the firm be valued at ₹ 1,50,000.

(ii) Land be revalued at ₹ 80,000 and building be depreciated by 6%.

(iii) Creditors of ₹ 6,000 were not likely to be claimed and hence be written-off.

Prepare revaluation account, partners' capital accounts and the balance sheet of the reconstituted firm.

9. P, Q and R are partners sharing profits and losses in the ratio of 2 : 2 : 1. On 1st April, 2024, they decided to share future profits equally. Following revaluation account and capital accounts were drawn, in which some values are missing

Revaluation Account

Dr | | | | Cr

Particulars		Amt (₹)	Particulars	Amt (₹)
To Stock A/c		40,000	By Machinery A/c	...
To Provision for Doubtful Debts A/c		40,000	By Sundry Creditors A/c	40,000
To Outstanding Expenses A/c		...		
To Profit transferred to Capital A/cs				
P	...			
Q	...			
R	...	...		
		2,00,000		2,00,000

Dr **Partners' Capital Account** Cr

Particulars	P (₹)	Q (₹)	R (₹)	Particulars	P (₹)	Q (₹)	R (₹)
To Advertisement Suspense A/c	...	...	...	By Balance b/d	...	...	...
To Balance c/d	6,00,000	5,60,000	5,20,000	By Revaluation A/c	32,000	32,000	16,000
	6,16,000	5,76,000	5,28,000		6,16,000	5,76,000	5,28,000

You are required to complete the accounts.

Answers

If your answer matches with the answer given here then put (✓) in the box otherwise put (✗). In case you did not attempt the question leave the box blank.

Multiple Choice Questions

1. B ☐ 2. C ☐
3. B ☐ 4. D ☐
5. B ☐ 6. D ☐
7. C ☐ 8. C ☐
9. D ☐ 10. B ☐
11. B ☐ 12. C ☐
13. A ☐ 14. D ☐
15. D ☐ 16. D ☐
17. D ☐ 18. B ☐
19. C ☐ 20. D ☐
21. D ☐ 22. A ☐
23. A ☐ 24. D ☐
25. C ☐ 26. A ☐
27. B ☐ 28. D ☐
29. D ☐ 30. A ☐
31. C ☐ 32. D ☐

Your Score__________ (*No. of Correct Answers*)

Assertion-Reason Questions

1. A ☐ 2. B ☐ 3. B ☐
4. A ☐ 5. B ☐ 6. C ☐
7. B ☐ 8. B ☐

Your Score__________ (*No. of Correct Answers*

Correct/Incorrect Statements

1. A ☐ 2. B ☐ 3. B ☐
4. B ☐ 5. A ☐ 6. B ☐
7. A ☐

Your Score__________ (*No. of Correct Answers*)

Case Based Questions

1. (i) B ☐ (ii) C ☐
(iii) C ☐
2. (i) C ☐ (ii) D ☐
(iii) B ☐

Your Score__________ (*No. of Correct Answers*)

Explanations

Multiple Choice Questions

1. (B) It is shown in balance sheet as an asset
2. (C) Income from investment must be added to net profit
3. (B) Average Profit

$$= \frac{(1,30,000 + 20,000) + 1,50,000 + 1,90,000 + (1,80,000 - 30,000)}{4} = ₹\ 1,60,000$$

4. (D) 2019-20 ₹ 82,000

2020-21 $66,400 + 30,000 - 3,000 = ₹\ 93,400$

2021-22 $70,000 - 5,400 = ₹\ 64,600$

$$\text{Average Profit} = \frac{2,40,000}{3} = ₹\ 80,000$$

5. (B) 1,50,000

$$= \frac{(60,000 + 80,000 + x + 50,000 + 70,000)}{5} \times 3$$

$$\frac{1,50,000 \times 5}{3} = 2,60,000 + x$$

$$2,50,000 = 2,60,000 + x$$

$\therefore$ Loss of 2020-21 $(x) = ₹\ (10,000)$

6. (D) Capital Employed = Assets − Outside Liabilities

Capital Employed = 2,00,000 + 40,000 − 20,000 = ₹ 2,20,000

$$\text{Normal Profit} = \text{Capital Employed} \times \frac{\text{Normal Rate of Return}}{100}$$

$$= 2,20,000 \times \frac{8}{100} = ₹\ 17,600$$

Now, Goodwill = Super Profit × Number of Years Purchase

1,20,000 = Super Profit × 4

$$\therefore \text{Super Profit} = \frac{1,20,000}{4} = ₹\ 30,000$$

Now, Super Profit = Average Profit − Normal Profit

30,000 = Average Profit − 17,600

$\therefore$ Average Profit = 30,000 + 17,600 = ₹ 47,600

7. (C) $3,50,000 = \left(60,000 \times \frac{100}{10}\right) - (9,50,000 - \text{Outside Liabilities})$

3,50,000 = 6,00,000 − 9,50,000 + Outside Liabilities

$\therefore$ Outside Liabilities = ₹ 7,00,000

8. (C) Dissolution of partnership firm
9. (D) When purchased goodwill is written-off from the books
10. (B) balance sheet, liability side
11. (B) all partners, old partners
12. (C) P's New Share $= \frac{1}{3} + \frac{1}{6} = \frac{3}{6} \times \frac{2}{2} = \frac{6}{12}$

Q's New Share $= \frac{1}{3} - \frac{1}{12} = \frac{4-1}{12} = \frac{3}{12}$

R's New Share $= \frac{1}{3} - \frac{1}{12} = \frac{3}{12}$

New Ratio = 6 : 3 : 3 *or* 2 : 1 : 1

13. (A) B's Sacrifice = P's Gain + O's Gain

$$\frac{8}{30} = \frac{2}{15} + \text{O's Gain}$$

$$\text{O's Gain} = \frac{8}{30} - \frac{2}{15} = \frac{8-4}{30} = \frac{4}{30}$$

$$\text{O's New Share} = \frac{1}{5} + \frac{4}{30} = \frac{6+4}{30} = \frac{10}{30} = \frac{1}{3}$$

14. (D) Niva $= \frac{4}{9} - \frac{1}{9} = \frac{3}{9}$; Naman $= \frac{3}{9} - \frac{1}{9} = \frac{2}{9}$

Nityam $= \frac{2}{9} + \frac{1}{9} + \frac{1}{9} = \frac{4}{9}$

15. (D) B's Sacrifice/Gain $= \frac{2}{5} - \frac{3}{5} = \left(\frac{1}{5}\right)$ (Gain)

B's Goodwill Share $= 15,000 \times \frac{1}{5} = ₹\ 3,000$

B's account will be debited by ₹ 3,000

16. (D) Since C is sacrificing and M is gaining, the journal entry will be

M's Capital A/c Dr	375	
To C's Capital A/c		375

Goodwill $= 3,750 \times \frac{1}{10} = ₹\ 375$

17. (D) Vishal's Old Share $= \frac{2}{10}$

Debit balance of profit and loss account = ₹ 50,000

Vishal's share of loss $= 50,000 \times \frac{2}{10} = ₹\ 10,000$

18. (B) Investment Fluctuation Reserve A/c Dr 40,000
To Investment A/c 30,000
To X's Capital A/c 5,000
To Y's Capital A/c 3,333
To Z's Capital A/c 1,667

19. (C) Aarti's Share $= \frac{2}{5} - \frac{3}{5} = -\frac{1}{5}$ (Gain)

Bharti's Share $= \frac{3}{5} - \frac{2}{5} = \frac{1}{5}$ (Sacrificing)

JOURNAL

Date	Particulars	Amt (Dr)	Amt (Cr)
	Aarti's Capital A/c $\left(40{,}000 \times \frac{1}{5}\right)$ Dr	8,000	
	To Bharti's Capital A/c		8,000
	(Being adjustment entry passed)		

20. (D) Gaining ratio

Malika $= \frac{7}{15} - \frac{2}{5} = \frac{1}{15}$; Meera $= \frac{5}{15} - \frac{2}{5} = \left(\frac{1}{15}\right)$

Madhu $= \frac{3}{15} - \frac{1}{5} =$ Nil

Amount to be compensated by Malika

$= 30{,}000 \times \frac{1}{15} = ₹\ 2{,}000$

21. (D) Revaluation loss $= 5{,}000 \times \frac{9}{3} = ₹\ 15{,}000$

Outstanding workmen claim transferred to revaluation account = ₹ 15,000

Total workmen claim = 65,000 + 15,000
= ₹ 80,000

22. (A) **Sacrificing /(Gaining) Ratio**

Arun $= \frac{3}{8} - \frac{1}{3} = \frac{1}{24}$; Babita $= \frac{3}{8} - \frac{1}{3} = \frac{1}{24}$

Charu $= \frac{2}{8} - \frac{1}{3} = \left(\frac{2}{24}\right)$

23. (A) **Calculation of Gaining/Sacrificing Ratio**

Samiksha $= \frac{5}{10} - \frac{2}{10} = \frac{3}{10}$ (Sacrifice)

Arshiya $= \frac{3}{10} - \frac{5}{10} = \left(\frac{2}{10}\right)$ (Gain)

Divya $= \frac{2}{10} - \frac{3}{10} = \left(\frac{1}{10}\right)$ (Gain)

Calculation of Profit/Loss on Revaluation Amt (₹)

Debit Balance of Profit and Loss Account	=	(50,000)
Investment Fluctuation Fund (40,000 – 20,000)	=	20,000
Loss	=	(30,000)

Share of loss between partners in their sacrificing/gaining ratio

Samiksha $= (30{,}000) \times \frac{3}{10} = ₹\ (9{,}000)$

Arshiya $= (30{,}000) \times \frac{2}{10} = ₹\ 6{,}000$

Divya $= 30{,}000 \times \frac{1}{10} = ₹\ 3{,}000$

24. (D) Partner taking firm's assets will be debited to partners capital account.

25. (C) Stock is taken over by a partner at ₹ 2,000 less value. Therefore, this loss will be transferred to debit side of revaluation account.

26. (A) **Profit/Loss on Revaluation Amt (₹)**

Furniture	5,000
Printers	(3,500)
Machinery	(6,000)
Stock	10,000
Creditors	500
Profit	6,000

Gaining/Sacrificing Ratio

P $= \frac{3}{6} - \frac{1}{3} = \frac{1}{6}$ (Sacrifice)

Q $= \frac{2}{6} - \frac{1}{3} = 0$

R $= \frac{1}{6} - \frac{1}{3} = \left(\frac{1}{6}\right)$ (Gain)

JOURNAL

Date	Particulars	Amt (Dr)	Amt (Cr)
	R's Capital A/c Dr	1,000	
	To P's Capital A/c (6,000 ×1/6)		1,000

27. (B) Increase in land = ₹ 2,00,000
Decrease in machinery = ₹ (3,00,000)
Loss on revaluation = ₹ (1,00,000)

28. (D) Value of machinery $= \frac{40,000}{133.33} \times 100$

$= ₹ 30,000$

29. (D) A. Net Profit = 2,50,000 – 5,000 = ₹ 2,45,000

B. Net Profit = 2,50,000 –10,000 = ₹ 2,40,000

C. Net Profit = 2,50,000 + 10,000 = ₹ 2,60,000

D. Net Prfoit = 2,50,000 – 20,000 = ₹ 2,30,000

30. (A) A. Goodwill = Average Profit × No. of Years Purchase

= 3,00,000 × 4 = ₹ 12,00,000

B. I. Capitalised Value of the Firm

$= \frac{\text{Average Profit} \times 100}{\text{Normal Rate of Return}}$

$= \frac{3,00,000 \times 100}{10} = ₹\ 30,00,000$

II. Net Assets = ₹ 10,00,000

Goodwill = I – II

= 30,00,000 – 10,00,000= ₹ 20,00,000

C. Goodwill = Super Profit* × No. of Years Purchase

= 2,00,000 × 4 = ₹ 8,00,000

Average Profit = ₹ 3,00,000

Normal Profit

$= \text{Capital Employed} \times \frac{\text{Normal Rate of Return}}{100}$

$= 10,00,000 \times \frac{10}{100} = ₹\ 1,00,000$

∴ *Super Profit = 3,00,000 – 1,00,000

= ₹ 2,00,000

31. (C) (iii) (ii) (i)

32. (D) (iii) (i) (iv) (ii)

Assertion-Reason Questions

1. (A) Both Assertion (A) and Reason (R) are true and Reason (R) is the correct explanation of Assertion (A)
2. (B) Both Assertion (A) and Reason (R) are true, but Reason (R) is not the correct explanation of Assertion (A)
3. (B) Both Assertion (A) and Reason (R) are true, but Reason (R) is not the correct explanation of Assertion (A)
4. (A) Both Assertion (A) and Reason (R) are true and Reason (R) is the correct explanation of Assertion (A)
5. (B) Both Assertion (A) and Reason (R) are true, but Reason (R) is not the correct explanation of Assertion (A)
6. (C) Assertion (A) is true, but Reason (R) is false
7. (B) Both Assertion (A) and Reason (R) are true, but Reason (R) is not the correct explanation of Assertion (A)
8. (B) Both Assertion (A) and Reason (R) are true, but Reason (R) is not the correct explanation of Assertion (A)

Correct/Incorrect Statements

1. (A) Both statements are correct
2. (B) Goodwill is the "present value" of a firm's anticipated excess earnings.
3. (B) Change in profit sharing ratio does affect the relationship of the partners as the old agreement comes to an end and new agreement is created.
4. (B) Accumulated profits are distributed among the partners in their old ratio.
5. (A) Both statements are correct
6. (B) Employees provident fund is a liability and not a reserve.
7. (A) Both statements are correct

Case Based Questions

1. (i) (B) 2021= 6,00,000 – 50,000 – 40,000 + 4,000 – 4,800 = ₹ 5,09,200

(ii) (C) 2020 = 5,00,000 + 40,000 + 4,000 – 4,800 = ₹ 5,39,200

(iii) (C) 2019 = 4,00,000 + 50,000 – 4,800 – 40,000 + 1,000 = ₹ 4,06,200

2022 = 7,00,000 + 4,000 – 4,800 = ₹ 6,99,200

Average Profit $= \frac{21,53,800}{4}$

= ₹ 5,38,450

2. (i) (C) M = 2/10 – 1/5 = Nil

(ii) (D) Balance in Workmen Compensation Fund = 1,35,000 – 60,000 = ₹ 75,000

M's Share in Workmen Compensation = 75,000 × 2/10 = ₹ 15,000

(iii) (B) Revaluation Gain = ₹ 60,000

S's Share = 60,000 × 3/10 = ₹ 18,000

Subjective Questions

1. Average Profit = 3,60,000 – 1,20,000 (Salary) = ₹ 2,40,000

Normal Profit = $(5,00,000 + 3,00,000 + 1,50,000 - 50,000 + 1,00,000) \times \frac{15}{100}$ = ₹ 1,50,000

So, Super Profit = 2,40,000 – 1,50,000 = ₹ 90,000

∴ Goodwill = 90,000 × 2 = ₹ 1,80,000

2. **JOURNAL**

Date	Particulars		Amt (Dr)	Amt (Cr)
	Sam's Capital A/c	Dr	25,000	
	Arsh's Capital A/c	Dr	15,000	
	Dona's Capital A/c	Dr	10,000	
	To Profit and Loss A/c			50,000
	(Being loss distributed)			
	Investment Fluctuation Fund A/c	Dr	40,000	
	To Investment A/c			20,000
	To Sam's Capital A/c			10,000
	To Arsh's Capital A/c			6,000
	To Dona's Capital A/c			4,000
	(Being investment fluctuation fund distributed among partners)			
	Dona's Capital A/c	Dr	21,000	
	To Sam's Capital A/c			21,000
	(Being goodwill adjustment made)			

3. A's share = $\frac{2}{9} - \frac{4}{9} = -\frac{2}{9}$ (Gain) ; B's share = $\frac{3}{9} - \frac{3}{9} = 0$; C's share = $\frac{4}{9} - \frac{2}{9} = \frac{2}{9}$ (Sacrificing)

JOURNAL

Date	Particulars		Amt (Dr)	Amt (Cr)
	A's Capital A/c $\left(45,000 \times \frac{2}{9}\right)$	Dr	10,000	
	To C's Capital A/c $\left(45,000 \times \frac{2}{9}\right)$			10,000
	(Being adjustment of reserve, profit and loss and advertisement suspense)			

4. A's Share = $\frac{5}{12} - \frac{4}{9} = \frac{15-16}{36} = \left(\frac{1}{36}\right)$ (Gain) ; B's Share = $\frac{4}{12} - \frac{3}{9} = \frac{12-12}{36} = 0$

C's Share = $\frac{3}{12} - \frac{2}{9} = \frac{9-8}{36} = \frac{1}{36}$ (Sacrificing)

JOURNAL

Date	Particulars		LF	Amt (Dr)	Amt (Cr)
	A's Capital A/c $\left(82,000 \times \frac{1}{36}\right)$	Dr		2,278	
	To C's Capital A/c				2,278

Dr **Partners' Capital Account** Cr

Particulars	A (₹)	B (₹)	C (₹)	Particulars	A (₹)	B (₹)	C (₹)
To C's Capital A/c	2,278	—	—	By Balance b/d	1,00,000	2,00,000	3,00,000
To Balance c/d	97,722	2,00,000	3,02,278	By A's Capital A/c	—	—	2,278
	1,00,000	2,00,000	3,02,278		1,00,000	2,00,000	3,02,278

5. Sacrificing/(Gaining) Share = Old Share – New Share

Mehak $= \frac{5}{10} - \frac{4}{10} = \frac{1}{10}$ Sacrificing; Ayush $= \frac{3}{10} - \frac{3}{10} =$ Nil

Anshu $= \frac{2}{10} - \frac{3}{10} = \frac{2-3}{10} = \left(\frac{1}{10}\right)$ Gain

JOURNAL

Date	Particulars		LF	Amt (Dr)	Amt (Cr)
	General Reserve A/c	Dr		80,000	
	To Mehak's Capital A/c				40,000
	To Ayush's Capital A/c				24,000
	To Anshu's Capital A/c				16,000
	(Being general reserve transferred to partners in their old ratio)				
	Mehak's Capital A/c	Dr		25,000	
	Ayush's Capital A/c	Dr		15,000	
	Anshu's Capital A/c	Dr		10,000	
	To Revaluation A/c				50,000
	(Being loss on revaluation transferred to partners capital account)				
	Anshu's Capital A/c (3,00,000 × 1/ 10)	Dr		30,000	
	To Mehak's Capital A/c (3,00,000 × 1/ 10)				30,000
	(Being treatment of goodwill due to change in profit sharing ratio)				

6. **Calculation of Sacrificing/Gaining Ratio**

Sacrificing Ratio = Old Ratio – New Ratio

Asha $= \frac{2}{5} - \frac{1}{3} = \frac{6-5}{15} = \frac{1}{15}$; Rina $= \frac{2}{5} - \frac{1}{3} = \frac{6-5}{15} = \frac{1}{15}$; Chahat $= \frac{1}{5} - \frac{1}{3} = \frac{3-5}{15} = \left(\frac{2}{15}\right)$

JOURNAL

Date	Particulars		LF	Amt (Dr)	Amt (Cr)
	Chahat's Capital A/c	Dr		20,000	
	To Asha's Capital A/c				10,000
	To Rina's Capital A/c				10,000
	(Being amount of goodwill adjusted)				
	Provision for Doubtful Debts A/c	Dr		20,000	
	Revaluation A/c	Dr		20,000	
	To Debtors A/c				40,000
	(Being bad debts written-off)				

Date	Particulars		LF	Amt (Dr)	Amt (Cr)
	Revaluation A/c	Dr		11,000	
	To Provision for Doubtful Debts				11,000
	(Being 5% PFDD created)				
	Asha's Capital A/c	Dr		12,400	
	Rina's Capital A/c	Dr		12,400	
	Chahat Capital A/c	Dr		6,200	
	To Revaluation A/c				31,000
	(Being revaluation loss transferred to partner's capital account)				

Working Note

Dr **Revaluation Account** Cr

Particulars	Amt (₹)	Particulars		Amt (₹)
To Debtors A/c	20,000	By Revaluation Loss transferred to Capital A/c		
To Provision for Doubtful Debts	11,000	Asha	12,400	
		Rina	12,400	
		Chahat	6,200	31,000
	31,000			31,000

7. **JOURNAL**

Date	Particulars		LF	Amt (Dr)	Amt (Cr)
	Profit and Loss A/c	Dr		75,000	
	To Hari's Capital A/c				37,500
	To Kunal's Capital A/c				22,500
	To Uma's Capital A/c				15,000
	(Being balance of profit and loss distributed among partners in old ratio)				
	Kunal's Capital A/c $\left(3{,}00{,}000 \times \frac{2}{10}\right)$	Dr		60,000	
	Uma's Capital A/c $\left(3{,}00{,}000 \times \frac{1}{10}\right)$	Dr		30,000	
	To Hari's Capital A/c $\left(3{,}00{,}000 \times \frac{3}{10}\right)$				90,000
	(Being amount of goodwill adjusted)				
	Investment Fluctuation Fund A/c	Dr		15,000	
	To Investment A/c				15,000
	(Being investment loss adjusted through investment fluctuation fund)				
	Revaluation A/c	Dr		5,000	
	To Stock A/c				5,000
	(Being value of stock depreciated)				
	Hari's Capital A/c	Dr		2,500	
	Kunal's Capital A/c	Dr		1,500	
	Uma's Capital A/c	Dr		1,000	
	To Revaluation A/c				5,000
	(Being loss on revaluation transferred to old partners' capital account in old ratio)				

Working Note

Calculation of Gaining or Sacrificing Ratio

Sacrificing Ratio = Old Ratio – New Ratio

Hari $= \frac{5}{10} - \frac{2}{10} = \frac{3}{10}$; Kunal $= \frac{3}{10} - \frac{5}{10} = \left(\frac{2}{10}\right)$; Uma $= \frac{2}{10} - \frac{3}{10} = \left(\frac{1}{10}\right)$

8. Dr **Revaluation Account** Cr

Particulars		Amt ₹	Particulars	Amt ₹
To Building A/c		3,000	By Land A/c	30,000
To Profit transferred to Capital A/cs			By Creditors A/c	6,000
R	5,500			
S	11,000			
T	16,500	33,000		
		36,000		36,000

Dr **Partners' Capital Account** Cr

Particulars	R (₹)	S (₹)	T (₹)	Particulars	R (₹)	S (₹)	T (₹)
To T's Capital A/c (Goodwill)	25,000	—	—	By Balance b/d	1,00,000	50,000	25,000
				By Revaluation A/c (Profit)	5,500	11,000	16,500
To Balance c/d	85,500	71,000	81,500				
				By R's Capital A/c	—	—	25,000
				By General Reserve A/c	5,000	10,000	15,000
	1,10,500	71,000	81,500		1,10,500	71,000	81,500

Balance Sheet
as at 1st April, 2024

Liabilities		Amt ₹	Assets		Amt ₹
Creditors	50,000		Land	50,000	
(–) Written-off	(6,000)	44,000	(+) Appreciation	30,000	80,000
Bills Payable		20,000	Building	50,000	
Capital A/cs			(–) Depreciation	(3,000)	47,000
R	85,500		Plant		1,00,000
S	71,000		Stock		40,000
T	81,500	2,38,000	Debtors		30,000
			Bank		5,000
		3,02,000			3,02,000

Working Note

Calculation of Sacrifice or Gain of Each Partner

Sacrificing/(Gaining) Share = Old Share – New Share

R $= \frac{1}{6} - \frac{1}{3} = \frac{1-2}{6} = \left(\frac{1}{6}\right)$ Gain ; S $= \frac{2}{6} - \frac{1}{3} = \frac{2-2}{6} =$ Nil ; T $= \frac{3}{6} - \frac{1}{3} = \frac{3-2}{6} = \frac{1}{6}$ Sacrifice

Firm's goodwill = ₹ 1,50,000

R will pay for goodwill = 1,50,000 × 1/6 = ₹25,000

R's Capital A/c	Dr	25,000	
To T's Capital A/c			25,000

9. Dr **Revaluation Account** Cr

Particulars		Amt (₹)	Particulars	Amt (₹)
To Stock A/c		40,000	By Machinery A/c	**1,60,000**
To Provision for Doubtful Debts A/c		40,000	By Sundry Creditors A/c	40,000
To Outstanding Expenses A/c		**40,000**		
To Profit transferred to Capital A/cs				
P	**32,000**			
Q	**32,000**			
R	**16,000**	**80,000**		
		2,00,000		2,00,000

Dr **Partners' Capital Account** Cr

Particulars	P (₹)	Q (₹)	R (₹)	Particulars	P (₹)	Q (₹)	R (₹)
To Advertisement Suspense A/c	**16,000**	**16,000**	**8,000**	By Balance b/d	**5,84,000**	**5,44,000**	**5,12,000**
To Balance c/d	6,00,000	5,60,000	5,20,000	By Revaluation A/c	32,000	32,000	16,000
	6,16,000	5,76,000	5,28,000		6,16,000	5,76,000	5,28,000

CHAPTER-3

Reconstitution of a Partnership Firm : Admission of a Partner

Types & Nos. of Questions

Multiple Choice Questions	– 34
Assertion-Reason Questions	– 8
Correct/Incorrect Statements	– 9
Case Based Questions	– 2 Cases, *with 3/4 Questions*
Subjective Questions	– 9

Trend Analysis

On the basis of analysis of last 2 years' papers, it is found that on an average 3 Multiple Choice Questions and 1 Long Answer Type Question are asked from this chapter.

Focus Topics of the Chapter

- New Profit Sharing Ratio and Sacrificing Ratio
- Treatment of Goodwill
- Adjustment for Reserves and Accumulated Profits/Losses
- Revaluation of Asset and Reassessment of Liabilities
- Adjustment of Capital

Multiple Choice Questions

No. of Questions : **34** Suggested Time : **50 Minutes**

Direction Each of the question given below is Multiple Choice Question (MCQ) i.e. there are Four Options/Choices for answer, out of which ONLY ONE is correct. You have to select the correct option. A response box is given with each option, mark (✓) in the box of the correct option. For each correct answer you will get 1 mark, while there is no penalty for incorrect answer or missed out questions.

1. Raju and Bantu are partners in a firm sharing profits and losses in the ratio of 3 : 2. Chintu is admitted for 4/25 share. Raju agreed to contribute 3/25 of his share in favour of Chintu and remaining taken over by Bantu. The new profit sharing will be

(A) 4 : 3 : 2 ☐
(B) 3 : 2 : 4 ☐
(C) 48 : 66 : 11 ☐
(D) 66 : 39 : 20 ☐

2. A newly admitted partner has

(A) right to share asset of the firm ☐
(B) right to share future profit of the firm ☐
(C) Both (A) and (B) ☐
(D) None of the above ☐

3. Employees provident fund is not distributed among the partners because it is a

(A) statutory liability ☐
(B) accumulated profit ☐
(C) free reserve ☐
(D) fictitious asset ☐

4. X and Y were partners sharing profits and losses in the ratio of 7:3. Z was admitted for 1/5th share in the profits which he took 75% from X and remaining from Y. Sacrificing ratio of X and Y will be

(A) 1 : 1 ☐ (B) 3 : 2 ☐
(C) 7 : 3 ☐ (D) 3 : 1 ☐

5. A, B and C were partners sharing profits and losses in the ratio of 1/2, 1/3 and 1/6. D was admitted in the firm for 1/6th share. C would retain his original share. New ratio will be

(A) 1 : 1 : 1 : 1 ☐ (B) 3 : 2 : 1 : 1 ☐
(C) 12 : 8 : 5 : 3 ☐ (D) 12 : 8 : 5 : 5 ☐

6. A, B, C and D are partners. A and B share 2/3rd of profits equally while C and D share remaining profits in the ratio of 3 : 2. Profit sharing ratio of the partners will be

(A) 5 : 5 : 3 : 2 ☐
(B) 7 : 7 : 6 : 4 ☐
(C) 5 : 5 : 16 : 12 ☐
(D) 3 : 9 : 8 : 3 ☐

7. A and B are partners in the ratio of 3 : 2. C is admitted as a partner and he takes 1/16th of his share from A and 3/16th share from B. What is the share of C?

(A) 1/4 ☐ (B) 1/6 ☐
(C) 1/16 ☐ (D) 1/8 ☐

8. Ravi and Kishan are partners in a firm. Chitra admitted as new partner and new ratio is 5 : 3 : 4. If Ravi and Kishan made equal sacrifice to accommodate Chitra, the old profit sharing ratio was

(A) 1 : 1 ☐ (B) 7 : 5 ☐
(C) 4 : 3 ☐ (D) 5 : 7 ☐

9. Gupta and Sharma are partners in a firm sharing profits in the ratio of 4 : 1. They admitted Preeti as a new partner for 1/4th share in the profits, which she acquired wholly from Gupta.

New profit sharing ratio of Gupta, Sharma and Preeti will be *[CBSE 2024]*

(A) 2 : 1 : 1 ☐ (B) 11 : 4 : 5 ☐
(C) 3 : 3 : 2 ☐ (D) 7 : 5 : 4 ☐

10. Akshita and Anurag are partners in a firm sharing profits in the ratio of 2 :1. Akshat is admitted in the firm with 1/3 share in profits. Akshat acquires 2/3 of his share from Akshita and 1/3 of his share from Anurag. The new profit sharing ratio of Akshita, Anurag and Akshat will be *[CBSE 2023]*

(A) 3 : 2 : 4 ☐ (B) 4 : 3 : 2 ☐
(C) 2 : 1 : 1 ☐ (D) 4 : 2 : 3 ☐

11. Virat and Anushka share profits and losses equally. Their capital were ₹ 1,20,000 and ₹ 80,000 respectively. There was also a balance of ₹ 30,000 in general reserves and revaluation gain amounted to ₹ 7,500.

They admit their friend, Rohit with 1/5th share and he brings ₹ 1,50,000 as capital. Calculate the amount of goodwill of the firm.

(A) ₹ 1,00,000 ☐
(B) ₹ 3,62,500 ☐
(C) ₹ 20,000 ☐
(D) ₹ 7,50,000 ☐

12. A and B are partners sharing profits and losses in the ratio of 7 : 3. They decided to admit C as a new partner and new ratio will be 4 : 3 : 3. C paid ₹ 10,000 as his share of goodwill. Amount of goodwill transferred to the capital of B will be

(A) ₹ 1,200 ☐
(B) ₹ 4,800 ☐
(C) ₹ 3,600 ☐
(D) Nil ☐

13. Tarun and Bhushan are partners sharing profits and losses in the ratio of 5:2. They decided to admit Rishi as a new partner and new ratio is 3:3:1. Rishi paid ₹ 10,000 as his share of goodwill. Bhushan's capital account is to be credited/debited with

(A) debited by ₹ 10,000 ☐
(B) credited by ₹ 10,000 ☐
(C) debited by ₹ 2,850 ☐
(D) credited by ₹ 2,850 ☐

14. A and B are partners sharing profits and losses in the ratio of 5 : 3. They decided to admit C as a new partner and profit sharing ratio become 3 : 2 : 3.

On the date of admission, C's share of goodwill is ₹ 42,000 out of which C only bring ₹ 18,000 in cash. Capital accounts of A and B credited with

(A) A = ₹ 26,250; B = ₹ 15,750 ☐
(B) A = ₹ 12,000; B = ₹ 6,000 ☐
(C) A = ₹ 15,000; B = ₹ 9,000 ☐
(D) A = ₹ 28,000; B = ₹ 14,000 ☐

15. X, Y and Z are partners sharing profits in 2 : 1 : 1. On 1st April, 2023, they admitted A as a new partner. New profit sharing ratio decided 1 : 2 : 1 : 1.

Y's capital account was debited with ₹ 18,000. How much premium for goodwill was brought by A?

(A) ₹ 1,20,000 ☐
(B) ₹ 1,08,000 ☐
(C) ₹ 24,000 ☐
(D) ₹ 30,000 ☐

16. Karan and Laxmi are partners sharing profits and losses in the ratio of 3 : 2. Amit was admitted as a new partner with 1/5th share in the profits and brought in ₹ 4,000 as his share of goodwill premium that was credited to the capital accounts of Karan and Laxmi with ₹ 3,000 and ₹ 1,000 respectively. New ratio will be

(A) 3 : 2 : 1 ☐ (B) 1 : 1 : 1 ☐
(C) 9 : 4 : 7 ☐ (D) 9 : 7 : 4 ☐

17. Disha and Abha were partners in a firm. Farad was admitted as a new partner for 1/5th share in profit of firm. Farad brought proportionate capital. Capitals of Disha and Abha after all adjustments were ₹ 64,000 and ₹ 46,000 respectively. Capital brought by Farad was

(A) ₹ 22,000 ☐ (B) ₹ 27,500 ☐
(C) ₹ 55,000 ☐ (D) ₹ 28,000 ☐

18. Puneet and Deepak were in partnership sharing profits and losses in the ratio of 2 : 1. They admitted Manya as a new partner. Manya brought ₹ 1,00,000 as her share of goodwill premium, which was entirely credited to Puneet's capital account.

On the date of admission, goodwill of the firm was valued at ₹ 3,00,000. Calculate the new profit sharing ratio of Puneet, Deepak and Manya.

(A) 2 : 1 : 1 ☐ (B) 1 : 1 : 1 ☐
(C) 4 : 3 : 2 ☐ (D) 1 : 2 : 2 ☐

19. Amit and Sumit were partners in a firm with fixed capitals of ₹ 6,00,000 and ₹ 4,00,000 respectively. Kavi was admitted as a new partner for 1/5th share in the profit of the firm. Kavi brought ₹ 40,000 as his share of goodwill premium and ₹ 3,00,000 as his capital. The amount of goodwill premium credited to Sumit will be *[CBSE 2023]*

(A) ₹ 20,000 ☐ (B) ₹ 24,000 ☐
(C) ₹ 16,000 ☐ (D) ₹ 40,000 ☐

20. Ram and Krishna were partners sharing profits and losses in the ratio of 2 : 1. They admitted Shanker as a partner for 1/5th share in the profits. For this purpose the goodwill of the firm was to be valued on the basis of three times of last five years average profits. The profits for the last five years were

Year	2016-17	2017-18	2018-19	2019-20	2020-21
Profit (₹)	50,000	40,000	75,000	(25,000)	50,000

Profit of 2017-18 was calculated after charging ₹ 10,000 for abnormal loss of goods by fire.

The value of goodwill of the firm is

(A) ₹ 1,28,000 ☐ (B) ₹ 2,00,000 ☐
(C) ₹ 1,90,000 ☐ (D) ₹ 1,20,000 ☐

21. Angle and Circle were partners in a firm. Their balance sheet showed furniture at ₹ 2,00,000, Stock at ₹ 1,40,000, Debtors at ₹ 1,62,000 and Creditors at ₹ 60,000. Square was admitted and new profit sharing ratio was agreed at 2:3:5.

Stock was revalued at ₹ 1,00,000, Creditors of ₹ 15,000 are not likely to be claimed, debtors for ₹ 2,000 have become irrecoverable and provision for doubtful debts to be provided @ 10%. Angle's share in loss on revaluation amounted to ₹ 30,000. Revalued value of furniture will be

(A) ₹ 2,17,000 ☐ (B) ₹ 1,03,000 ☐
(C) ₹ 3,03,000 ☐ (D) ₹ 1,83,000 ☐

22. A and B are equal partners. C is admitted for 1/4th share in profit. Building (Book value ₹ 35,000) is decreased by 10%. Creditors are increased by ₹ 2,000. Bills payable decreased by ₹ 1,000. Trademark (Book value ₹ 3,000) are valueless. Profit/Loss on revaluation is

(A) ₹ 7,500 (Loss) ☐ (B) ₹ 8,500 (Loss) ☐
(C) ₹ 6,500 (Profit) ☐ (D) ₹ 5,500 (Profit) ☐

23. Sun and Moon were partners in a firm sharing profits and losses in the ratio of 2 : 1. Star was admitted as a new partner and new ratio decided at 4 : 3 : 3. Star will bring machine worth ₹ 50,000, Stock worth ₹ 10,000, Debtors worth ₹ 5,000 as his capital and goodwill.

If his share of capital is ₹ 50,000, find goodwill of the firm.

(A) ₹ 15,000 ☐ (B) ₹ 30,000 ☐
(C) ₹ 45,000 ☐ (D) ₹ 50,000 ☐

24. A and B are partners sharing profits and losses in the ratio of 2 : 3. Their balance sheet shows Machinery at ₹ 2,00,000, Stock at ₹ 80,000 and Debtors at ₹ 1,60,000. C was admitted and new profit sharing ratio is agreed at 6 : 9 : 5.

Machinery is revalued at ₹ 1,40,000 and a provision is made for doubtful debts @ 5%. A's share in loss on revaluation amount to ₹ 20,000. Revalued value of stock will be

(A) ₹ 62,000 ☐ (B) ₹ 1,00,000 ☐
(C) ₹ 60,000 ☐ (D) ₹ 98,000 ☐

25. Atul and Vipul are partners in a firm sharing profits and losses equally. They decided to admit Kavi as a new partner with 1/5th share in the firm. On admission, debtor whose dues of ₹ 15,000 were written-off as bad debt, paid ₹ 10,000 in full settlement. Entry for above will be

(A) Debit Cash and Credit Revaluation Account ☐
(B) Debit Bad Debt Recovered and Credit Bad Debt ☐
(C) Debit Cash and Credit Bad Debt Account ☐
(D) Debit Revaluation and Credit Bad Debt Recovered ☐

26. Amar and Akbar were partners sharing profits and losses in the ratio 3 : 2. They decided to admit Anthony into partnership with 1/5 share.

Workmen compensation reserve appears in balance sheet at ₹ 40,000. Claim against workmen compensation will be ₹ 50,000. It's effect will be

(A) distribute ₹ 10,000 among old partners ☐
(B) distribute ₹ 40,000 among old partners ☐
(C) debit ₹ 10,000 in revaluation account ☐
(D) credit ₹ 10,000 in revaluation account ☐

27. Choose the correct sequence from the following.

(i) Treatment of change in value of assets
(ii) Treatment of goodwill of new partner
(iii) Calculation of sacrifice ratio
(iv) Closing of capital account

Codes

(A) (i), (ii), (iii), (iv) ☐
(B) (i), (iii), (ii), (iv) ☐
(C) (iii), (ii), (i), (iv) ☐
(D) (ii), (iii), (i), (iv) ☐

28. Following balances were appearing in balance sheet Debtors ₹ 60,000, Provision for bad debts ₹ 5,000. Partners decided to maintain provision at 5% on debtors. What will be the effect of above adjustment?

(A) Debit revaluation account by ₹ 3,000 ☐
(B) Debit revaluation account by ₹ 5,000 ☐
(C) Credit revaluation account by ₹ 2,000 ☐
(D) Distribute ₹ 3,000 in partners' capital account ☐

29. Rohit and Mohit were partners sharing profits and losses in the ratio of 2 :1. Their capital accounts as on 31st March, 2021 had a credit balance of ₹ 1,09,000 and ₹ 66,000 respectively. They admitted Sahil as a new partner on 1st April, 2021 for 1/5th share in profits.

Sahil brought ₹ 25,000 as his share of goodwill premium. He agreed to contribute capital in new profit sharing ratio. The amount of capital brought by Sahil was *[CBSE 2023]*

(A) ₹ 40,000 ☐
(B) ₹ 32,000 ☐
(C) ₹ 12,50,000 ☐
(D) ₹ 50,000 ☐

30. At the time of admission of a partner, the balance sheet of the firm showed a workmen compensation reserve of ₹ 80,000. The claim for workmen compensation was estimated at ₹ 1,00,000. The shortfall of ₹ 20,000 will be *[CBSE 2024]*

(A) debited to revaluation account ☐
(B) credited to revaluation account ☐
(C) debited to partners' capital account ☐
(D) credited to partners' capital account ☐

31. Match the following

Column I	Column II
A. Goodwill appear in the books at the time of admission of a partner	(i) Is to be done in new ratio
B. When goodwill is brought by new partner in cash	(ii) Write-off among old partners in old ratio
C. Adjustment of capital	(iii) Distributed among old partners in sacrificing ratio

Codes

	A	B	C			A	B	C	
(A)	(ii)	(iii)	(i)	☐	(B)	(ii)	(i)	(iii)	☐
(C)	(i)	(iii)	(ii)	☐	(D)	(i)	(ii)	(iii)	☐

32. Match the following

Column I	Column II
A. Building undervalued	(i) Credit side of partners' capital account
B. Building overvalued	(ii) Debit side of revaluation account
C. Asset taken over by a partner	(iii) Credit side of revaluation account
D. Profit and loss account (Credit).	(iv) Debit side of partners' capital account

Codes

	A	B	C	D	
(A)	(iv)	(i)	(ii)	(iii)	☐
(B)	(iii)	(ii)	(iv)	(i)	☐
(C)	(iii)	(i)	(iv)	(ii)	☐
(D)	(i)	(iii)	(iv)	(ii)	☐

33. Match the following

Column I	Column II
A. Goodwill	(i) Real account
B. Partners' capital account	(ii) Personal account
C. Revaluation account	(iii) Nominal account

Codes

	A	B	C			A	B	C	
(A)	(i)	(iii)	(ii)	☐	(B)	(i)	(ii)	(iii)	☐
(C)	(ii)	(i)	(iii)	☐	(D)	(ii)	(iii)	(i)	☐

34. Match the following

Column I	Column II
A. Increase in the value of furniture	(i) Revaluation account credit
B. Sale of machinery	(ii) Not to be shown in revaluation account
C. Increase in provision	(iii) Revaluation account debit

Codes

	A	B	C			A	B	C	
(A)	(iii)	(ii)	(i)	☐	(B)	(i)	(ii)	(iii)	☐
(C)	(iii)	(i)	(ii)	☐	(D)	(ii)	(i)	(iii)	☐

Assertion-Reason Questions

No. of Questions : **8** Suggested Time : **15 Minutes**

Direction Each of the question given below consist of the two statements; one labelled as **Assertion** (A) and other as **Reason** (R) List of common options applicable for each question is given below

(A) Both Assertion (A) and Reason (R) are true and Reason (R) is the correct explanation of Assertion (A)

(B) Both Assertion (A) and Reason (R) are true, but Reason (R) is not the correct explanation of Assertion (A)

(C) Assertion (A) is true, but Reason (R) is false

(D) Assertion (A) is false, but Reason (R) is true

You have to select the codes as *A, B, C* or *D* as your answer to the question by marking ✓) in the response box given against each option.

1. Assertion (A) A new partner can be admitted, if it is agreed in the deed but in the absence of deed, a new partner can be admitted only if all the partners agree to admit that partner.

Reason (R) In the absence of deed, Section 31 of the Indian Partnership Act, 1932 will be applicable.

(A) ☐ (B) ☐

(C) ☐ (D) ☐

2. **Assertion (A)** A new partner should contribute towards goodwill on his/her admission.

Reason (R) The new partner has to compensate the existing partners for the sacrifice they make in his/her favour.

(A) ☐ (B) ☐
(C) ☐ (D) ☐

3. **Assertion (A)** Ajay and Vijay are partners sharing profits and losses in the ratio of 2 : 1. They admit Sujal into business for 1/4th share in profit. On this date, goodwill account appears in books for ₹ 10,000. Partners decided to value goodwill at ₹ 25,000 on admission of new partner. They divide difference of ₹ 15,000 in old ratio for treatment of goodwill.

Reason (R) Excess goodwill of ₹ 15,000 will be divided among partners in old ratio as new partner will compensate goodwill to old partners.

(A) ☐ (B) ☐ (C) ☐ (D) ☐

4. **Assertion (A)** At the time of admission of new partner, general reserve appearing in old balance sheet is distributed among old partners.

Reason (R) General reserve is a past profit and it will be used in contigency, hence it cannot be distributed among old partners.

(A) ☐ (B) ☐ (C) ☐ (D) ☐

5. **Assertion (A)** At the time of admission of a new partner, purchase of new asset will not be recorded in the revaluation account but if asset was written-off earlier and now it is brought back into the books, it will be shown in the credit side of revaluation account.

Reason (R) Revaluation account is prepared to record all types of assets whether assets are old or new, purchased or sold.

(A) ☐ (B) ☐
(C) ☐ (D) ☐

6. **Assertion (A)** Increase in the value of liabilities on reconstitution of a firm is debited to revaluation account.

Reason (R) Increase in the value of liabilities is a loss. *[CBSE 2023]*

(A) ☐ (B) ☐
(C) ☐ (D) ☐

7. **Assertion (A)** It is necessary to revalue assets and liabilities of a firm in case of admission of a partner.

Reason (R) It is because the incoming partner is neither put to an advantage nor to a disadvantage due to change in the value of assets and liabilities.

(A) ☐ (B) ☐
(C) ☐ (D) ☐

8. **Assertion (A)** Revaluation account is prepared at the time of admission of a partner.

Reason (R) It is required to adjust the values of assets and liabilities at the time of admission of a partner, so that the true financial position of the firm is reflected.

(A) ☐
(B) ☐
(C) ☐
(D) ☐

Correct/Incorrect Statements

No. of Questions : **9** Suggested Time : **15 Minutes**

Direction Each of the question given below consist of the two statements. List of common options applicable for each question is given below

(A) Both statements are correct
(B) Statement I is correct and Statement II is incorrect
(C) Statement I is incorrect and Statement II is correct
(D) Both statement are incorrect

You have to select the codes as *A, B, C* or *D* as your answer to the question by marking (✓) in the response box given against each option.

1. **Statement I** When a new partner is admitted, it is necessary to ascertain new profit sharing ratio for all partners.

   Statement II Profit sharing ratio among the old partners may change at the time of admission of a partner as they will compensate to new partner for his share in the business.

   (A) ☐ (B) ☐ (C) ☐ (D) ☐

2. **Statement I** Goodwill appearing in the balance sheet is transferred to partners' current account in case of fixed capitals.

   Statement II New partner acquires a right over the net assets when he brings capital into the firm.

   (A) ☐ (B) ☐ (C) ☐ (D) ☐

3. **Statement I** Old ratio + Sacrificing ratio = New ratio.

   Statement II If a partners' old share is less than new share, he is gaining.

   (A) ☐ (B) ☐ (C) ☐ (D) ☐

4. **Statement I** Unrecorded assets are debited and unrecorded liabilities are credited to revaluation account.

   Statement II Revaluation account shows gain or loss on revaluation of assets and liabilities which will be distributed among old partners in sacrificing ratio.

   (A) ☐ (B) ☐ (C) ☐ (D) ☐

5. **Statement I** Revaluation account is prepared at the time of admission of a partner only.

   Statement II Revaluation account shows the gain or loss arising due to change in value of any assets during reconstitution of the firm.

   (A) ☐ (B) ☐ (C) ☐ (D) ☐

6. **Statement I** Workmen reserve is transferred to revaluation account in case of admission of a partner.

   Statement II Employees provident fund is not distributed among the old partners.

   (A) ☐ (B) ☐ (C) ☐ (D) ☐

7. **Statement I** Increase in provision for doubtful debts will be recorded on the debit side of revaluation account.

   Statement II Machinery of ₹ 30,000 sold at ₹ 35,000 will not be recorded in the revaluation account.

   (A) ☐ (B) ☐ (C) ☐ (D) ☐

8. **Statement I** Loss on revaluation of assets will be debited to the partners' capital account.

   Statement II Goodwill appearing in the balance sheet will be written-off in sacrificing ratio.

   (A) ☐ (B) ☐
   (C) ☐ (D) ☐

9. **Statement I** An asset will be credited to partners' capital account if the asset is acquired by the partner.

Statement II If a furniture of ₹ 40,000 is taken over by X, a partner, at an agreed value of ₹ 45,000, then ₹ 45,000 will be credited to X's capital account.

(A) ☐ (B) ☐ (C) ☐ (D) ☐

Case Based Questions

No. of Questions : **2** Suggested Time : **10 Minutes**

Direction This section contains 2 cases each having 3/4 questions of 1 mark each. You have to write the answer of each question based on the context of the related case.

Case 1 Sterling Enterprises is a partnership business with Ryan, Williams and Sania as partners engaged in production and sales of electrical items and equipment.

Their capital contributions were ₹ 50,00,000, ₹ 50,00,000 and ₹ 80,00,000 respectively with the profit sharing ratio of 5 : 5 : 8. As they are now looking forward to expanding their business, it was decided that they would bring in sufficient cash to double their respective capitals.

This was duly followed by Ryan and Williams but due to unavoidable reasons Sania could not do so and ultimately it was agreed that to bridge the shortfall in the required capital a new partner should be admitted who would bring in the amount that Sania could not bring and that the new partner would get share of profits equal to half of Sania's share which would be sacrificed by Sania only.

Consequent to this agreement Ejaz was admitted and he brought in the required capital and ₹ 30,00,000 as premium for goodwill. Based on the above information you are required to answer the following questions. *[CBSE QB]*

Questions

(i) What will be the new profit sharing ratio of Ryan, Williams, Sania and Ejaz?

(A) 1 : 1 : 1 : 1 ☐
(B) 5 : 5 : 8 : 8 ☐
(C) 5 : 5 : 4 : 4 ☐
(D) None of the above ☐

(ii) What is the amount of capital brought in by the new partner Ejaz?

(A) ₹ 50,00,000 ☐ (B) ₹ 80,00,000 ☐
(C) ₹ 40,00,000 ☐ (D) ₹ 30,00,000 ☐

(iii) What is the value of the goodwill of the firm?

(A) ₹ 1,35,00,000 ☐
(B) ₹ 30,00,000 ☐
(C) ₹ 1,50,00,000 ☐
(D) Cannot be determined from the given data ☐

(iv) What will be correct journal entry for distribution of premium for goodwill brought in by Ejaz?

(A) Ejaz Capital A/c ...... Dr 30,00,000
To Sania's Capital A/c 30,00,000
(Being...............................) ☐

(B) Premium for Goodwill A/c... Dr 30,00,000
To Sania's Capital A/c 30,00,000
(Being...............................) ☐

(C) Premium for Goodwill A/c......

	Dr	30,00,000
To Ryan's Capital A/c		8,33,333
To William's Capital A/c		8,33,333
To Ejaz's Capital A/c		13,33,333
(Being...............................)		☐

(D) Premium for Goodwill A/c......

	Dr	30,00,000
To Ryan's Capital A/c		10,00,000
To William's Capital A/c		10,00,000
To Ejaz's Capital A/c		10,00,000
(Being...............................)		☐

Case 2 Jolly and Mayank are partners since last 5 years. Vinod gets 75% of the profit and Mayank gets 25%. Their capitals are fixed. They need more capital for the business so they decided to admit a new partner Yuvraj for 1/4th share.

Yuvraj brings ₹ 3,00,000 as his capital. He could bring only 40% of his share in cash and furniture of ₹ 16,000 for his share of goodwill. Goodwill of the firm was valued at ₹ 2,40,000.

Questions

(i) The new ratio of the partners will be

(A) 3 : 1 : 1 ☐ (B) 5 : 3 : 2 ☐
(C) 9 : 4 : 3 ☐ (D) 9 : 3 : 4 ☐

(ii) How much amount of premium for goodwill brought in cash by Yuvraj?

(A) ₹ 9,600 ☐ (B) ₹ 24,000 ☐
(C) ₹ 25,600 ☐ (D) ₹ 24,600 ☐

(iii) Yuvraj was unable to bring .... as his share of goodwill.

(A) ₹ 24,000 ☐ (B) ₹ 9,600 ☐
(C) ₹ 34,400 ☐ (D) ₹ 20,000 ☐

Subjective Questions

Free Response Questions, Open-ended Questions etc.

No. of Questions : **9** Suggested Time : **70 Minutes**

1. A, B and C are partners sharing profits and losses in the ratio of 3 : 2. A's capital is ₹ 48,000 and B's capital ₹ 32,000. C is admitted for 1/5th share in profits. Calculate the amount of capital which C should bring.

2. A and B are partners sharing profits and losses in the ratio 3 : 2. C is admitted for 1/5th share. Afterwards D enters for 25 paise in the rupee. Calculate the new ratio of A, B, C and D.

3. Asin and Shreya are partners in a firm. They admit Ajay as a new partner with 1/5th share in the profits of the firm. Ajay brings ₹ 5,00,000 as his share of capital. The value of total assets of the firm was ₹ 15,00,000 and outside liabilities were valued at ₹ 5,00,000 on that date.

   Give the necessary journal entry to record goodwill at the time of Ajay's admission.

4. Anubhav and Babita are partners in a firm sharing profits and losses in the ratio of 3 : 2. On 1st April, 2021 they admit Deepak as a new partner for 3/13 share in the profits.

   Deepak contributed the following assets towards his capital and for his share of goodwill land ₹ 90,000, machinery ₹ 70,000, stock ₹ 60,000 and debtors ₹ 40,000.

   On the date of admission of Deepak, the goodwill of the firm was valued at ₹ 5,20,000, which is not to appear in the books. Record necessary journal entries in the books of the firm. Show your calculations clearly.

5. A and B were partners in a firm sharing profits and losses in 4:3 ratio. On 1st April, 2022 they admitted C as a new partner.

On the date of C's admission, the balance sheet of A and B showed a general reserve of ₹ 70,000 and a debit balance of ₹ 7,000 in profit and loss account.

Pass the necessary journal entries for the treatment of these items on C's admission.

6. B and C were partners sharing profits and losses in the ratio of 3 : 2. Their balance sheet as on 31st March, 2021 was as follows

Balance Sheet
as at 31st March, 2021

Liabilities	Amt (₹)	Assets	Amt (₹)
B's Capital	60,000	Land and Building	80,000
C's Capital	40,000	Machinery	20,000
Prov. for Bad Debt	1,000	Furniture	10,000
Creditors	60,000	Debtors	25,000
		Cash	16,000
		Profit and Loss Account	10,000
	1,61,000		1,61,000

D was admitted to the partnership for 1/5th share in the profits on the following terms

(i) The new ratio was decided as 2 : 2 : 1.

(ii) D will bring ₹ 30,000 as his capital and ₹ 15,000 for his share of goodwill.

(iii) Half of goodwill was withdrawn by the partner who sacrificed his share of profit in favour of D.

(iv) A provision of 5% for bad and doubtful debt was to be maintained.

(v) An item of ₹ 500 included in creditors was not likely to be paid.

(vi) A provision of ₹ 800 was to be made for claim for damages against the firm.

(vii) After making above adjustments, the capital account of B and C were to be adjusted on the basis of D's capital. Actual cash was to be brought in or paid off as the case may be.

Prepare revaluation account and partners' capital account of the new firm.

7. Anikesh and Bhavesh are partners in a firm sharing profits in the ratio of 7 : 3. Their balance sheet as on 31st March, 2023 was a follows

Balance Sheet of Anikesh and Bhavesh
as at 31st March, 2023

Liabilities		Amt (₹)	Assets		Amt (₹)
Creditors		60,000	Cash		36,000
Outstanding Wages		9,000	Debtors	54,000	
General Reserve		15,000	(–) Provisions for Doubtful Debts	(6,000)	48,000
Capital A/cs			Stock		60,000
Anikesh	1,20,000		Furniture		1,20,000
Bhavesh	1,80,000	3,00,000	Machinery		1,20,000
		3,84,000			3,84,000

On 1st April, 2023 Chahat was admitted for 1/4th share in the profits on the following terms

(i) Chahat will bring ₹ 90,000 as her capital and ₹ 30,000 as her share of goodwill premium.

(ii) Outstanding wages will be paid.

(iii) Stock will be reduced by 10%.

(iv) A creditor of ₹ 6,300, not recorded in the books, was to be taken into account.

Pass necessary journal entries for the above transactions in the books of the firm. *[CBSE 2024]*

8. Bhumi and Chavi were partners in a firm sharing profits and losses in the ratio of 5 : 3. They admitted Aditi in the firm on 1st April, 2022. On that data their balance sheet was as follows

Balance Sheet of Bhumi and Chavi
as at 1st April, 2022

Liabilities		Amt (₹)	Assets	Amt (₹)
Capital A/cs			Machinery	3,80,000
Bhumi	3,20,000		Furniture	50,000
Chavi	3,40,000	6,60,000	Debtors	2,30,000
General Reserve		80,000	Stock	1,50,000
Bank Loan		60,000	Cash	50,000
Creditors		60,000		
		8,60,000		8,60,000

Aditi was admitted in the firm with 1/3 share in profits on the following terms
- (i) Aditi will bring ₹ 3,00,000 as her capital.
- (ii) Aditi will bring her share of goodwill premium in cash. Goodwill of the firm was valued on the basis of two years purchase of average profits of the last three years. Average profits of the last three years were ₹ 60,000.
- (iii) Machinery was revalued at ₹ 4,60,000.
- (iv) The capitals of Bhumi nad Chavi were adjusted on the basis of Aditi's capital by opening current accounts.

Prepare revaluation account and partner's capital accounts. [CBSE 2023]

9. Nand and Deepak are partners and profit is divided as 1/2 to Nand, 1/3 to Deepak and 1/6 carried to general reserve account. They admit Dev as a partner on 1st April, 2021 on which date the balance sheet was as under

Liabilities	Amt (₹)	Assets	Amt (₹)
Creditors	80,000	Cash at Bank	10,000
Outstanding Expenses	6,000	Debtors	1,10,000
Workmen's Compensation Fund	45,000	Stock	90,000
Nand's Capital	1,59,000	Plant and Machine	75,000
Deepak's Capital	1,00,000	Buildings	1,00,000
		Advertisement Expenditure	5,000
	3,90,000		3,90,000

The following adjustments were agreed upon
- (i) Stock is undervalued by 10%.
- (ii) Depreciation of ₹ 15,000 had been omitted on plant and machine for the year ended 31st March, 2021.

(iii) Creditors include a contingent liability of ₹ 25,000 which has been decided by the court at ₹ 21,500.

(iv) In respect of debtors, the following debts proved bad or doubtful
₹ 7,500 due from Aman – Bad to full extent.

₹ 10,000 due from Danny — Insolvent, estate expected to pay only 40%.

(v) Goodwill of the firm valued at ₹ 30,000. However, Dev is unable to bring his share of goodwill in cash.

(vi) Dev is given 1/5th share of profits which he acquires equally from Nand and Deepak. Dev is to bring in capital ₹ 72,500 proportionate to his share of profits in the firm.

Prepare revaluation account and partners' capital account.

Answers

If your answer matches with the answer given here then put (✓) in the box otherwise put (✗). In case you did not attempt the question leave the box blank.

Multiple Choice Questions

1. D ☐	2. C ☐
3. A ☐	4. D ☐
5. D ☐	6. A ☐
7. A ☐	8. B ☐
9. B ☐	10. D ☐
11. B ☐	12. D ☐
13. A ☐	14. D ☐
15. C ☐	16. D ☐
17. B ☐	18. B ☐
19. A ☐	20. D ☐
21. D ☐	22. A ☐
23. D ☐	24. D ☐
25. A ☐	26. C ☐
27. C ☐	28. C ☐
29. D ☐	30. A ☐
31. A ☐	32. B ☐
33. B ☐	34. A ☐

Your Score__________ *(No. of Correct Answers)*

Assertion-Reason Questions

1. A ☐	2. A ☐
3. D ☐	4. C ☐
5. C ☐	6. A ☐
7. A ☐	8. A ☐

Your Score__________ *(No. of Correct Answers)*

Correct/Incorrect Statements

1. A ☐	2. A ☐
3. A ☐	4. D ☐
5. C ☐	6. C ☐
7. B ☐	8. B ☐
9. D ☐	

Your Score__________ *(No. of Correct Answers)*

Case Based Questions

1. (i) C ☐	(ii) B ☐
(iii) A ☐	(iv) B ☐
2. (i) D ☐	(ii) B ☐
(iii) D ☐	

Your Score__________ *(No. of Correct Answers)*

Explanations

Multiple Choice Questions

1. (D) Raju's Sacrifice $= \frac{3}{25} \times \frac{3}{5} = \frac{9}{125}$

Bantu's Sacrifice $= \frac{4}{25} - \frac{9}{125} = \frac{20-9}{125} = \frac{11}{125}$

Raju's New $= \frac{3}{5} - \frac{9}{125} = \frac{75-9}{125} = \frac{66}{125}$

Bantu's New $= \frac{2}{5} - \frac{11}{125} = \frac{50-11}{125} = \frac{39}{125}$

Chintu's New $= \frac{4}{25} \times \frac{5}{5} = \frac{20}{125}$

66 : 39 : 20

2. (C) Both (A) and (B)

3. (A) statutory liability

4. (D) X = 75%

Y = 25%

75 : 25 *or* 3 : 1

5. (D) A : B : C

Old Ratio 3 : 2 : 1

Remaining Share $= 1 - \frac{1}{6} - \frac{1}{6} = \frac{6-1-1}{6} = \frac{4}{6}$

So, new ratio will be

A's Share $= \frac{4}{6} \times \frac{3}{5} = \frac{12}{30}$; B's Share $= \frac{4}{6} \times \frac{2}{5} = \frac{8}{30}$

C's Share $= \frac{1}{6} \times \frac{5}{5} = \frac{5}{30}$; D's Share $= \frac{1}{6} \times \frac{5}{5} = \frac{5}{30}$

⇒ 12 : 8 : 5 : 5

6. (A) A's New $= \frac{2}{3} \times \frac{1}{2} = \frac{2}{6} \times \frac{5}{5} = \frac{10}{30}$

B's New $= \frac{2}{3} \times \frac{1}{2} = \frac{2}{6} \times \frac{5}{5} = \frac{10}{30}$

C's New $= \frac{1}{3} \times \frac{3}{5} = \frac{3}{15} \times \frac{2}{2} = \frac{6}{30}$

D's New $= \frac{1}{3} \times \frac{2}{5} = \frac{2}{15} \times \frac{2}{2} = \frac{4}{30}$

⇒ 10 : 10 : 6 : 4

or 5 : 5 : 3 : 2

7. (A) A's Sacrifice $= \frac{1}{16}$

B's Sacrifice $= \frac{3}{16}$

C's Share $= \frac{1}{16} + \frac{3}{16} = \frac{4}{16} = \frac{1}{4}$

8. (B) Ravi's Old $= \frac{5}{12} + \left[\frac{4}{12} \times \frac{1}{2}\right] = \frac{5}{12} + \frac{4}{24}$

$= \frac{10+4}{24} = \frac{14}{24}$

Kishan's Old $= \frac{3}{12} + \left[\frac{4}{12} \times \frac{1}{2}\right] = \frac{3}{12} + \frac{4}{24}$

$= \frac{6+4}{24} = \frac{10}{24}$

14 : 10 *or* 7 : 5

9. (B) Preeti's share $= \frac{1}{4}$th share, which she acquired from Gupta

Gupta's New Share $= \frac{4}{5} - \frac{1}{4} = \frac{16-5}{20} = \frac{11}{20}$

Sharma's Share $= \frac{1}{5}$

∴ New profit sharing ratio of Gupta, Sharma and Preeti $= \frac{11}{20} : \frac{1}{5} : \frac{1}{4} = 11 : 4 : 5$

10. (D) Share Sacrifice by Akshita $= \frac{1}{3} \times \frac{2}{3} = \frac{2}{9}$

Share Sacrifice by Anurag $= \frac{1}{3} \times \frac{1}{3} = \frac{1}{9}$

New Share of Akshita $= \frac{2}{3} - \frac{2}{9} = \frac{6-2}{9} = \frac{4}{9}$

New Share of Anurag $= \frac{1}{3} - \frac{1}{9} = \frac{3-1}{9} = \frac{2}{9}$

Akshat Share $= \frac{1}{3} \times \frac{3}{3} = \frac{3}{9}$

New profit sharing ratio = 4 : 2 : 3

11. (B)

Total Capital	=	7,50,000
(–) Capitals of All (1,20,000 + 80,000 + 30,000 + 7,500 + 1,50,000)	=	(3,87,500)
Goodwill of Firm	=	3,62,500

12. (D) A's Sacrifice $= \frac{7}{10} - \frac{4}{10} = \frac{3}{10}$

B's Sacrifice $= \frac{3}{10} - \frac{3}{10} = 0$

B's Share in Goodwill = Nil

13. (A) Tarun's Sacrifice $= \frac{5}{7} - \frac{3}{7} = \frac{2}{7}$

Bhushan's Sacrifice $= \frac{2}{7} - \frac{3}{7} = (-)\ \frac{1}{7}$

Bhushan's capital debited by

$70{,}000 \times \frac{1}{7} = ₹\,10{,}000$

14. (D) A's Sacrifice $= \frac{5}{8} - \frac{3}{8} = \frac{2}{8}$

B's Sacrifice $= \frac{3}{8} - \frac{2}{8} = \frac{1}{8}$

Sacrificing ratio = 2 : 1

C's Share of ₹ 42,000 in 2 : 1 i.e. ₹ 28,000 and ₹ 14,000.

15. (C) Y's Sacrifice $= \frac{1}{4} - \frac{2}{5} = \frac{5-8}{20} = (-)\frac{3}{20}$ (Gain)

Total Goodwill $\times \frac{3}{20}$ = ₹ 18,000

∴ Total Goodwill $= 18{,}000 \times \frac{20}{3}$ = ₹ 1,20,000

A's Share $= 1{,}20{,}000 \times \frac{1}{5}$ = ₹ 24,000

16. (D) Karan's New $= \frac{3}{5} - \left[\frac{1}{5} \times \frac{3}{4}\right]$

$= \frac{3}{5} - \frac{3}{20} = \frac{12-3}{20} = \frac{9}{20}$

Laxmi's New $= \frac{2}{5} - \left[\frac{1}{5} \times \frac{1}{4}\right] = \frac{2}{5} - \frac{1}{20} = \frac{8-1}{20} = \frac{7}{20}$

Amit's New $= \frac{1}{5} \times \frac{4}{4} = \frac{4}{20}$ ⇒ 9 : 7 : 4

17. (B) Adjusted Capital of Disha and Abha = 64,000 + 46,000 = ₹ 1,10,000

Total Capital $= 1{,}10{,}000 \times \frac{5}{4}$ = ₹ 1,37,500

Fahad Share $= 1{,}37{,}500 \times \frac{1}{5}$ = ₹ 27,500

18. (B) Manya's Share

$= \frac{\text{Share of Goodwill She Brought}}{\text{Firm's Total Goodwill}} = \frac{1{,}00{,}000}{3{,}00{,}000} = \frac{1}{3}$

Puneet and Deepak's old share = 2 : 1

Puneet's New Share = Old Share − Sacrificing Share

$= \frac{2}{3} - \frac{1}{3} = \frac{1}{3}$

New ratio of Puneet, Deepak and Manya

⇒ $\frac{1}{3} : \frac{1}{3} : \frac{1}{3}$ i.e. 1 : 1 : 1

19. (A) Assuming that the old profit sharing ratio between Amit and Sumit is 1 : 1

Remaining share of profit in the firm $= 1 - \frac{1}{5} = \frac{4}{5}$

New Profit Share of Amit $= \frac{1}{2} \times \frac{4}{5} = \frac{2}{5}$

New Profit Share of Sumit $= \frac{1}{2} \times \frac{4}{5} = \frac{2}{5}$

Sacrificing Ratio ⇒ Amit $= \frac{1}{2} - \frac{2}{5} = \frac{5-4}{10} = \frac{1}{10}$

Sumit $= \frac{1}{2} - \frac{2}{5} = \frac{5-4}{10} = \frac{1}{10}$ ⇒ 1 : 1

20. (D) Goodwill = 3 × Last Five Years' Average Profit*

= 3 × 40,000 = ₹ 1,20,000

*Average profit (last 5 years)

$= \frac{50{,}000 + (40{,}000 + 10{,}000) + 75{,}000 - 25{,}000 + 50{,}000}{5}$

$= \frac{2{,}00{,}000}{5}$ = ₹ 40,000

21. (D)

Dr **Revaluation Account** Cr

Particulars	Amt (₹)	Particulars		Amt (₹)
To Stock A/c	40,000	By Creditors A/c		15,000
To Debtor's A/c	2,000	By Revaluation Loss		
To Provision for Doubtful Debts	16,000	Angle	30,000	
		Circle	30,000	60,000
To Furniture A/c (Balancing Figure)	17,000			
	75,000			75,000

Value of Furniture = 2,00,000 − 17,000 = ₹ 1,83,000

22. (A)

Dr **Revaluation Account** Cr

Particulars	Amt (₹)	Particulars	Amt (₹)
To Building	3,500	By Bills Payable	1,000
To Creditors	2,000	By Loss	7,500
To Trademark	3,000		
	8,500		8,500

23. (D) Star's Goodwill = ₹ 15,000

Firm's Goodwill $= 15{,}000 \times \frac{10}{3}$ = ₹ 50,000

24. (D)

Dr **Revaluation Account** Cr

Particulars	Amt (₹)	Particulars		Amt (₹)
To Machine	60,000	By Stock		18,000
To Provision for Bad Debt	8,000	By Loss		
		A's Capital	20,000	
		B's Capital	30,000	50,000
	68,000			68,000

Revalued Value of Stock = 80,000 + 18,000 = ₹ 98,000

25. (A) Debit Cash and Credit Revaluation Account

26. (C) debit ₹ 10,000 in revaluation account

27. (C) (iii), (ii), (i), (iv)

28. (C) New Provision $= 60,000 \times \frac{5}{100} =$ ₹ 3,000

Existing Provisions = ₹ 5,000

∴ Decrease in Provisions = ₹ 2,000

29. (D) Remaining share of a firm $= 1 - \frac{1}{5} = \frac{4}{5}$

Total capital of a firm

$= (1,09,000 + 66,000 + 25,000) \times \frac{5}{4} =$ ₹ 2,50,000

Capital brought by new partner Sahil

$= 2,50,000 \times \frac{1}{5} =$ ₹ 50,000

30. (A) debited to revaluation account

31. (A) (ii) (iii) (i)

32. (B) (iii) (ii) (iv) (i)

33. (B) (i) (ii) (iii)

34. (A) (iii) (ii) (i)

Assertion-Reason Questions

1. (A) Both Assertion (A) and Reason (R) are true and Reason (R) is the correct explanation of Assertion (A)
2. (A) Both Assertion (A) and Reason (R) are true and Reason (R) is the correct explanation of Assertion (A)
3. (D) Assertion (A) is false, but Reason (R) is true
4. (C) General reserve is the part of profit saved by old partners therefore in case of admission of a partner, it will be distributed among old partners.
5. (C) Purchase and sale of assets is not recorded in revaluation account.
6. (A) Both Assertion (A) and Reason (R) are true and Reason (R) is the correct explanation of Assertion (A)
7. (A) Both Assertion (A) and Reason (R) are true and Reason (R) is the correct explanation of Assertion (A)
8. (A) Both Assertion (A) and Reason (R) are true and Reason (R) is the correct explanation of Assertion (A)

Correct/Incorrect Statements

1. (A) Both statements are correct
2. (A) Both statements are correct
3. (A) Both statements are correct
4. (D) Unrecorded assets are credited and unrecorded liabilities are debited. Profit/Loss on revaluation is distributed in old ratio.
5. (C) Revaluation account is prepared at the time of reconstitution of partnership, i.e. change in profit sharing ratio, admission of a partner, retirement/death of partner.
6. (C) Workmen reserve is distributed among old partners in case of admission of a partner.
7. (B) Since there is a change in the value of machinery, the increase/decrease will be recorded in the revaluation account, i.e. ₹ 5,000.
8. (B) Goodwill appearing in the balance sheet will be written-off in old ratio.
9. (D) An asset will be debited to partners' capital account if the asset is acquired by the partner.

Case Based Questions

1. (i) (C) Sania sacrificed $\frac{8}{18} \times \frac{1}{2} = \frac{2}{9}$ in favour of Ejaz

Ryan $= \frac{5}{18}$; Williams $= \frac{5}{18}$

Sania $= \frac{8}{18} - \frac{2}{9} = \frac{8-4}{18} = \frac{4}{18}$; Ejaz $= \frac{2}{9}$

New profit sharing ratio

= Ryan : Williams : Sania : Ejaz

$= \frac{5}{18} : \frac{5}{18} : \frac{4}{18} : \frac{2}{9}$ *or* 5 : 5 : 4 : 4

(ii) (B) Sania to bring ₹ 80,00,000 to double her capital. Thus Ejaz would bring ₹ 80,00,000 as his share of capital.

(iii) (A) Goodwill of firm = ₹ 30,00,000

Ejaz's share = 4/18 for which he bought ₹ 30,00,000 as his share of goodwill

Firm's Goodwill = 30,00,000 × 18/4

= ₹ 1,35,00,000

(iv) (B) Premium for Goodwill A/c Dr 30,00,000

To Sania's Capital A/c 30,00,000

2. (i) (D) Jolly's New $= \frac{3}{4} \times \frac{3}{4} = \frac{9}{16}$

Mayank's New $= \frac{3}{4} \times \frac{1}{4} = \frac{3}{16}$

Yuvraj's New $= \frac{1}{4} \times \frac{4}{4} = \frac{4}{16}$

9 : 3 : 4

(ii) (B) Yuvraj's share of goodwill

$$= 2,40,000 \times \frac{1}{4} = ₹\ 60,000$$

$$\text{Goodwill brought in cash} = 60,000 \times \frac{40}{100}$$

$$= ₹\ 24,000$$

(iii) (D) Goodwill unable to bring in cash

$$= 60,000 - 24,000 - 16,000 = ₹\ 20,000$$

Subjective Questions

1. $C\text{'s Capital} = (48,000 + 32,000) \times \frac{5}{4} \times \frac{1}{5} = ₹\ 20,000$

2. $\text{Remaining Share} = 1 - \frac{1}{5} = \frac{4}{5}$

$A' \text{ Share} = \frac{4}{5} \times \frac{3}{5} = \frac{12}{25}$; $B' \text{ Share} = \frac{4}{5} \times \frac{2}{5} = \frac{8}{25}$

$C' \text{ Share} = \frac{1}{5} \times \frac{5}{5} = \frac{5}{25}$

New ratio of A : B : C = 12 : 8 : 5

Now, D admit for $\frac{25}{100} = \frac{1}{4}$

$A' \text{ Share} = \frac{3}{4} \times \frac{12}{25} = \frac{36}{100}$

$B' \text{ Share} = \frac{3}{4} \times \frac{8}{25} = \frac{24}{100}$

$C' \text{ Share} = \frac{3}{4} \times \frac{5}{25} = \frac{15}{100}$; $D' \text{ Share} = \frac{1}{4} \times \frac{25}{25} = \frac{25}{100}$

∴ New ratio of A : B : C : D = 36 : 24 : 15 : 25

3. Total Capital = 25,00,000
(–) Capital of All = (15,00,000)
(5,00,000 + 10,00,000)
Goodwill of Firm 10,00,000

$\text{Ajay' Share} = 10,00,000 \times \frac{1}{5}$

$= ₹\ 2,00,000$

JOURNAL

Particulars		Amt (Dr)	Amt (Cr)
Cash A/c	Dr	5,00,000	
To Ajay's Capital A/c			5,00,000
(Being capital brought by Ajay)			
Ajay's Current A/c	Dr	2,00,000	
To Asin's Capital A/c			1,00,000
To Shreya's Capital A/c			1,00,000
(Being goodwill not brought by Ajay)			

4. **JOURNAL**

Particulars		Amt (Dr)	Amt (Cr)
Land A/c	Dr	90,000	
Machinery A/c	Dr	70,000	
Stock A/c	Dr	60,000	
Debtors A/c	Dr	40,000	
To Deepak's Capital A/c			1,40,000
To Premium for Goodwill A/c			1,20,000
(Being goodwill brought by partner)			
Premium for Goodwill A/c	Dr	1,20,000	
To Anubhav's Capital A/c			72,000
To Babita's Capital A/c			48,000
(Being goodwill brought by new partner)			

5. **JOURNAL**

Particulars		Amt (Dr)	Amt (Cr)
General Reserve A/c	Dr	70,000	
To A's Capital A/c			40,000
To B's Capital A/c			30,000
(Being general reserve distributed)			
A's Capital A/c	Dr	4,000	
B's Capital A/c	Dr	3,000	
To Profit and Loss A/c			7,000
(Being profit and loss distributed)			

6. Dr **Revaluation Account** Cr

Particulars	Amt (₹)	Particulars		Amt (₹)
To Provision for Bad Debt	250	By Creditors		500
To Claim for Damages	800	By Loss transferred to Capital A/cs		
		B	330	
		C	220	550
	1,050			1,050

Partners' Capital Account

Dr | | | | | | | | Cr

Particulars	A (₹)	B (₹)	C (₹)	Particulars	A (₹)	B(₹)	C (₹)
To Profit and Loss A/c	6,000	4,000	—	By Balance b/d	60,000	40,000	—
To Revaluation A/c	330	220	—	By Cash A/c	—	—	30,000
To Cash A/c	7,500	—	—	By Premium for Goodwill	15,000	—	—
To Cash A/c	1,170	—	—	By Cash A/c (Balancing figure)	—	24,220	—
To Balance c/d	60,000	60,000	30,000				
	75,000	64,220	30,000		75,000	64,220	30,000

Working Notes

1. Sacrifice Ratio = Old Ratio – New Ratio

$$B = \frac{3}{5} - \frac{2}{5} = \frac{1}{5}; \quad C = \frac{2}{5} - \frac{2}{5} = 0$$

2. **Calculation of Total Capital**

D's Capital = 30,000 for 1/5 share

$$\therefore \text{ Total Capital} \times \frac{1}{5} = 30,000$$

So, Total Capital = ₹ 1,50,000

7. **JOURNAL**

Date	Particulars		LF	Amt (Dr)	Amt (Cr)
(i)	Bank A/c	Dr		1,20,000	
	To Chahat's Capital A/c				90,000
	To Premium for Goodwill A/c				30,000
	(Being the amount of capital and premium for goodwill introduced by Chahat)				
(ii)	Premium for Goodwill A/c	Dr		30,000	
	To Anikesh's Capital A/c				21,000
	To Bhavesh's Caital A/c				9,000
	(Being premium for goodwill transferred in sacrificing ratio 7 : 3)				
(iii)	General Reserve A/c	Dr		15,000	
	To Anikesh's Capital A/c				10,500
	To Bhavesh's Capital A/c				4500
	(Being general reserve distributed between the old partners in their old ratio 7 : 3)				
(iv)	Outstanding Wages A/c	Dr		9,000	
	To Cash A/c				9,000
	(Being outstanding wages paid)				
(v)	Revaluation A/c	Dr		12,300	
	To Stock A/c				6,000
	To Creditors A/c				6,300
	(Being decrease in the value of assets and increase in value of liabilities)				
(vi)	Anikesh's Capital A/c	Dr		8,610	
	Bhavesh's Capital A/c	Dr		3,690	
	To Revaluation A/c				12,300
	(Being transfer of loss on revaluation)				

Working Notes

1. New Profit Sharing Ratio

   Chahat's share = 1/4

   Remaining share $= 1 - \frac{1}{4} = \frac{4-1}{4} = \frac{3}{4}$

   $\therefore$ Anikesh's share $= \frac{3}{4} \times \frac{7}{10} = \frac{21}{40}$; Bhavesh's share $= \frac{3}{4} \times \frac{3}{10} = \frac{9}{40}$

   So, new profit sharing ratio = 21 : 9 : 10

2. Sacrificing Ratio = Old Share – New Share

   Anikesh $= \frac{7}{10} - \frac{21}{40} = \frac{28-21}{40} = \frac{7}{40}$; Bhavesh $= \frac{3}{10} - \frac{9}{40} = \frac{12-9}{40} = \frac{3}{40} = 7 : 3$

8. Dr **Revaluation Account** Cr

Particulars		**Amt (₹)**	**Particulars**	**Amt (₹)**
To Revaluation Profit transferred to Capital A/c			By Machinery A/c	80,000
Bhumi	50,000			
Chavi	30,000	80,000		
		80,000		80,000

Dr **Partners' Capital Account** Cr

Particulars	**Bhumi (₹)**	**Chavi (₹)**	**Aditi (₹)**	**Particulars**	**Bhumi (₹)**	**Chavi (₹)**	**Aditi (₹)**
To Bhumi's Current A/c	70,000	1,90,000	—	By Balance b/d	3,20,000	3,40,000	—
To Balance c/d (WN2)	3,75,000	2,25,000	3,00,000	By Revaluation A/c	50,000	30,000	—
				By General Reserve	50,000	30,000	—
				By Cash A/c	—	—	3,00,000
				By Premium for Goodwill A/c	25,000	15,000	—
	4,45,000	4,15,000	3,00,000		4,45,000	4,15,000	3,00,000

Working Notes

1. **Calculation of Goodwill brought in by Aditi**

   Goodwill of firm = 60,000 × 2 = ₹ 1,20,000; Aditi's share of goodwill $= 1{,}20{,}000 \times \frac{1}{3} =$ ₹ 40,000

2. Calculation of the proportionate capital of Bhumi and Chavi on the basis of Aditi's capital.

   New profit sharing ratio

   Remaining share of profits in a firm $= 1 - \frac{1}{3} = \frac{2}{3}$

   Bhumi $= \frac{5}{8} \times \frac{2}{3} = \frac{10}{24}$; Chavi $= \frac{3}{8} \times \frac{2}{3} = \frac{6}{24}$; Aditi $= \frac{1}{3} \times \frac{8}{8} = \frac{8}{24}$

   New profit sharing ratio = 10 : 6 : 8 *or* 5 : 3 : 4

   Total capital of a firm $= 3{,}00{,}000 \times \frac{3}{1} =$ ₹ 9,00,000

   Bhumi's Capital $= 9{,}00{,}000 \times \frac{5}{12} =$ ₹ 3,75,000; Chavi's Capital $= 9{,}00{,}000 \times \frac{3}{12} =$ ₹ 2,25,000

   Aditi's Capital $= 9{,}00{,}000 \times \frac{4}{12} =$ ₹ 3,00,000

3. When the new partner gets his share of profits in a firm and sacrificing ratio is not given then the sacrificing ratio is same as old profit sharing ratio.

9. Dr **Revaluation Account** Cr

Particulars	Amt (₹)	Particulars		Amt (₹)
To Depreciation	15,000	By Stock		10,000
To Bad Debt	13,500	By Creditors		3,500
		By Loss transferred to Capital A/cs		
		Nand	9,000	
		Deepak	6,000	15,000
	28,500			28,500

Dr **Partners' Capital Account** Cr

Particulars	Nand (₹)	Deepak (₹)	Dev (₹)	Particulars	Nand (₹)	Deepak (₹)	Dev (₹)
To Advertisement Expense A/c	3,000	2,000	—	By Balance b/d	1,59,000	1,00,000	—
To Revaluation	9,000	6,000	—	By Workmen Compensation Reserve	27,000	18,000	—
To Balance c/d	1,77,000	1,13,000	72,000				
				By Bank A/c	—	—	72,000
				By Dev's Current A/c	3,000	3,000	—
	1,89,000	1,21,000	72,000		1,89,000	1,21,000	72,000

CHAPTER -4

Reconstitution of a Partnership Firm : Retirement/Death of a Partner

Types & Nos. of Questions

Multiple Choice Questions	-	34
Assertion-Reason Questions	-	8
Correct/Incorrect Statements	-	8
Case Based Questions	-	2 Cases, *with 2/3 Questions*
Subjective Questions	-	10

Trend Analysis

On the basis of analysis of last 2 years' papers, it is found that on an average 3 Multiple Choice Questions, 1 Short Answer Type Question and 2 Long Answer Type Questions are asked from this chapter.

Focus Topics of the Chapter

- New Profit Sharing Ratio and Gaining Ratio
- Treatment of Goodwill
- Computation of Amount due to Retiring Partner
- Adjustment of Capital
- Death of Partner

Multiple Choice Questions

No. of Questions : **34**

Suggested Time : **50 Minutes**

Direction Each of the question given below is Multiple Choice Question (MCQ) i.e. there are Four Options/ Choices for answer, out of which ONLY ONE is correct. You have to select the correct option.
A response box is given with each option, mark (✓) in the box of the correct option. For each correct answer you will get 1 mark, while there is no penalty for incorrect answer or missed out questions.

1. In the absence of any agreement, the rate of interest payable on the amount remaining unpaid to the executor of deceased partner is

(A) 8% p.a. ☐ (B) 6% p.a. ☐
(C) 9% p.a. ☐ (D) 12% p.a. ☐

2. David, Tony and Bhavishya are sharing profits and losses in the ratio 3/8, 1/2 and 1/8. Tony retired and surrenders 1/2th share in the favour of David and remaining share in the favour of Bhavishya. New ratio will be

(A) 4 : 5 ☐ (B) 5 : 4 ☐
(C) 5 : 3 ☐ (D) 4 : 3 ☐

3. P, Q, R and S are partners sharing profits and losses in the ratio of 3 : 3 : 2 : 2. On P's retirement, Q decided to retain his original share while R and S decided to take P's share in the ratio 3 : 2. The new ratio will be

(A) 19 : 15 : 16 ☐ (B) 15 : 19 : 16 ☐
(C) 16 : 19 : 15 ☐ (D) 1 : 1 : 1 ☐

4. A, B and C are partners in a firm. C retires and A and B decided to share future profits and losses in the ratio of 5 : 3. A gained 1/9th and B gained 2/9th share from C. Old ratio of A : B : C was

(A) 5 : 3 : 1 ☐ (B) 5 : 3 : 2 ☐
(C) 37 : 11 : 24 ☐ (D) 37 : 24 : 11 ☐

5. Gopal, Krishna and Govind were partners sharing profits and losses in the ratio of 5 : 4 : 3. Krishna retired on 1st April, 2022. Gopal and Govind purchased his share of profit by giving him ₹ 1,20,000, ₹ 80,000 was pass by Gopal and ₹ 40,000 by Govind. Gaining ratio is *[CBSE 2023]*

(A) 1 : 2 ☐ (B) 5 : 3 ☐
(C) 1 : 1 ☐ (D) 2 : 1 ☐

6. Pooja, Nita and Anita were partners in a firm sharing profits and losses in the ratio of 3 : 2 : 1. Pooja retired and her share is taken up by Nita and Anita equally. The new profit sharing ratio of Nita and Anita will be *[CBSE 2023]*

(A) 2 : 1 ☐ (B) 7 : 5 ☐
(C) 1 : 1 ☐ (D) 3 : 2 ☐

7. P, Q and R were partners sharing profits or losses equally. R retires and the goodwill is appearing in the books at ₹ 15,000. Goodwill of the firm is valued at ₹ 60,000. Calculate the net amount to be credited to R's capital account

(A) ₹ 30,000 ☐
(B) ₹ 25,000 ☐
(C) ₹ 20,000 ☐
(D) ₹ 15,000 ☐

8. A, B and C are partners in a firm sharing profits and losses in the ratio of 5 : 3 : 2. The following journal entry was made for treatment of goodwill on B's retirement

C's Capital A/c	Dr	48,000	
To B's Capital A/c			36,000
To A's Capital A/c			12,000

What will be the new profit sharing ratio?

(A) 5 : 2 ☐ (B) 1 : 1 ☐
(C) 3 : 1 ☐ (D) 2 : 3 ☐

9. A, B and C are partners sharing profits and losses in the ratio of 3 : 2 : 1. A retires and sell his share to B and C for ₹ 30,000 (₹ 20,000 paid by B and ₹ 10,000 by C). Calculate the new ratio.

(A) 3 : 2 ☐ (B) 17 : 11 ☐
(C) 2 : 1 ☐ (D) 19 : 11 ☐

10. P, Q and R have been sharing profits in the ratio of 8 : 3 : 5. P retires. Q takes 3/16th share from P and R takes 5/16th share from P. New profit sharing ratio will be

(A) 3 : 5 ☐ (B) 10 : 6 ☐
(C) 9 : 7 ☐ (D) 5 : 3 ☐

11. A, B and C are partners in a firm. C decided to retire and following entries were passed

A's Capital A/c	Dr	50,000	
B's Capital A/c	Dr	25,000	
C's Capital A/c	Dr	25,000	
To Goodwill A/c			1,00,000
(Being goodwill appear in books)			
A's Capital A/c	Dr	10,000	
B's Capital A/c	Dr	50,000	
To C's Capital A/c			60,000
(Being C's share of goodwill adjusted)			

New ratio of partners will be

(A) 1 : 5 ☐ (B) 13 : 11 ☐
(C) 11 : 13 ☐ (D) 2 : 1 ☐

12. Nidhi, Kunal and Kabir are partners in a firm sharing profits in the ratio of 2 : 1 : 2. Kunal retired and the balance in his capital account after making necessary adjustments on account of reserves, revaluation of assets and reassessment of liabilities was ₹ 80,000. Nidhi and Kabir agreed to pay him ₹ 1,00,000 in full settlement of his claim. Kunal's share of goodwill of the firm, on his retirement was *[CBSE 2023]*

(A) ₹ 4,000 ☐
(B) ₹ 20,000 ☐
(C) ₹ 16,000 ☐
(D) ₹ 1,80,000 ☐

13. Suresh, Ramesh and Tushar were partners of a firm sharing profit in the ratio of 6:5:4. Ramesh retired and his capital after making adjustments on account of reserves, revaluation of assets and reassessment of liabilities stood at ₹ 2,50,400.

Suresh and Tushar agreed to pay him ₹ 2,90,000 in full settlement of his claim. For the treatment of goodwill, Suresh's capital account will be

(A) debited by ₹ 23,760 ☐
(B) credited by ₹ 23,760 ☐
(C) debited by ₹ 25,500 ☐
(D) credited by ₹ 25,500 ☐

14. A, B and C were sharing profits and losses in the ratio of 5 : 3 : 2. B decided to retire and his share was taken by A and C in the ratio of 5 : 2. On retirement, an old machine which was unrecorded, was sold for ₹ 4,000. B's capital account will be

(A) ₹ 1,200 debit ☐
(B) ₹ 1,200 credit ☐
(C) ₹ 4,000 debit ☐
(D) ₹ 4,000 credit ☐

15. A, B and C are partners sharing profits and losses in the ratio of 3:1:1 with a capital of ₹ 2,00,000, ₹ 1,00,000 and ₹ 1,00,000 respectively. On C's retirement, building is increased by 5,00,000. Balance of capital of C will be

(A) ₹ 1,00,000 ☐ (B) ₹ 1,50,000 ☐
(C) ₹ 2,00,000 ☐ (D) ₹ 6,00,000 ☐

16. Following balances appears in balance sheet of a company. Debtors ₹ 10,000 and provision for bad debts ₹ 3,000. If all debtors are good, then what will be the effect of above transaction on revaluation?

(A) Debtors will be debited by ₹ 10,000 ☐
(B) Debtors will be credited by ₹ 10,000 ☐
(C) Provision for bad debt will be debited by ₹ 3,000 ☐
(D) Provision for bad debt will be credited by ₹ 3,000 ☐

17. Rosy, Daisy and Charles are partners sharing profits and losses in the ratio of 3 : 2 : 1. Rosy retired and on that day, stock and patents stood at ₹ 80,000 and ₹ 10,000 respectively. The stock was found undervalued by 20%, patents were valueless and provision for legal damages was to be made for ₹ 10,000.

What amount will be credited/debited in Rosy's capital account on profit or loss on revaluation?

(A) Debited by ₹ 18,000 ☐
(B) Debited by ₹ 2,000 ☐
(C) Credited by ₹ 5,000 ☐
(D) Nil ☐

18. A, B and C were partners in a firm sharing profits and losses in the ratio of 5 : 3 : 2. C retired and his capital balance after adjustments regarding reserves, accumulated profits/losses and his share of gain on revaluation was ₹ 2,50,000. C was paid ₹ 3,22,000 including his share of goodwill. The amount credited to C's capital account on his retirement, for goodwill will be

(A) ₹ 72,000 ☐ (B) ₹ 7,200 ☐
(C) ₹ 14,000 ☐ (D) ₹ 3,22,000 ☐

19. Amay, Bina and Chander are partners in a firm with capital balances of ₹ 50,000, ₹ 70,000 and ₹ 80,000 respectively on 31st March, 2022. Amay decides to retire from the firm on 31st March, 2022. With the help of the information provided, calculate the amount to be paid to Amay on his retirement.

There existed a general reserve of ₹ 7,500 in the balance sheet on that date. The goodwill of the firm was valued at ₹ 30,000. Gain on revaluation was ₹ 24,000.

(A) ₹ 88,500 ☐
(B) ₹ 90,500 ☐
(C) ₹ 65,375 ☐
(D) ₹ 70,500 ☐

20. A, B and C were partners in a firm sharing profits and losses in the ratio of 2 : 2 : 1. The capital balance are ₹ 50,000 for A, ₹ 70,000 for B and ₹ 35,000 for C. B decided to retire from the firm and balance in reserve on the date was ₹ 25,000.

If goodwill of the firm was valued at ₹ 30,000 and profit on revaluation was ₹ 7,500, then, what amount will be payable to B?

(A) ₹ 70,820 ☐ (B) ₹ 76,000 ☐
(C) ₹ 75,000 ☐ (D) ₹ 95,000 ☐

21. A, B and C are partners sharing profits and losses in the ratio of 3 : 2 : 1. B retires and the balance of his capital after all adjustments was ₹ 2,40,000.

The remaining partners gave B an unrecorded vehicle valued at ₹ 60,000 and the balance payable to B was discharged by giving a bank draft. What will be the amount of the bank draft?

(A) ₹ 1,80,000 ☐ (B) ₹ 2,40,000 ☐
(C) ₹ 2,60,000 ☐ (D) ₹ 2,00,000 ☐

22. G, S and T were partners sharing profits in the ratio 3 : 2 : 1. G retired and his dues towards the firm including capital balance, accumulated profits and losses share, revaluation gain amounted to ₹ 5,80,000.

G was being paid ₹ 7,00,000 in full settlement. For giving that additional amount of ₹ 1,20,000, S was debited for ₹ 40,000. Determine goodwill of the firm.

(A) ₹ 1,20,000 ☐ (B) ₹ 80,000 ☐
(C) ₹ 2,40,000 ☐ (D) ₹ 3,60,000 ☐

23. Ravi, Vani and Toni were equal partners in a firm. After the retirement of Vani, the capital balances of Ravi and Toni were ₹ 1,56,000 and ₹ 1,08,000 respectively.

The new capital of the firm was determined at ₹ 2,80,000. It was decided that the capital will be in proportion of the profit sharing ratio of the remaining partners.

Toni will bring .... for deficiency of his new capital. [CBSE 2024]

(A) ₹ 40,000 ☐ (B) ₹ 12,000 ☐
(C) ₹ 20,000 ☐ (D) ₹ 32,000 ☐

24. Deceased partner is entitled to

(A) share of profit from beginning of accounting year till date of death ☐
(B) interest on capital as per deed ☐
(C) his share in goodwill of the firm ☐
(D) None of the above ☐

25. A, B and C are partners in a firm. A died on 31st March and partners close book of accounts on 31st March. Calculated amount of A's profit till the date of death is ₹ 10,000. Which account will be debited for transfer of profit?

(A) Profit and loss account ☐
(B) Profit and loss appropriation account ☐
(C) Profit and loss suspense account ☐
(D) Revaluation account ☐

26. Aditya, Vishesh and Nimesh were partners in a firm sharing profits and losses equally. Aditya died on 1st July, 2023. Remaining partners decided to continue the business of the firm and decided to share future profits in the ratio of 4 : 3. The gaining ratio of Vishesh and Nimesh will be [CBSE 2024]

(A) 4 : 3 ☐ (B) 3 : 2 ☐
(C) 5 : 2 ☐ (D) 1 : 1 ☐

27. A, B and C were partners in a firm sharing profits and losses in the ratio of 4 : 3 : 2. A died on 10th April, 2023. Sales and profit of previous year were ₹ 3,00,000 and ₹ 45,000 respectively.

If sales from 1st January to 10th April was ₹ 1,20,000, A's share of profit would be

(A) ₹ 8,000 ☐ (B) ₹ 10,000 ☐
(C) ₹ 12,000 ☐ (D) ₹ 16,000 ☐

28. P, Q and R were sharing profits and losses in the ratio of 4 : 3 : 1. P died on 1st July, 2023.

Her share of profit till the date of death was to be calculated on the basis of sales. The profit for the year ended 31st March, 2023 was ₹ 96,000.

Sales for the year ended 31st March, 2023 was ₹ 12,00,000. For the period 1st April, 2023 to 30th June 2023, firm's sales were ₹ 1,00,000. P's share of profit will be

(A) ₹ 4,000 ☐
(B) ₹ 4,800 ☐
(C) ₹ 6,000 ☐
(D) ₹ 6,400 ☐

29. X, Y and Z were partners sharing profits and losses in the ratio of 2 : 2 : 1. On 1st July, 2023, Z died. The books of accounts were closed on March 31 every year. Sales for the year 2022-23 amounted to ₹ 5,00,000 and that from 1st April to 30th June, 2023 were ₹ 1,40,000.

The rate of profit during the past 3 years had been 10% of sales. But, it was decided to calculate Z's profit as 20% on sales. Z's share of profit till date of death will be

(A) ₹ 900 ☐
(B) ₹ 1,800 ☐
(C) ₹ 3,600 ☐
(D) ₹ 5,600 ☐

30. P, Q and R were partners in a firm sharing profits and losses in the ratio of 4 : 3 : 1. P died on 1st September, 2022. On the date of P's death, the profits of the firm were calculated as ₹ 80,000. [CBSE 2023]

P's share of profit will be adjusted by

(A) debiting profit and loss account with ₹ 40,000 ☐
(B) debiting profit and loss appropriation account by ₹ 40,000 ☐
(C) debiting profit and loss suspense account with ₹ 80,000 ☐
(D) debiting profit and loss suspense account with ₹ 40,000 ☐

31. A, B and C are partners. C expired on 18th December, 2019 and as per agreement surviving partners A and B directed the accountant to prepare financial statements as on 18th December, 2019 and accordingly the share of profits of C (deceased partner) was calculated as ₹ 12,00,000.

Which account will be debited to transfer C's share of profits?

(A) Profit and loss suspense account ☐
(B) Profit and loss appropriation account ☐
(C) Profit and loss account ☐
(D) None of the above ☐

32. Match the Column I with Column II in the following information

Column I	Column II
A. At the end of accounting year, profit and loss suspense account is closed by transferring its balance to the	(i) Executor's Account
B. Balance of profit and loss account appearing in the balance sheet is transferred to	(ii) Profit and Loss Appropriation Account
C. Balance in deceased partners capital account is transferred to	(iii) Capital Account

Codes

	A	B	C
(A)	(iii)	(ii)	(i) ☐
(B)	(iii)	(i)	(ii) ☐
(C)	(ii)	(iii)	(i) ☐
(D)	(i)	(ii)	(iii) ☐

33. Match the following

Column I	Column II
A. Bills receivables omitted to be recorded earlier, will now be recorded on	(i) Debit side of revaluation account
B. Creditors of ₹ 1,000 were not likely to be claimed	(ii) Credit side of revaluation account
C. Workmen compensation fund	(iii) Debit partners capital account
D. Goodwill appearing in the balance sheet	(iv) Credit partners capital account

Codes

	A	B	C	D
(A)	(i)	(ii)	(iv)	(iii) ☐
(B)	(i)	(iii)	(iv)	(ii) ☐
(C)	(ii)	(iii)	(iv)	(i) ☐
(D)	(ii)	(iv)	(i)	(iii) ☐

34. Match the following

Column I	Column II
A. A, B and C are partners sharing profits and losses in the ratio of 5 : 3 : 2. B retires and the new ratio between A and C is 4 : 1. Which partner gain?	(i) B and C both gain
B. A, B and C are partners sharing in 6 : 4 : 5. B retires and new ratio becomes 2 : 3. Which partner gain?	(ii) Only A gains
C. A, B and C are sharing profits in 5 : 3 : 2. A retired and B and C decided to share future profits in 2 : 3.	(iii) Only C gains
D. A, B and C are sharing profits in 5 : 3 : 2. B retired and A and C decided to share profits in 2 : 3 ratio.	(iv) A and B both sacrifice

Codes

	A	B	C	D
(A)	(i)	(iv)	(ii)	(iii) ☐
(B)	(i)	(ii)	(iii)	(iv) ☐
(C)	(ii)	(iii)	(i)	(iv) ☐
(D)	(iii)	(iv)	(i)	(ii) ☐

Assertion-Reason Questions

No. of Questions : **8** Suggested Time : **15 Minutes**

Direction Each of the question given below consist of the two statements; one labelled as **Assertion** (A) and other as **Reason** (R). List of common options applicable for each question is given below

(A) Both Assertion (A) and Reason (R) are true and Reason (R) is the correct explanation of Assertion (A)

(B) Both Assertion (A) and Reason (R) are true, but Reason (R) is not the correct explanation of Assertion (A)

(C) Assertion (A) is true, but Reason (R) is false

(D) Assertion (A) is false, but Reason (R) is true

You have to select the codes as *A, B, C* or *D* as your answer to the question by marking (✓) in the response box given against each option.

1. **Assertion (A)** Retirement of a partner leads to dissolution of partnership.

   Reason (R) In the absence of deed, if one partner retires, this will dissolve the firm compulsorily.

   (A) ☐ (B) ☐ (C) ☐ (D) ☐

2. **Assertion (A)** In retirement of a partner, usually remaining partner gains and retiring partner sacrifices.

   Reason (R) Gaining ratio is determined because the gaining partner compensates the retiring partner by paying goodwill.

   (A) ☐ (B) ☐ (C) ☐ (D) ☐

3. **Assertion (A)** Gaining ratio is required to be calculated at the time of retirement of a partner.

   Reason (R) The remaining partner acquires the retiring or deceased partner's share of profit in gaining ratio.

   (A) ☐ (B) ☐ (C) ☐ (D) ☐

4. **Assertion (A)** Remaining partner's capital account is debited with the share of goodwill of the retiring partner in the gaining ratio.

   Reason (R) Gaining ratio is calculated by deducting new profit sharing ratio from the old profit sharing ratio of a partner.

   (A) ☐ (B) ☐ (C) ☐ (D) ☐

5. **Assertion (A)** The retiring partner is entitled to his share of reserves, profits and losses.

   Reason (R) The existing profits and reserves are earned with the efforts of all the partners.

   (A) ☐ (B) ☐ (C) ☐ (D) ☐

6. **Assertion (A)** At the time of retirement of a partner, the profit on revaluation is credited to partners' capital account.

   Reason (R) Revaluation profit is distributed among all partners in their old ratio.

   (A) ☐ (B) ☐ (C) ☐ (D) ☐

7. **Assertion (A)** At the time of retirement of a partner, advertisement suspense is written-off by transferring it to the debit side of partners' capital account.

   Reason (R) Advertisement suspense is a fictitious asset and will be written-off in case of reconstitution of a partnership.

   (A) ☐ (B) ☐ (C) ☐ (D) ☐

8. **Assertion (A)** Deceased partner is entitled to his share of profit from the beginning of an accounting year till date of his death.

   Reason (R) The share of profit is credited to the deceased partner's capital account and debited to profit and loss suspense account.

   (A) ☐ (B) ☐ (C) ☐ (D) ☐

Correct/Incorrect Statements

No. of Questions : **8** Suggested Time : **15 Minutes**

Direction Each of the question given below consist of the two statements. List of common options applicable for each question is given below.

(A) Both the statements are correct
(B) Statement I is correct and Statement II is incorrect
(C) Statement II is correct and Statement I is incorrect
(D) Both statements are incorrect

You have to select the codes as *a, b, c* or *d* as your answer to the question by marking (✓) in the response box given against each option.

1. **Statement I** Section 37 of the Indian Partnership Act, 1932 states that the retiring partner has an option to receive either interest @ 6% p.a. till the date of payment or such share of profits which has been earned with his/her money (i.e. based on capital ratio).

   Statement II The total amount due to the retiring partner, which is ascertained after all adjustments have been made, has to be paid immediately to the retiring partner in all cases.

   (A) ☐ (B) ☐ (C) ☐ (D) ☐

2. **Statement I** A partner can only retire from the firm with the consent of managing partners.

   Statement II Revaluation account is prepared when the partnership is dissolved.

   (A) ☐ (B) ☐ (C) ☐ (D) ☐

3. **Statement I** A retiring partner can nominate any member of his family as new partner in the firm.

   Statement II Retiring partner will receive his share of goodwill from the gaining partners.

   (A) ☐ (B) ☐ (C) ☐ (D) ☐

4. **Statement I** The representatives of deceased partners will receive the balance amount of deceased partner.

   Statement II The balance amount of deceased partner will be transferred to his loan account.

   (A) ☐ (B) ☐ (C) ☐ (D) ☐

5. **Statement I** On retirement of a partner, the retiring partner's capital will be credited with goodwill of the firm.

   Statement II If the firm had paid any excess amount from what is due to him, it shall be treated as his share of goodwill.

   (A) ☐ (B) ☐
   (C) ☐ (D) ☐

6. **Statement I** On death of a partner, revaluation account is prepared in order to ascertain net gain (loss) on revaluation of assets and reassessment of liabilities in remaining partners in gaining ratio.

   Statement II Partners cannot retire without the consent of all partners.

   (A) ☐ (B) ☐ (C) ☐ (D) ☐

7. **Statement I** The amount payable to deceased partner can either be paid in cash or can be transferred to his executor's loan account.

   Statement II Retiring partner will receive interest at 6% p.a. on his loan in the absence of deed.

   (A) ☐ (B) ☐
   (C) ☐ (D) ☐

8. **Statement I** The balance amount of deceased partner is always settled in cash.

Statement II The executor of deceased partner will receive interest at 6% p.a. if the amount is transferred to executor's loan account.

(A) ☐ (B) ☐ (C) ☐ (D) ☐

Case Based Questions

No. of Questions : **2** Suggested Time : **10 Minutes**

Direction This section contains 2 cases having 2/3 Questions of 1 mark each. You have to write the answer of each question based on the context of the related case.

Case 1 A, B, C and D were partners sharing profits and losses in the ratio of 4:3:2:1. A retired on 31st March, 2023 and his share was acquired by C and D equally. On the retirement of A, goodwill is valued at 3 years purchase of average profit of last 4 years.

The profit/loss of last 4 years were 20,000 (loss), 50,000, 70,000 and 60,000

On the date of retirement, balance sheet shows a reserve of ₹ 1,30,000.

Questions

(i) A's share of goodwill

(A) ₹ 1,20,000 ☐

(B) ₹ 48,000 ☐

(C) ₹ 24,000 ☐

(D) Nil ☐

(ii) For accounting of goodwill, at the time of A's retirement, C's account will be debited/credited with

(A) credit by ₹ 24,000 ☐

(B) debit by ₹ 24,000 ☐

(C) debit by ₹ 48,000 ☐

(D) credit by ₹ 48,000 ☐

(iii) A's share in general reserve will be

(A) ₹ 13,000 ☐

(B) ₹ 26,000 ☐

(C) ₹ 39,000 ☐

(D) ₹ 52,000 ☐

Case 2 Rohit, Karan and Karim are partners sharing profits and losses in the ratio of 14 : 5 : 6 respectively. Karan retires and surrenders his entire share in favour of Rohit. The goodwill of the firm is valued at 2 years' purchase of super profit based on average profits of last three years.

The profits for the last three years are ₹ 50,000, ₹ 55,000 and ₹ 60,000, respectively. The normal profits for the similar firm are ₹ 30,000. Goodwill already appears in the books of the firm at ₹ 75,000.

Questions

(i) What is the value of goodwill determined by using super profit method?

(A) ₹ 50,000 ☐

(B) ₹ 10,000 ☐

(C) ₹ 30,000 ☐

(D) ₹ 75,000 ☐

(ii) In which ratio, existing goodwill of ₹ 75,000 be written-off?

(A) 14 : 5 : 6 ☐

(B) New ratio, after Karan retirement ☐

(C) In gaining ratio ☐

(D) None of the above ☐

Subjective Questions

Free Response Questions, Open-ended Questions etc.

No. of Questions : **10** Suggested Time : **80 Minutes**

1. Kavi, Ravi, Kumar and Guru were partners in a firm sharing profits in the ratio of 3 : 2 : 2 : 1. On 1st February, 2024, Guru retired and the new profit sharing ratio decided between Kavi, Ravi and Kumar was 3 : 1 : 1. On Guru's retirement, the goodwill of the firm was valued at ₹ 3,60,000. Showing your working notes clearly, pass necessary journal entry in the books of the firm for the treatment of goodwill on Guru's retirement.

2. Arjun, Bheem and Nakul are partners sharing profits and losses in the ratio of 14 : 5 : 6 respectively. Bheem retires and surrenders his 5/25th share in favour of Arjun. The goodwill of the firm is valued at 2 years' purchase of super profits based on average profits of last 3 years. The profits of the last three years are ₹ 50,000, ₹ 55,000 and ₹ 60,000 respectively.

   The normal profits of the similar firms are ₹ 30,000. Goodwill already appears in the books of the firm at ₹ 75,000. The profit for the first year after the Bheem's retirement was ₹ 1,00,000. Give necessary journal entries to adjust goodwill and distribute profits showing your workings.

3. Raman, Ratan and Rajan were partners sharing profits in the ratio of 4:2:1 respectively. Following was their balance sheet as at 31st March, 2013

Balance Sheet
as at 31st March, 2013

Liabilities		Amt (₹)	Assets	Amt (₹)
Creditors		30,000	Cash	14,000
Bills Payable		4,000	Stock	30,000
General Reserve		21,000	Debtors	22,000
Capitals A/cs			Building	40,000
Raman	60,000		Plant	53,000
Ratan	40,000		Motor Van	26,000
Rajan	30,000	1,30,000		
		1,85,000		1,85,000

On the above date, Raman retired and following were agreed

(i) The assets and liabilities were valued as: stock ₹ 24,000, debtors ₹ 21,000, building ₹ 45,200, plant ₹ 50,000 and creditors ₹ 28,000.

(ii) Amount due to Raman will be transferred to Raman's loan account.

Prepare revaluation account and Raman's capital account.

4. Nandan, John and Rosa are partners sharing profits in the ratio of 4 : 3 : 2. On 1st April, 2024, John gave a notice to retire from the firm. Nandan and Rosa decided to share future profits in the ratio of 1 : 1. The capital accounts of Nandan and Rosa after all adjustments showed a balance of ₹ 43,000 and ₹ 80,500 respectively. The total amount to be paid to John was ₹ 95,500. This amount was to be paid by Nandan and Rosa in such a way that their capitals become proportionate to their new profit sharing ratio. Pass necessary journal entries in the books of the firm for the above transactions. Show your workings clearly.

5. Reyansh, Aayushman and Sabhya were partners in a firm sharing profits and losses in the ratio of 5 : 3 : 2. Their balance sheet as at 31st March, 2022 was as under

Balance Sheet of Reyansh, Aayushman and Sabhya
as at 31st March, 2022

Liabilities		Amt (₹)	Assets		Amt (₹)
Sundry Creditors		2,20,000	Cash		1,60,000
General Reserve		1,20,000	Debtors	1,80,000	
Capital A/cs			(–) Provision for Doubtful Debts	(20,000)	1,60,000
Reyansh	6,00,000		Stock		2,00,000
Aayushman	5,00,000		Machinery		6,00,000
Sabhya	3,00,000	14,00,000	Building		4,00,000
			Patents		1,20,000
			Profit and Loss A/c		1,00,000
		17,40,000			17,40,000

Reyansh retired on the above date and it was agreed that

(i) Goodwill of the firm on Reyansh's retirement was valued at ₹ 12,00,000.
(ii) Aayushman and Sabhya will share future profits in the ratio of 2 : 3.
(iii) An unrecorded creditor of ₹ 40,000 will be taken into account.
(iv) Debtors of ₹ 30,000 will be written-off as bad debts.
(v) Amount payable to Reyansh was to be transferred to his loan account.

Pass necessary journal entries for the above transactions in the books of the firm. *[CBSE 2023]*

6. Prina, Qadir and Kian were partners in a firm sharing profits in the ratio of 7 : 2 : 1. On 31st March, 2023 their balance sheet was as follows

Balance Sheet of Prina, Qadir and Kian
as at 31st March, 2023

Liabilities		Amt (₹)	Assets		Amt (₹)
Capital A/cs			Land		12,00,000
Prina	9,60,000		Building		9,00,000
Qadir	8,40,000		Furniture		3,60,000
Kian	9,00,000	27,00,000	Stock		6,60,000
General Reserve		3,00,000	Debtors	6,00,000	
Workmen's Compensation Reserve		5,40,000	(–) Provision for Doubtful Debts	(30,000)	5,70,000
Creditors		3,60,000	Cash at Bank		2,10,000
		39,00,000			39,00,000

On the above date, Qadir retired on the following terms

(i) Goodwill of the firm was valued at ₹ 12,00,000.
(ii) Land was to be appreciated by 30% and building was to be depreciated by ₹ 3,54,000.
(iii) A provision of 6% is to be maintained on debtors.
(iv) Liability for workmen's compensation was determined at ₹ 1,40,000.
(v) Amount payable to Qadir was transferred to his loan account.
(vi) Total capital of the new firm was fixed at ₹ 16,00,000 which will be adjusted according to their new profit ratio by opening current accounts.

Prepare revaluation account and partners' capital account. *[CBSE 2024]*

7. Anna, Bina and Teena were partners sharing profits and losses in the ratio of 5 : 3 : 2. Their balance sheet on 31st March, 2022 was as follows

Balance Sheet of Anna, Bina and Teena
as at 31st March, 2022

Liabilities		Amt (₹)	Assets		Amt (₹)
Creditors		66,000	Furniture		1,12,000
Bills Payable		59,000	Stock		1,77,000
Capital A/cs			Debtors	2,80,000	
Anna	2,00,000		(–) Provision for Bad Debts	(7,000)	2,73,000
Bina	2,00,000		Cash		63,000
Teena	1,00,000	5,00,000			
		6,25,000			6,25,000

On the above date, Anna retried on the following terms

(i) Goodwill of the firm was valued at ₹ 60,000 and Anna's share of goodwill was adjusted through the capital accounts of remaining partners.
(ii) Furniture was depreciated by ₹ 10,000.
(iii) Anna was to be paid through cash brought in by Bina and Teena is such a way as to make their capitals proportionate to their new profits sharing ratio of 1 : 1.

Prepare revaluation and partner's capital accounts. [CBSE 2023]

8. Nirmala, Divisha and Sara were partners in a firm sharing profits and losses in the 3 : 4 : 3. Books were closed on 31st March every year. Sara died on 1st February, 2022. As per the partnership deed, Sara's executors are entitled to her share of profit till the date of death on the basis of sales turnover.

Sales for the year ended 31st March, 2021 was ₹ 10,00,000 and profit for the same year was ₹ 1,20,000. Sales show a positive trend of 20% and percentage of profit earning is reduced by 2%.

Journalise the transaction along with the working notes.

9. Ashok, Babu and Chetan were partners in a firm sharing profits in the ratio of 4 : 3 : 3. The firm closes its books on 31st March every year. On 31st December, 2016, Ashok died. The partnership deed provided that on the death of a partner, his executors will be entitled to the following

(i) Balance in his capital account. On 1st April, 2016, there was a balance of ₹ 90,000 in Ashok's capital account.
(ii) Interest on capital @ 12% per annum.
(iii) His share in the profits of the firm in the year of his death will be calculated on the basis of rate of net profit on sales of the previous year, which was 25%. The sales of the firm till 30th December, 2016 were ₹ 4,00,000.
(iv) His share in the goodwill of the firm. The goodwill of the firm on Ashok's death was valued at ₹ 4,50,000.

The partnership deed also provided for the following deductions from the amount payable to the executor of the deceased partner.

(i) His drawings in the year of his death. Ashok's drawings till 31st December, 2016 were ₹ 15,000.
(ii) Interest on drawing @ 12% per annum which was calculated as ₹ 1,500.

The accountant of the firm prepared Ashok's capital account to be presented to the executor of Ashok but in a hurry, he left it incomplete. Ashok's capital account as prepared by the firm's accountant is given below

Dr **Ashok's Capital Account** Cr

Date	Particulars	Amt (₹)	Date	Particulars	Amt (₹)
2016			2016		
Dec 31	....	15,000	Apr 1	....	90,000
Dec 31	....	...	Dec 31	....	8,100
Dec 31	....	...	Dec 31	....	40,000
			Dec 31	....	90,000
			Dec 31	....	90,000
		3,18,100			3,18,100

You are required to complete Ashok's capital account.

10. Ram, Ravi and Rohan were partners sharing profits in the ratio of 2 : 3 : 1. On 31st March, 2023 their balance sheet was as follows

Balance Sheet of Ram, Ravi and Rohan
as at 31st March, 2023

Liabilities		Amt (₹)	Assets		Amt (₹)
Creditors		3,62,000	Cash		14,000
General Reserve		18,000	Bank		2,96,000
Capital A/cs			Stock		80,000
Ram	1,00,000		Debtors	3,00,000	
Ravi	2,00,000		(–) Provision for Doubtful Debts	(10,000)	2,90,000
Rohan	3,00,000	6,00,000	Investments		50,000
			Land		2,50,000
		9,80,000			9,80,000

Rohan died on 30th September, 2023. On the death of a partner the partnership deed provided for the following

(i) Goodwill was to be valued at two years purchase of average profit of last three years. The profits for the last three years were 2020-21 – ₹ 45,000, 2021-22 – ₹ 90,000 and 2022-23 – ₹ 1,35,000.

(ii) Deceased partner's share of profit till the date of his death will be calculated on the basis of average profit of last thre years.

Prepare Rohan's capital account to be rendered to his executors. [CBSE 2024]

Answers

If your answer matches with the answer given here then put (✓) in the box otherwise put (✗). In case you did not attempt the question leave the box blank.

Multiple Choice Questions

1. B ☐ 2. C ☐
3. B ☐ 4. C ☐
5. D ☐ 6. B ☐
7. D ☐ 8. D ☐
9. C ☐ 10. A ☐
11. B ☐ 12. B ☐
13. A ☐ 14. B ☐
15. C ☐ 16. D ☐
17. D ☐ 18. A ☐
19. D ☐ 20. D ☐
21. A ☐ 22. C ☐
23. D ☐ 24. D ☐
25. B ☐ 26. C ☐
27. A ☐ 28. A ☐
29. D ☐ 30. D ☐
31. A ☐ 32. C ☐
33. A ☐ 34. C ☐

Your Score__________ *(No. of Correct Answers)*

Assertion-Reason Questions

1. C ☐ 2. B ☐
3. A ☐ 4. C ☐
5. A ☐ 6. B ☐
7. A ☐ 8. B ☐

Your Score__________ *(No. of Correct Answers)*

Correct/Incorrect Statements

1. B ☐ 2. C ☐
3. C ☐ 4. B ☐
5. C ☐ 6. D ☐
7. A ☐ 8. C ☐

Your Score__________ *(No. of Correct Answers)*

Case Based Questions

1. (i) B ☐ (ii) B ☐
(iii) D ☐
2. (i) A ☐ (ii) A ☐

Your Score__________ *(No. of Correct Answers)*

Explanations

Multiple Choice Questions

1. (B) 6% p.a.

2. (C) David's New Share

$$= \frac{3}{8} + \left[\frac{1}{2} \times \frac{1}{2}\right] = \frac{3}{8} + \frac{1}{4} = \frac{3+2}{8} = \frac{5}{8}$$

Bhavishya's New Share

$$= \frac{1}{8} + \left[\frac{1}{2} \times \frac{1}{2}\right] = \frac{1}{8} + \frac{1}{4} = \frac{1+2}{8} = \frac{3}{8}$$

∴ New Ratio = 5 : 3

3. (B) $Q\text{'s New} = \frac{3}{10} \times \frac{5}{5} = \frac{15}{50}$

$$R\text{'s New} = \frac{2}{10} + \left[\frac{3}{10} \times \frac{3}{5}\right] = \frac{2}{10} + \frac{9}{50}$$

$$= \frac{10+9}{50} = \frac{19}{50}$$

$$S\text{'s New} = \frac{2}{10} + \left[\frac{3}{10} \times \frac{2}{5}\right] = \frac{2}{10} + \frac{6}{50} = \frac{10+6}{50} = \frac{16}{50}$$

∴ New Ratio = 15 : 19 : 16

4. (C) $A\text{'s old share} = \frac{5}{8} - \frac{1}{9} = \frac{45-8}{72} = \frac{37}{72}$

$$B\text{'s old share} = \frac{3}{8} - \frac{2}{9} = \frac{27-16}{72} = \frac{11}{72}$$

$$C\text{'s Share} = \frac{3}{9} \times \frac{8}{8} = \frac{24}{72}$$

∴ Old Ratio = 37 : 11 : 24

5. (D) $\frac{\text{Gopal}}{\text{Govind}} = \frac{80{,}000}{40{,}000} = \frac{2}{1}$

∴ Gaining ratio = 2 : 1

6. (B) $\text{Nita} = \frac{2}{6} + \frac{3}{6} \times \frac{1}{2} = \frac{4+3}{12} = \frac{7}{12}$

Anita $= \frac{1}{6} + \frac{3}{6} \times \frac{1}{2} = \frac{2+3}{12} = \frac{5}{12}$

New profit sharing ratio = 7 : 5

7. (D) Amount debited to R's account

$$= 15,000 \times \frac{1}{3} = ₹\ 5,000$$

Amount credited to R $= 60,000 \times \frac{1}{3} = ₹\ 20,000$

∴ Net credit in R's capital account

$$= 20,000 - 5,000 = ₹\ 15,000$$

8. (D) Firm's Goodwill $= 36,000 \times \frac{10}{3} = ₹\ 1,20,000$

C's Goodwill = Firm's Goodwill × C's Gain

48,000 = 1,20,000 × C's Gain

C's Gain $= \frac{48,000}{1,20,000} = \frac{2}{5}$

C's New share $= \frac{2}{10} + \frac{2}{5} = \frac{6}{10}$

A's Goodwill = Firm's Goodwill × A's Sacrifice

12,000 = 1,20,000 × A's Sacrifice

A's Sacrifice $= \frac{12,000}{1,20,000} = \frac{1}{10}$

A's New Ratio $= \frac{5}{10} - \frac{1}{10} = \frac{4}{10}$

∴ New profit sharing ratio = 4 : 6 *or* 2 : 3

9. (C)

	A	:	B	:	C
Old ratio	3	:	2	:	1

A's Share $= \frac{3}{6}$

B's New Share

$$= \frac{2}{6} + \left(\frac{3}{6} \times \frac{2}{3}\right) = \frac{2}{6} + \frac{6}{18} = \frac{6+6}{18} = \frac{12}{18}$$

C's New Share $= \frac{1}{6} + \left(\frac{3}{6} \times \frac{1}{3}\right) = \frac{3+3}{18} = \frac{6}{18}$

∴ New ratio = 12 : 6 *or* 2 : 1

10. (A) Q's New Share $= \frac{3}{16} + \frac{3}{16} = \frac{6}{16}$

[change option A as 3 : 5]

R's New Share $= \frac{5}{16} + \frac{5}{16} = \frac{10}{16}$

= 6 : 10 *or* 3 : 5

11. (B) Old Ratio = 2 : 1 : 1

Gain Ratio = 1 : 5

A's New Share

$$= \frac{2}{4} + \left[\frac{1}{4} \times \frac{1}{6}\right] = \frac{2}{4} + \frac{1}{24} = \frac{12+1}{24} = \frac{13}{24}$$

B's New Share

$$= \frac{1}{4} + \left[\frac{1}{4} \times \frac{5}{6}\right] = \frac{1}{4} + \frac{5}{24} = \frac{6+5}{24} = \frac{11}{24}$$

12. (B) If the amount paid to the retiring partner is excess of capital account after all adjustments, then the difference is for goodwill amount.

13. (A) New ratio between Suresh and Tushar = 6 : 4

Gaining ratio of Suresh $= \frac{6}{15} - \frac{6}{10} = \frac{60-90}{150} = \left(\frac{30}{150}\right)$

Tushar $= \frac{4}{15} - \frac{4}{10} = \frac{40-60}{150} = \left(\frac{20}{150}\right)$

Gaining ratio = 3 : 2

Goodwill of Ramesh = 2,90,000 – 2,50,400

= ₹ 39,600

∴ Suresh will be debited by $39,600 \times \frac{3}{5} = ₹\ 23,760$

14. (B) Unrecorded asset is credited to revaluation account

∴ Revaluation profit = ₹ 4,000

So, B's share $= 4,000 \times \frac{3}{10} = ₹\ 1,200$

(Credited to B's account)

15. (C) C's Capital

$$= 1,00,000 + \left[5,00,000 \times \frac{1}{5}\right] = ₹\ 2,00,000$$

16. (D) Provision for bad debt will be credited by ₹ 3,000

17. (D)

Dr **Revaluation Account** Cr

Particulars	Amt (₹)	Particulars	Amt (₹)
To Patents	10,000	By Stock	20,000
To Damages	10,000		
	20,000		20,000

18. (A) C's balance for all the adjustments but before goodwill = ₹ 2,50,000

Final payment made to C = ₹ 3,22,000

∴ C's goodwill = 3,22,000 – 2,50,000 = ₹ 72,000

19. (D)

Amay's Capital Account Balance	₹ 50,000
(+) General Reserve $\left(7,500 \times \frac{1}{3}\right)$	₹ 2,500
(+) Goodwill $\left(30,000 \times \frac{1}{3}\right)$	₹ 10,000
(+) Revaluation Profit $\left(24,000 \times \frac{1}{3}\right)$	₹ 8,000
	₹ 70,500

20. (D) B's Share = 70,000 + 10,000 + 12,000 + 3,000
(Capital) (Reserve) (Goodwill) (Reserve)
= ₹ 95,000

21. (A) Total amount payable to B = ₹ 2,40,000
Amount of bank overdraft = 2,40,000 – 60,000
= ₹ 1,80,000

22. (C) Gaining ratio of T = $\frac{1}{3}$
Amount of G's goodwill paid by T = ₹ 80,000
Goodwill of the firm = 80,000 × $\frac{3}{1}$ = ₹ 2,40,000

23. (D)

	Amt (₹)
New Capital (2,80,000 × 1/2)	1,40,000
(–) Old Capital	(1,08,000)
Toni will bring	32,000

24. (D) Since the partner is dead, only his legal representatives are entitled to receive the outstanding balance of deceased partner.

25. (B) Profit and loss appropriation account

26. (C) Gaining Ratio = New Ratio – Old Ratio
Vishesh = $\frac{4}{7} - \frac{1}{3} = \frac{12-7}{21} = \frac{5}{21}$
Nimesh = $\frac{3}{7} - \frac{1}{3} = \frac{9-7}{21} = \frac{2}{21}$

27. (A) A's Share in Profit = $\left(\frac{45,000}{3,00,000} \times 1,20,000\right) \times \frac{4}{9}$
= ₹ 8,000

28. (A) P's share of profit
= $\left[\frac{96,000}{12,00,000} \times 1,00,000\right] \times \frac{4}{8}$ = ₹ 4,000

29. (D) Z's Profit = $\left(1,40,000 \times \frac{20}{100}\right) \times \frac{1}{5}$ = ₹ 5,600

30. (D) P's Share = 80,000 × $\frac{4}{8}$ = ₹ 40,000

31. (A) Profit and loss suspense account

32. (C) (ii) (iii) (i)

33. (A) (i) (ii) (iv) (iii)

34. (C) (ii) (iii) (i) (iv)

Assertion-Reason Questions

1. (C) Assertion (A) is true, but Reason (R) is false
2. (B) Both Assertion (A) and Reason (R) are true, but Reason (R) is not the correct explanation of Assertion (A)
3. (A) Both Assertion (A) and Reason (R) are true and Reason (R) is the correct explanation of Assertion (A)
4. (C) Assertion (A) is true, but Reason (R) is false
5. (A) Both Assertion (A) and Reason (R) are true and Reason (R) is the correct explanation of Assertion (A)
6. (B) Both Assertion (A) and Reason (R) are true, but Reason (R) is not the correct explanation of Assertion (A)
7. (A) Both Assertion (A) and Reason (R) are true and Reason (R) is the correct explanation of Assertion (A)
8. (B) Both Assertion (A) and Reason (R) are true, but Reason (R) is not the correct explanation of Assertion (A)

Correct/Incorrect Statements

1. (B) The amount due to retiring partner is either paid-off immediately or is transferred to his loan account.
2. (C) A partner can retire from the firm if either there is an agreement to that effect or all partners must agree in the absence of deed.
3. (C) A retiring partner cannot nominate any member of his family as new partner in the firm.
4. (B) The balance amount of deceased partner will be transferred to his executor's account.
5. (C) Statement II is correct and Statement I is incorrect
6. (D) Both statements are incorrect
7. (A) Both the statements are correct
8. (C) The balance amount of deceased partner can either transferred to his executor's account or settled in cash.

Case Based Questions

1. (i) (B) C's Gain = $\frac{4}{10} \times \frac{1}{2} = \frac{4}{20}$

D's Gain = $\frac{4}{10} \times \frac{1}{2} = \frac{4}{20}$

Goodwill
= $\left(\frac{-20,000 + 50,000 + 70,000 + 60,000}{4}\right) \times 3$
= 1,20,000

A's share = 1,20,000 × $\frac{4}{10}$ = ₹ 48,000 (Cr)

(ii) (B) **Goodwill of the Firm**

$$\text{Average Profit} = \frac{(20{,}000) + 50{,}000 + 70{,}000 + 60{,}000}{4} = ₹\ 40{,}000$$

Goodwill = 40,000 × 3 = ₹ 1,20,000

$$\text{A's share in goodwill} = 1{,}20{,}000 \times \frac{4}{10} = ₹\ 48{,}000$$

$$\text{C's gain} = \frac{1}{2};\quad \text{C's share in goodwill} = 48{,}000 \times \frac{1}{2} = 24{,}000\ (\text{Dr})$$

(iii) (D) ₹ 52,000

2. (i) (A) $$\text{Super Profit} = \left[\frac{50{,}000 + 55{,}000 + 60{,}000}{3}\right] - [30{,}000] = ₹\ 25{,}000$$

∴ Goodwill = 25,000 × 2 = ₹ 50,000

(ii) (A) 14 : 5 : 6

Subjective Questions

1. **JOURNAL**

Date	Particulars		LF	Amt (Dr)	Amt (Cr)
2024					
Feb 1	Kavi's Capital A/c	Dr		81,000	
	To Ravi's Capital A/c				18,000
	To Kumar's Capital A/c				18,000
	To Guru's Capital A/c				45,000
	(Being amount of goodwill adjusted)				

Working Notes

1. **Calculation of Gaining Ratio**

Gaining Ratio = New Share – Old Share

$$\text{Kavi} = \frac{3}{5} - \frac{3}{8} = \frac{24-15}{40} = \frac{9}{40};\quad \text{Ravi} = \frac{1}{5} - \frac{2}{8} = \frac{8-10}{40} = \left(\frac{2}{40}\right)\text{Sacrifice}$$

$$\text{Kumar} = \frac{1}{5} - \frac{2}{8} = \frac{8-10}{40} = \left(\frac{2}{40}\right)\text{Sacrifice}$$

2. **Calculation of Share of Goodwill**

$$\text{Guru's share of goodwill} = 3{,}60{,}000 \times \frac{1}{8} = ₹\ 45{,}000$$

$$\text{Kavi gains} = 3{,}60{,}000 \times \frac{9}{40} = ₹\ 81{,}000;\quad \text{Ravi sacrifices} = 3{,}60{,}000 \times \frac{2}{40} = ₹\ 18{,}000$$

$$\text{Kumar sacrifices} = 3{,}60{,}000 \times \frac{2}{40} = ₹\ 18{,}000$$

2. **JOURNAL**

Date	Particulars		LF	Amt (Dr)	Amt (Cr)
	Arjun's Capital A/c (75,000× 14/25)	Dr		42,000	
	Bheem's Capital A/c (75,000× 5/25)	Dr		15,000	
	Nakul's Capital A/c (75,000× 6/25)	Dr		18,000	
	To Goodwill A/c				75,000
	(Being amount of goodwill written-off in old ratio)				

Date	Particulars		LF	Amt (Dr)	Amt (Cr)
	Arjun's Capital A/c	Dr		10,000	
	To Bheem's Capital A/c				10,000
	(Being amount of goodwill adjusted in gaining ratio)				
	Profit and Loss Appropriation A/c	Dr		1,00,000	
	To Arjun's Capital A/c (1,00,000 × 19/25)				76,000
	To Nakul's Capital A/c (1,00,000 × 6/25)				24,000
	(Being profit distributed among partners)				

Working Notes

1. **Calculation of New Profit Sharing Ratio and Gaining Ratio**

Old ratio of Arjun, Bheem and Nakul = 14 : 5 : 6

Bheem surrenders in favour of Arjun = $\frac{5}{25}$th share, Arjun's new share = $\frac{14}{25} + \frac{5}{25} = \frac{19}{25}$

New ratio of Arjun and Nakul = 19 : 6

Gaining Ratio = New Share – Old Share

Arjun = $\frac{19}{25} - \frac{14}{25} = \frac{19-14}{25} = \frac{5}{25}$; Nakul = $\frac{6}{25} - \frac{6}{25} = \frac{6-6}{25}$ = Nil

2. **Calculation of Bheem's Share of Goodwill**

Actual average profit = $\frac{50{,}000 + 55{,}000 + 60{,}000}{3}$ = ₹ 55,000

Normal profit = ₹ 30,000

Super Profit = Average Profit – Normal Profit = 55,000 – 30,000 = ₹ 25,000

Firm's goodwill = 25,000 × 2 = ₹ 50,000

Bheem's share of goodwill = 50,000 × $\frac{5}{25}$ = ₹ 10,000 (to be contributed by Arjun alone)

3. Dr **Revaluation Account** Cr

Particulars	Amt (₹)	Particulars		Amt (₹)
To Stock A/c	6,000	By Building A/c		5,200
To Debtors A/c	1,000	By Creditors A/c		2,000
To Plant A/c	3,000	By Loss on Revaluation Transferred to Capital A/cs		
		Raman	1,600	
		Ratan	800	
		Rajan	400	2,800
	10,000			10,000

Dr **Raman's Capital Account** Cr

Date	Particulars	Amt (₹)	Date	Particulars	Amt (₹)
2013			2013		
Mar 31	To Revaluation A/c (Loss)	1,600	Mar 31	By Balance b/d	60,000
Mar 31	To Raman's Loan A/c	70,400	Mar 31	By General Reserve (21,000 × 4/7)	12,000
		72,000			72,000

4. JOURNAL

Date	Particulars		LF	Amt (Dr)	Amt (Cr)
2024					
Apr 1	Cash A/c	Dr		95,500	
	To Nandan's Capital A/c				66,500
	To Rosa's Capital A/c				29,000
	(Being cash to be paid to John brought in by Nandan and Rosa)				
Apr 1	John's Capital A/c	Dr		95,500	
	To Cash A/c				95,500
	(Being cash paid to John for his capital)				

Working Notes

Particulars	Amt (₹)
Adjusted Capitals of Nandan and Rosa (43,000 + 80,500)	1,23,500
(+) Amount to be Paid to John	95,500
Total Capital of New Firm	2,19,000

Amount to be Brought in or Withdrawn

Particulars	Nandan (₹)	Rosa (₹)
New Firm's Capital (2,19,000) in New Ratio, i.e. 1:1	1,09,500	1,09,500
(–) Existing Capitals	(43,000)	(80,500)
Cash to be Brought in	66,500	29,000

5. JOURNAL

Date	Particulars		LF	Amt (Dr)	Amt (Cr)
	General Reserve A/c	Dr		1,20,000	
	To Reyansh's Capital A/c				60,000
	To Aayushman's Capital A/c				36,000
	To Sabhya's Capital A/c				24,000
	(Being general reserve distributed in old profit sharing ratio)				
	Reyansh's Capital A/c	Dr		50,000	
	Aayushman's Capital A/c	Dr		30,000	
	Sabhya's Capital A/c	Dr		20,000	
	To Profit and Loss A/c				1,00,000
	(Being loss distributed in old profit sharing ratio)				
	Aayushman's Capital A/c	Dr		1,20,000	
	Sabhya's Capital A/c	Dr		4,80,000	
	To Reyansh's Capital A/c				6,00,000
	(Being goodwill adjusted in the gaining ratio 1: 4)				
	Revaluation A/c	Dr		40,000	
	To Creditors A/c				40,000
	(Being unrecorded creditors now recorded)				

Date	Particulars		LF	Amt (Dr)	Amt (Cr)
	Revaluation A/c	Dr		10,000	
	Provision of Doubtful Debts A/c	Dr		20,000	
	To Debtors A/c				30,000
	(Being the debtors written-off as bad debts)				
	Reyansh's Capital A/c	Dr		25,000	
	Aayushman's Capital A/c	Dr		15,000	
	Sabhya's Capital A/c	Dr		10,000	
	To Revaluation A/c				50,000
	(Being revaluation loss distributed)				
	Reyansh's Capital A/c	Dr		11,85,000	
	To Reyansh's Loan A/c				11,85,000
	(Being the balance of Reyansh's capital account transferred to his loan account (6,00,000 + 60,000 – 50,000 + 6,00,000 – 25,000)				

Working Notes

1. Calculation of Gaining/Sacrificing Ratio

   Aayushman $= \frac{3}{10} - \frac{2}{5} = \frac{3-4}{10} = -\frac{1}{10}$ (Gain) ; Sabhya $= \frac{2}{10} - \frac{3}{5} = \frac{2-6}{10} = -\frac{4}{10}$ (Gain)

   Gaining ratio is 1 : 4

2. Calculation of Reyansh Share of Goodwill = 1,20,000 × $\frac{5}{10}$ = ₹ 6,00,000

6. Dr **Revaluation Account** Cr

Particulars	Amt (₹)	Particulars	Amt (₹)
To Building A/c	3,54,000	By Land A/c	3,60,000
To Provision for Doubtful Debts	6,000		
	3,60,000		3,60,000

Dr **Partners' Capital Account** Cr

Particulars	Prina (₹)	Qadir (₹)	Kian (₹)	Particulars	Prina (₹)	Qadir (₹)	Kian (₹)
To Qadir's Capital A/c	2,10,000	—	30,000	By Balance b/d	9,60,000	8,40,000	9,00,000
To Qadir's Loan A/c	—	12,20,000	—	By Prina's Capital A/c	—	2,10,000	—
To Balance c/d	14,00,000	—	2,00,000	By Kian's Capital A/c	—	30,000	—
To Bank A/c	—	—	7,40,000	By Workmen Compensation Reserve A/c	2,80,000	80,000	40,000
				By General Reserve A/c	2,10,000	60,000	30,000
				By Bank A/c	1,60,000	—	—
	16,10,000	12,20,000	9,70,000		16,10,000	12,20,000	9,70,000

Working Notes

1. **Entry for Goodwill**

Prina's Capital A/c	Dr	2,10,000	
Kian's Capital A/c	Dr	30,000	
To Qadir's Capital A/c			2,40,000

2. **Capitals of Partners in New Firm**

   Prina's Capital (16,00,000 × 7/8) = ₹ 14,00,000 ; Kian's Capital (16,00,000 × 1/8) = ₹ 2,00,000

7. Dr **Revaluation Account** Cr

Particulars	Amt (₹)	Particulars		Amt (₹)
To Furniture A/c	10,000	By Revaluation Loss Transfer to Capital A/c		
		Anna	5,000	
		Bina	3,000	
		Teena	2,000	10,000
	10,000			10,000

Dr **Partners' Capital Account** Cr

Particulars	Anna (₹)	Bina (₹)	Teena (₹)	Particulars	Anna (₹)	Bina (₹)	Teena (₹)
To Revaluation A/c	5,000	3,000	2,000	By Balance b/d	2,00,000	2,00,000	1,00,000
To Anna's Capital A/c	—	12,000	18,000	By Bina's Capital A/c	12,000	—	—
To Balance c/d	2,25,000	1,85,000	80,000	By Teena's Capital A/c	18,000	—	—
	2,30,000	2,00,000	1,00,000		2,30,000	2,00,000	1,00,000
To Cash A/c	2,25,000	—	—	By Balance b/d	2,25,000	1,85,000	80,000
To Balanced c/d	—	2,13,500	2,13,500	By Cash A/c (B/F)	—	28,500	1,33,500
	2,25,000	2,13,500	2,13,500		2,25,000	2,13,500	2,13,500

Working Notes

1. Calculation of Gaining Ratio

Bina $= \frac{3}{10} - \frac{1}{2} = \frac{3-5}{10} = \left(\frac{2}{10}\right)$ Gain; Teena $= \frac{2}{10} - \frac{1}{2} = \frac{2-5}{10} = \left(\frac{3}{10}\right)$ Gain ; Gaining ratio = 2 : 3

2. Calculation of Anna Share of Goodwill $= 60{,}000 \times \frac{5}{10} =$ ₹ 30,000

3. Calculation of total capital of the firm after Anna's retirement

(i) Balance of Capital Account of Bina and Teena after all adjustment

Bina	1,85,000
Teena	80,000
	2,65,000

(ii) Shortage of cash to be brought in by Bina and Teena in order to make payment to Anna

Anna's Balance in Capital A/c	2,25,000
(–) Cash available	(63,000)
	1,62,000

Total capital of a firm (i) + (ii) = 2,65,000 + 1,62,000 = ₹ 4,27,000

New capital of Bina and Teena in ratio of 1 : 1= 4,27,000 × 1/2 = ₹ 2,13,500

8. **JOURNAL**

Date	Particulars		LF	Amt (Dr)	Amt (Cr)
2022					
Feb 1	Profit and Loss Suspense A/c	Dr		30,000	
	To Sara's Capital A/c				30,000
	(Being Sara's share of profit allowed till the date of her death				

Working Notes

1. Profit % to sales turnover for the year ended 31st March, 2021 = 1,20,000/10,00,000 × 100 = 12%
2. Estimated sales for the year ended 31st March, 2022 = 10,00,000 + 20% of ₹ 10,00,000 = ₹ 12,00,000
3. Estimated sales till 1st February, 2022 = 12,00,000 × 10/12 = ₹ 10,00,000

4. Profit percentage 12 – 2 = 10%

   Profit amount till 1st February, 2022 = 10% of ₹ 10,00,000 = ₹ 1,00,000

   Sara's share of profit till 1st February, 2022 = $\frac{1,00,000 \times 3}{10}$ = ₹ 30,000

9. Dr **Ashok's Capital Account** Cr

Date	Particulars	Amt (₹)	Date	Particulars	Amt (₹)
2016			2016		
Dec 31	**To Drawings A/c**	15,000	April 1	**By Balance b/d**	90,000
Dec 31	**To Interest on Drawings A/c**	**1,500**	Dec 31	**By Interest on Capital A/c**	8,100
Dec 31	**To Ashok's Executor A/c**	**3,01,600**	Dec 31	**By Profit and Loss Suspense A/c**	40,000
			Dec 31	**By Babu's Capital A/c**	90,000
			Dec 31	**By Chetan's Capital A/c**	90,000
		3,18,100			3,18,100

Working Notes

1. Calculation of Interest on Capital = 90,000 × 12/100 × 9/12 = ₹ 8,100
2. Calculation of Profit = 4,00,000 × 25/100 × 4/10 = ₹ 40,000
3. Calculation of Ashok's Share of Goodwill

   Ashok's share of goodwill = 4,50,000 × 4/10 = ₹ 1,80,000 to be contributed by Babu and Chetan in gaining ratio, i.e. 3 : 3 *or* 1 : 1.

10. Dr **Rohan's Capital Account** Cr

Particulars	Amt (₹)	Particulars	Amt (₹)
To Rohan's Executor A/c	3,40,500	By Balance b/d	3,00,000
		By Ram's Capital A/c (30,000 × 2/5)	12,000
		By Ravi's Capital A/c (30,000 × 3/5)	18,000
		By Profit and Loss Suspense A/c (WN2)	7,500
		By General Reserve A/c (18,000 × 1/6)	3,000
	3,40,500		3,40,500

Working Notes

1. Average Profit = $\frac{45,000 + 90,000 + 1,35,000}{3}$ = ₹ 90,000

   Goodwill = 90,000 × 2 = ₹ 1,80,000

   Rohan's share of goodwill = 1,80,000 × 1/6 = 30,000, to be contributed by Ram and Ravi in their gaining ratio i.e. 2 : 3.

2. Rohan's share in profit = 90,000 × $\frac{1}{6} \times \frac{6}{12}$ = ₹ 7,500

CHAPTER-5

Dissolution of Partnership Firm

Types & Nos. of Questions

Multiple Choice Questions	-	36
Assertion-Reason Questions	-	8
Correct/Incorrect Statements	-	8
Case Based Question	-	1 Case, *with 3 Questions*
Subjective Questions	-	9

Trend Analysis

On the basis of analysis of last 2 years' papers, it is found that on an average 2 Multiple Choice Questions and 1 Long Answer Type Question are asked from this chapter.

Focus Topics of the Chapter

- Meaning and Types of Dissolution of Partnership Firm
- Settlement of Accounts
- Accounting Procedure of Dissolution of Partnership Firm

Multiple Choice Questions

No. of Questions : **36** Suggested Time : **55 Minutes**

Direction Each of the question given below is Multiple Choice Question (MCQ) i.e. there are Four Options/Choices for answer, out of which ONLY ONE is correct. You have to select the correct option. A response box is given with each option, mark (✓) in the box of the correct option. For each correct answer you will get 1 mark, while there is no penalty for incorrect answer or missed out questions.

1. On dissolution of partnership firm, realisation loss is first of all met

(A) out of the capital of the partners ☐
(B) out of the loan given by outsiders ☐
(C) out of private asset of partners ☐
(D) out of loan taken from partner ☐

2. A partnership firm can be dissolved in the following situations except

(A) By mutual agreement ☐
(B) When all partners become insolvent except one partner ☐
(C) When all partners become insolvent except two partners ☐
(D) Dissolution by court ☐

3. State the order of payment of the following in case of dissolution of partnership firm.

(i) Partners' loan
(ii) Debt of outside parties
(iii) Partners' capital

Codes

(A) (i) (ii) (iii) ☐ (B) (ii) (iii) (i) ☐
(C) (iii) (ii) (i) ☐ (D) (ii) (i) (iii) ☐

4. When realisation expenses are paid by the firm on behalf of a partner, such expenses are debited to

(A) realisation account ☐
(B) partners' capital account ☐
(C) partner's loan account ☐
(D) None of the above ☐

5. If a firm had a balance of ₹ 50,000 in creditor's account; capital ₹ 48,000; cash balance ₹ 3,000, what will be the amount of loss on realisation if assets of the firm are realised at a loss of 12%?

(A) ₹ 6,000 ☐ (B) ₹ 11,760 ☐
(C) ₹ 11,400 ☐ (D) ₹ 3,600 ☐

6. In the balance sheet, total debtors appear at ₹ 50,000 and provision for doubtful debts appear at ₹ 1,500. How much amount will be realised from debtors, if bad debts amount to ₹ 10,000 and remaining debtors are realised at a discount of 5%?

(A) ₹ 38,000 ☐ (B) ₹ 36,500 ☐
(C) ₹ 36,575 ☐ (D) ₹ 39,500 ☐

7. Investments valued ₹ 5,00,000 were not shown in the books. One of the creditors took over these investments in full satisfaction of his debt of ₹ 5,20,000. How much amount will be deducted from creditors?

(A) ₹ 20,000 ☐ (B) ₹ 5,20,000 ☐
(C) ₹ 4,20,000 ☐ (D) ₹ 5,00,000 ☐

8. Atul and Vipul are partners sharing profits and losses in the ratio of 5:3. They decided to dissolve the firm and on that date Vipul has taken over all the sundry assets at ₹ 3,85,000 which is more than 10% of their book value.

Amount of realisation gain/loss to be transferred to Vipul's account will be

(A) ₹ 13,125 (gain) ☐ (B) ₹ 13,125 (loss) ☐
(C) ₹ 14,438 (gain) ☐ (D) ₹ 14,438 (loss) ☐

9. One of the creditors of ₹ 25,000 took away some part of the stock worth ₹ 12,000 and cash ₹10,000 in full settlement of his claim. What will be the journal entry for the above?
   (A) Debit creditor's account and credit realisation account by ₹ 10,000 ☐
   (B) Debit realisation account and credit bank account by ₹ 10,000 ☐
   (C) Debit realisation account and credit creditors account by ₹ 10,000 ☐
   (D) No entry is required ☐

10. At the time of dissolution of firm, debtors appear on the asset side amounted to ₹ 60,000. One of the debtors of ₹ 25,000 become bad and could realise only 40%. Balance of the debtors realised at 80%.

    State the amount credited to realisation account on account of amount realised from debtors.
    (A) ₹ 43,000 ☐ (B) ₹ 17,000 ☐
    (C) ₹ 22,000 ☐ (D) ₹ 38,000 ☐

11. At the time of dissolution, goodwill appears in the books ₹ 10,000. Goodwill is transferred to realisation account but there is no realisable value is given. What will be the treatment of goodwill?
    (A) ₹ 10,000 will be transferred to credit side of realisation account ☐
    (B) ₹ 10,000 will transferred to credit of partner's capital account ☐
    (C) ₹ 10,000 will transferred to debit of partner's capital account ☐
    (D) No treatment as realised value is not given ☐

12. At the time of dissolution, stock appearing in balance sheet amounting to ₹ 60,000. A, one of the partners, took some of the stock at 18,000 (being 10% less than book value). Calculate value of remaining stock.
    (A) ₹ 42,000 ☐
    (B) ₹ 43,200 ☐
    (C) ₹ 40,000 ☐
    (D) ₹ 54,000 ☐

13. On dissolution of partnership firm, stock appearing in balance sheet was ₹ 1,00,000. 50% of the stock was taken by partner at ₹ 35,000 and balance sold at 20% less than book value. The amount transferred to realisation account will be
    (A) ₹ 35,000 ☐ (B) ₹ 40,000 ☐
    (C) ₹ 85,000 ☐ (D) ₹ 75,000 ☐

14. Creditors in the balance sheet were ₹ 2,00,000. Half of the creditors accepted stock worth ₹ 1,20,000 at 10% less than book value in full settlement of their claim and remaining creditors allowed 10% discount.

    Amount debited in realisation account for payment of creditors will be
    (A) ₹ 90,000 ☐ (B) ₹ 1,00,000 ☐
    (C) ₹ 1,20,000 ☐ (D) ₹ 1,08,000 ☐

15. On dissolution of firm, an unrecorded asset worth ₹ 2,000 was taken by partner for ₹ 2,500 against cash payment. Which account will be credited with what amount?
    (A) Partners' capital account by ₹ 2,000 ☐
    (B) Partners' capital account by ₹ 2,500 ☐
    (C) Cash account by ₹ 2,500 ☐
    (D) Realisation account by ₹ 2,000 ☐

16. X and Y are partners sharing profits and losses in the ratio of 2 : 1. In dissolution, firm earned a profit of ₹ 15,000 and X took over investment of ₹ 10,000.

    Final payments made to X and Y are ₹1,20,000 and ₹1,00,000 respectively. Capitals of X and Y at the time of dissolution will be
    (A) X – ₹ 1,05,000; Y – ₹ 95,000 ☐
    (B) X – ₹ 1,15,000; Y – ₹ 95,000 ☐
    (C) X – ₹ 1,15,000; Y – ₹ 1,00,000 ☐
    (D) X – ₹ 1,05,000; Y – ₹ 1,00,000 ☐

17. On dissolution, firm had a balance of ₹ 1,00,000 in machine account. One partner took half of machine at book value and remaining at 20% more than book value. Calculate realisation gain or loss.
    (A) ₹ 50,000 ☐ (B) ₹ 60,000 ☐
    (C) ₹ 1,10,000 ☐ (D) ₹ 10,000 ☐

18. On the dissolution of a partnership firm there were debtors of ₹ 34,000. Debtors of ₹ 1,000 became bad and 60% was realised from the remaining debtors. Which account will be debited and by how much amount on the realisation from debtors? *[CBSE 2024]*

(A) Realisation account by ₹ 33,000 ☐
(B) Profit and loss account by ₹ 1,000 ☐
(C) Cash account by ₹ 19,800 ☐
(D) Debtors account by ₹ 14,200 ☐

19. On dissolution of a partnership firm, furniture appearing in the balance sheet was ₹ 2,00,000. 50% of the furniture was taken over by a partner at ₹ 65,000 and balance 50% was sold at 20% less than the book value. The amount debited to bank account was *[CBSE 2023]*

(A) ₹ 1,45,000 ☐ (B) ₹ 80,000 ☐
(C) ₹ 65,000 ☐ (D) ₹ 1,85,000 ☐

20. At the time of dissolution of a firm, creditors are ₹ 70,000, firm's capital is ₹ 1,20,000, cash balance is ₹ 10,000. Other assets realised ₹ 1,50,000. Gain/Loss in the realisation account will be

(A) ₹ 30,000 (Gain) ☐
(B) ₹ 40,000 (Gain) ☐
(C) ₹ 40,000 (Loss) ☐
(D) ₹ 30,000 (Loss) ☐

21. On the basis of the following data, how much final payment will be made to a partner on firm's dissolution? Credit balance of capital account of the partner was ₹ 50,000. Share of loss on realisation amounted to ₹ 10,000. Firm's liability taken over by him was for ₹ 8,000.

(A) ₹ 32,000 ☐ (B) ₹ 48,000 ☐
(C) ₹ 40,000 ☐ (D) ₹ 52,000 ☐

22. A and B are partners sharing profits and losses in the ratio of 2:1. On the date of dissolution of the firm, workmen compensation reserve is stood in the books and there is no liability towards workmen compensation reserve.

Amount of workmen compensation reserve transferred to A's capital is ₹ 1,00,000. Total amount of workmen compensation reserve was

(A) ₹ 50,000 ☐ (B) ₹ 1,00,000 ☐
(C) ₹ 1,50,000 ☐ (D) ₹ 2,00,000 ☐

23. On dissolution of a firm, a partner's capital account has a credit balance of ₹ 42,000. His share of profit in realisation account is ₹ 9,000.

He has paid firm's realisation expenses ₹ 3,000. He will finally get a payment of

(A) ₹ 39,000 ☐ (B) ₹ 42,000 ☐
(C) ₹ 54,000 ☐ (D) ₹ 48,000 ☐

24. If dissolution expenses are paid by a partner and he had to bear the expenses, how it will be recorded?

(A) Debit realisation account and credit bank account ☐
(B) Debit realisation account and credit partners' capital account ☐
(C) Debit partners' capital account and credit bank account ☐
(D) Not recorded ☐

25. Raman, a partner is to carry out dissolution for which he gets ₹ 70,000 as remuneration. Realisation expenses of ₹ 45,000 were paid by the firm. Realisation account will be debited with

(A) ₹ 70,000 ☐ (B) ₹ 45,000 ☐
(C) ₹ 25,000 ☐ (D) ₹ 1,15,000 ☐

26. On the day of dissolution of the firm 'Roop Brothers' had partner's capital amounting to ₹ 1,50,000, external liabilities ₹ 35,000, cash balance ₹ 8,000 and profit and loss (debit) ₹ 7,000.

If realisation expense and loss on realisation amounted to ₹ 5,000 and ₹ 25,000 respectively, the amount realised by sale of assets is

(A) ₹ 1,64,000 ☐ (B) ₹ 1,45,000 ☐
(C) ₹ 1,57,000 ☐ (D) ₹ 1,50,000 ☐

27. On dissolution of the firm of Ramesh, Suresh and Naresh, Naresh had agreed to bear all realisation expenses for which he was paid ₹ 14,500. Actual expenses on realisation amounted to ₹ 11,000 which were paid by Naresh. The journal entry passed will be

(A) Debit Cash A/c and Credit Naresh by ₹ 11,000 ☐

(B) Debit Naresh and Credit Cash A/c by ₹ 14,500 ☐

(C) Debit Realisation A/c and Credit Naresh by ₹ 14,500 ☐

(D) Debit Realisation A/c and Credit Cash A/c by ₹ 14,500 ☐

28. Total assets of a partnership firm which was dissolved were ₹ 30,00,000 and its total liabilities were ₹ 6,00,000. Assets were realised at 80% and liabilities were settled at 5% less. If dissolution expenses were ₹ 30,000 profit or loss on dissolution were *[CBSE 2023]*

(A) Profit ₹ 18,00,000 ☐

(B) Loss ₹ 6,00,000 ☐

(C) Profit ₹ 6,00,000 ☐

(D) Loss ₹ 18,00,000 ☐

29. X, a partner, was appointed to look after the dissolution work, for which he was allowed a remuneration of ₹ 8,000. X agreed to bear the dissolution expenses. Actual dissolution expenses ₹ 9,500 were paid by X. How much amount will be debited to realisation account?

(A) ₹ 8,000 ☐ (B) ₹ 9,500 ☐

(C) ₹ 1,500 ☐ (D) ₹ 6,500 ☐

30. In case of dissolution, A one of the partners was paid only ₹ 5,000 for his loan to the firm which amounted to ₹ 5,500. ₹ 500 will be recorded in which account and on which side?

(A) Realisation account, credit side ☐

(B) Realisation account, debit side ☐

(C) Loan account, debit side ☐

(D) All of the above ☐

31. If firm had given loan to any partner, than at the time of dissolution, the loan will be settled by

(A) transferring it to the debit side of realisation account ☐

(B) transferring it to the credit side of realisation account ☐

(C) transferring it to the debit side of respective partners' capital account ☐

(D) transferring it to the credit side of realisation account ☐

32. At the time of dissolution of partnership firm, journal entry for the settlement of loan advanced by the firm to a partner would be

(A) Bank A/c Dr
To Loan to Partner A/c ☐

(B) Loan to Partner A/c Dr
To Bank A/c ☐

(C) Realisation A/c Dr
To Loan to Partner A/c ☐

(D) None of the above ☐

33. Match the following

	Column I		Column II
A.	Realisation expenses of ₹ 10,000 paid by firm, out of which 4,000 was to be borne by a partner.	(i)	Partners' capital will be credited by ₹ 4,000
B.	Realisation expenses paid ₹ 10,000 by partner, out of which 6,000 is to be borne by firm.	(ii)	Partners' capital will be debited by ₹ 4,000
C.	Realisation expenses of ₹ 4,000 paid by a partner.	(iii)	Partners' capital will be credited by ₹ 6,000
D.	Realisation expenses of ₹ 6,000 borne by a partner, but paid by the firm.	(iv)	Partners' capital will be debited by ₹ 6,000

Codes

	A	B	C	D	
(A)	(iii)	(ii)	(i)	(iv)	☐
(B)	(ii)	(iii)	(i)	(iv)	☐
(C)	(i)	(iv)	(ii)	(iii)	☐
(D)	(iii)	(iv)	(ii)	(i)	☐

34. Match the following

	Column I		Column II
A.	A's wife loan taken over by A	(i)	Realisation account
B.	Investment fluctuation reserve	(ii)	Partner's loan account and bank account
C.	Payment of partner's loan	(iii)	Realisation account and partners' capital account

Codes

	A	B	C
(A)	(ii)	(i)	(iii)
(B)	(iii)	(ii)	(i)
(C)	(iii)	(i)	(ii)
(D)	(ii)	(iii)	(i)

35. Match the following

	Column I		Column II
A.	Workman compensation reserve appears in balance sheet at ₹ 20,000 and liability arise for ₹ 12,000	(i)	Debit realisation account by ₹ 30,000
B.	Workman compensation reserve appears in balance sheet at ₹ 20,000 and liability arise at ₹ 30,000	(ii)	Debit realisation account by ₹ 12,000
C.	Workman compensation reserve appears in balance sheet at ₹ 40,000 and liability arise at ₹ 10,000	(iii)	Debit realisation account by ₹ 8,000
D.	Workman compensation reserve appears in balance sheet at ₹ 20,000 and liability arise at ₹ 8,000	(iv)	Debit realisation account by ₹ 10,000

Codes

	A	B	C	D
(A)	(iii)	(i)	(iv)	(ii)
(B)	(ii)	(i)	(iv)	(iii)
(C)	(iii)	(iv)	(i)	(ii)
(D)	(ii)	(iii)	(i)	(iv)

36. Match the following

	Column I		Column II
A.	X, Y and Z are in partnership. Y become insolvent. This is a case of	(i)	Dissolution of partnership firm
B.	X, Y and Z are partners. X is found guilty of misconduct by court.	(ii)	Dissolution by court
C.	X, Y and Z are in partnership. X and Z become insolvent.	(ii)	Compulsory dissolution of partnership firm

Codes

	A	B	C
(A)	(i)	(ii)	(iii)
(B)	(iii)	(i)	(ii)
(C)	(i)	(iii)	(ii)
(D)	(ii)	(i)	(iii)

Assertion-Reason Questions

No. of Questions : **8** Suggested Time : **15 Minutes**

Direction Each of the question given below consist of the two statements; one labelled as **Assertion** (A) and other as **Reason** (R). List of common options applicable for each question is given below

(A) Both Assertion (A) and Reason (R) are true and Reason (R) is the correct explanation of Assertion (A)

(B) Both Assertion (A) and Reason (R) are true, but Reason (R) is not the correct explanation of Assertion (A)

(C) Assertion (A) is true, but Reason (R) is false

(D) Assertion (A) is false, but Reason (R) is true

You have to select the codes as *A, B, C* or *D* as your answer to the question by marking (✓) in the response box given against each option.

1. **Assertion** (A) A firm is dissolved compulsorily when all the partners or all but one partner, become insolvent.

   Reason (R) Dissolution of partnership and dissolution of firm both are the same.

   (A) ☐ (B) ☐ (C) ☐ (D) ☐

2. **Assertion** (A) Dissolution of a partnership firm cannot take place without the intervention of court.

   Reason (R) A firm will compulsorily dissolve if the business of the firm becomes unlawful.

   (A) ☐ (B) ☐ (C) ☐ (D) ☐

3. **Assertion** (A) The private property of any partner will be applied first in payment of his private debts.

   Reason (R) If the assets of the firm are not adequate enough to pay-off the firm's liabilities, the partners have to contribute out of their net private assets.

   (A) ☐ (B) ☐ (C) ☐ (D) ☐

4. **Assertion** (A) Dissolution expenses paid by the firm on behalf of a partner are recorded on the debit side of realisation account.

   Reason (R) Such expenses are a non-business expense.

   (A) ☐ (B) ☐ (C) ☐ (D) ☐

5. **Assertion** (A) If a partners pays the liability of the firm, his capital account is debited.

   Reason (R) A liability can be either paid-off in cash, or paid by a partner.

   (A) ☐ (B) ☐ (C) ☐ (D) ☐

6. **Assertion** (A) The gross amount of debtors is transferred to the debit side of the realisation account whereas the provision for bad debts is transferred to the credit side of this account.

   Reason (R) Debtors and provision for bad debts are two different accounts.

   (A) ☐ (B) ☐ (C) ☐ (D) ☐

7. **Assertion** (A) On dissolution, goodwill account is transferred to realisation account.

   Reason (R) Goodwill is an asset which cannot be seen or touched.

   (A) ☐ (B) ☐ (C) ☐ (D) ☐

8. **Assertion** (A) At the time of dissolution of partnership firm, the amount received from realisation of all the assets of the firm is used first of all to pay the external liabilities of the firm.

   Reason (R) As per the Partnership Act, outside liability should be paid first, at the time of dissolution of partnership firm.

   (A) ☐ (B) ☐ (C) ☐ (D) ☐

Correct/Incorrect Statements

No. of Questions : **8** Suggested Time : **15 Minutes**

Direction Each of the question given below consist of the two statements. List of common options applicable for each question is given below

(A) Both statements are correct
(B) Statement I is correct and Statement II is incorrect
(C) Statement II is correct and Statement I is incorrect
(D) Both statements are incorrect

You have to select the codes as *A, B, C* or *D* as your answer to the question by marking (✓) in the response box given against each option.

1. **Statement I** A firm is dissolved when all partners give consent to it.

   Statement II A firm is compulsorily dissolved when a partner decides to retire.

   (A) ☐ (B) ☐ (C) ☐ (D) ☐

2. **Statement I** Realisation account is a real account.

   Statement II In dissolution of a partnership firm, the operations of the business comes to an end.

   (A) ☐ (B) ☐ (C) ☐ (D) ☐

3. **Statement I** On dissolution of firm, partner's loan is not recorded in the realisation account.

   Statement II On dissolution of firm, partner's current accounts are transferred to respective partner's capital account.

   (A) ☐ (B) ☐ (C) ☐ (D) ☐

4. **Statement I** On dissolution of firm, all assets (except cash and fictitious assets) are transferred to the debit side of partners' capital account.

   Statement II On dissolution, all external liabilities are transferred to the credit side of realisation account.

   (A) ☐ (B) ☐ (C) ☐ (D) ☐

5. **Statement I** Unrecorded assets sold are debited to cash account.

   Statement II Cash account from the balance sheet is not transferred to realisation account.

   (A) ☐ (B) ☐ (C) ☐ (D) ☐

6. **Statement I** If an asset is taken over by a creditors, no journal entry is passed.

   Statement II Loan by a partner to the firm is transferred to credit side of realisation account.

   (A) ☐ (B) ☐ (C) ☐ (D) ☐

7. **Statement I** Loan provided by the firm to the partner is transferred to the debit side of cash account.

   Statement II Expenses on realisation are debited to realisation account.

   (A) ☐ (B) ☐
   (C) ☐ (D) ☐

8. **Statement I** There will be nil balance in cash account after the process of dissolution is completed.

   Statement II Goodwill will be considered as valueless if its realised value is not provided.

   (A) ☐ (B) ☐
   (C) ☐ (D) ☐

Case Based Question

No. of Question : **1** Suggested Time : **5 Minutes**

Direction This section contains 1 case having 3 Questions of 1 mark each. You have to write the answer of each question based on the context of the related case.

Case 1 Morris and Angel are partners since last 15 years. They share profits in the proportion to their capitals. Their capitals on 31st March, 2021, stood at ₹ 6,00,000 and ₹ 4,00,000 respectively. On this date, the firm had ₹ 1,00,000 in its workmen compensation reserve and its outside liabilities amounted to ₹ 6,00,000, which included creditors of ₹ 2,00,000 and bills payable of ₹ 60,000.

The firm was dissolved on 31st March, 2021, on that date, the assets, apart from cash of ₹ 70,000, realised ₹ 14,00,000 and the liabilities were discharged as follows

(i) Creditors due on 31st May, 2021 were paid-off at a discount of 3% per annum.
(ii) Bills payable were discharged at a rebate of ₹ 1,000.
(iii) Workmen compensation claim of ₹ 40,000 was met.
(iv) Expenses of dissolution amounting to ₹ 30,000 were paid.

Questions

(i) What amount is paid to the creditors?

(A) ₹ 1,00,000 ☐ (B) ₹ 1,99,000 ☐
(C) ₹ 2,99,000 ☐ (D) ₹ 3,99,000 ☐

(ii) How much amount of workmen compensation reserve was credited to Angel?

(A) ₹ 24,000 ☐ (B) ₹ 20,000 ☐
(C) ₹ 48,000 ☐ (D) ₹ 34,000 ☐

(iii) Give the journal entry for dissolution expenses.

(A) Cash A/c Dr 30,000
To Realisation A/c 30,000 ☐

(B) Realisation A/c Dr 30,000
To Cash A/c 30,000 ☐

(C) Realisation A/c Dr 30,000
To Partners' Capital A/c 30,000 ☐

(D) No entry ☐

Subjective Questions

Free Response Questions, Open-ended Questions etc.

No. of Questions : **9** Suggested Time : **70 Minutes**

1. Arun and Varun are partners in a firm sharing profits and losses equally. On 31st March, 2023, their firm dissolved and all the assets (except cash) transferred to realisation account. Pass journal entries for the following transactions

(i) Arun took over 30% of stock at 30% discount (Book value of stock ₹ 20,000).
(ii) 30% of total stock was taken over by creditors of ₹ 8,000 in full settlement of his claim (Book value of creditors ₹ 15,000).
(iii) Remaining stock was sold for cash at a discount of 10%.
(iv) Remaining creditors were paid at a discount of 10%.

2. Radha and Mudit were partners in a firm sharing profits and losses in the ratio of 3 : 2. The firm was dissolved on 31st March, 2019. Pass the necessary journal entries for the following transactions after various assets (other than cash in hand and cash at bank) and third party liabilities have been transferred to realisation account

(i) A creditor of ₹ 70,000 accepted furniture valued at ₹ 1,50,000 and paid to the firm ₹ 80,000.

(ii) Bank loan of ₹ 90,000 was settled along with interest ₹ 9,000.

(iii) Realisation expenses amounting to ₹ 8,000 were paid by Mudit.

(iv) Loss on realisation was ₹ 20,000.

3. Pass necessary journal entries on the dissolution of partnership firm in the following cases

(i) Dissolution expenses were ₹ 800.

(ii) Dissolution expenses ₹ 800 were paid by Prem, a partner.

(iii) Geetu, a partner, was appointed to look after the dissolution work, for which she was allowed a remuneration of ₹ 10,000. Geetu agreed to bear the dissolution expenses. Actual expenses ₹ 9,500 were paid by Geetu.

(iv) Jaskirat, a partner, agreed to look after the dissolution work for commission of ₹ 5,000. Jaskirat agreed to bear dissolution expenses. Actual expenses ₹ 5,500 were paid by Amar, another partner, on behalf of Jaskirat.

(v) A debtor, Arjun, for ₹ 10,000 agreed to pay the dissolution expenses which were ₹ 8,000 in full settlement of his debt.

4. Pass the necessary journal entries for the following transactions on the dissolution of the partnership firm of Tina and Rina after the various assets (other than cash and bank) and external liabilities have been transferred to realisation account

(i) There was an outstanding bill for repairs for which ₹ 20,000 were paid.

(ii) The firm had stock of ₹ 80,000. Tina took over 50% of the stock at a discount of 20% while the remaining stock was sold off for ₹ 52,000.

(iii) The firm had 100 shares of ₹ 10 each which were taken over by the partners at market value of ₹ 20 per share in their profit sharing ratio of 3 : 2.

(iv) Realisation expenses of ₹ 4,000 were paid by Rina.

(v) Tina had given a loan of ₹ 40,000 to the firm which was duly paid.

(vi) Rina agreed to pay-off her husband's loan of ₹10,000 at a discount of 10%.

[CBSE 2024]

5. Haneef and Jubed were partners in a firm sharing profits and losses in their capital. On 31st March, 2023, their balance sheet was as follows

Liabilities		Amt (₹)	Assets	Amt (₹)
Creditors		1,50,000	Bank	2,00,000
Workmen Compensation Reserve		3,00,000	Debtors	3,40,000
			Stock	1,50,000
			Furniture	4,60,000
General Reserve		75,000	Machinery	8,20,000
Hanif's Current A/c		25,000	Jubed's Current A/c	80,000
Capital A/cs				
Hanif's	10,00,000			
Jubed	5,00,000	15,00,000		
		20,50,000		20,50,000

On the above date the firm dissolved and the following transactions took place

(i) Debtors were realised at a discount of 5%. 50% of the stock was taken over by Hanif at 10% less than the book value. Remaining stock was sold for ₹ 65,000.

(ii) Furniture was taken over by Jubed for ₹ 1,35,000. Machinery was sold as scrap for ₹ 74,000.

(iii) Creditors were paid in full.

(iv) Expenses on realisation ₹ 8,000 were paid by Hanif.

Prepare realisation account.

6. Verma and Sharma were partners sharing profits in the ratio of 3 : 1. On 31st March, 2023, their balance sheet was as follows

Balance Sheet
as at 31st March, 2023

Liabilities		Amt (₹)	Assets	Amt (₹)
Creditors		70,000	Land and Building	70,000
Capital A/cs			Machinery	60,000
Verma	1,20,000		Debtors	80,000
Sharma	80,000	2,00,000	Bank	60,000
		2,70,000		2,70,000

The firm was dissolved on 1st April, 2023 and the assets and liabilities were settled as follows

(i) Creditors of ₹ 50,000 took over land and building in full settlement of their claim.
(ii) Remaining creditors were paid in cash.
(iii) Machinery was sold at a depreciation of 30%.
(iv) Debtors were collected at a cost of ₹ 500.
(v) Expenses on realisation were ₹ 1,700.

Pass necessary journal entries for dissolution of the firm.

7. X, Y and Z were partners sharing profits and losses in the ratio of 2:2:1. Their balance sheet as on 31st March 2023, the date on which they dissolve their firm, was as follows

Liabilities		Amt (₹)	Assets		Amt (₹)
Bank Loan		11,500	Other Sundry Assets		1,17,000
Creditors		16,000	Furniture		11,000
Capital A/cs			Debtors	1,24,200	
X	1,27,500		(−) Provision for Bad Debts	(1,200)	1,23,000
Y	1,10,000		Stock		17,800
Z	17,000	2,54,000	Cash		13,200
		2,82,000			2,82,000

Following transactions took place at the time of dissolution

(i) X took over furniture at ₹ 8,000, debtors amounting to ₹ 1,20,000 at ₹ 1,17,000 and the creditors of ₹ 16,000 were to be paid by him at this figure.

(ii) Y is to take over all stock for ₹ 17,000 and some sundry assets at ₹ 72,000 (being 10% less than the book value).

(iii) Z to take over remaining sundry assets at 80% of the book value and assume the responsibility of discharge of loan together with interest of ₹ 2,300.

(iv) The expenses of dissolution were ₹ 2,700. The remaining debtors were sold to a debt collection agency at 50% of the book value.

Prepare realisation account and partners' capital account.

8. Aadish and Shreyansh were partners in a firm sharing profits and losses in the ratio of 3 : 2. On 31st March, 2022 their balance sheet was as follows

Balance Sheet of Aadish and Shreyansh
as at 31st March, 2022

Liabilities		Amt (₹)	Assets		Amt (₹)
Creditors		90,000	Cash at Bank		20,000
Mrs. Aadish's Loan		30,000	Stock		24,000
Shreyansh's Loan		30,000	Investments		30,000
General Reserve		45,000	Debtors	20,000	
Capital A/cs			(−) Provision for Doubtful Debts	(2,000)	18,000
Aadish	1,00,000		Plant		1,00,000
Shreyansh	97,000	1,97,000	Advertisement Suspense A/c		2,00,000
		3,92,000			3,92,000

The firm was dissolved on 31st March, 2022 on the following terms

(i) Debtors realised ₹ 17,000 and plant realised 10% more than the book value.

(ii) Aadish promised to pay Mrs. Aadish's loan and took away stock at ₹ 20,000.

(iii) Shreyansh took away half of the investments at a discount of 10%. Remaining investments realised ₹ 4,500.

(iv) Creditors were paid-off at a discount of 10%.

(v) Expenses of realisation amounted to ₹ 7,000.

Prepare realisation account. [CBSE 2023]

9. Mala, Neela and Kala were partners sharing profits in the ratio of 3 : 2 : 1. On 1st March, 2015, their firm was dissolved. The assets were realised and liabilities were paid-off. The accountant prepared realisation account, partners' capital account and cash account, but forgot to post few amounts in these accounts.

You are required to complete these below given accounts by posting correct amounts.

Dr **Realisation Account** Cr

Particulars		Amt (₹)	Particulars		Amt (₹)
To Sundry Assets A/c			By Provision for Doubtful Debts A/c		1,000
Machinery	10,000		By Sundry Creditors A/c		15,000
Stock	21,000		By Sheela's Loan A/c		13,000
Debtors	20,000		By Repairs and Renewals Reserve A/c		1,200
Prepaid Insurance	400		By Cash A/c (Assets sold)		
Investments	3,000	54,400	Machinery	8,000	
To Mala's Capital A/c (Sheela's loan)		13,000	Stock	14,000	
To Cash A/c (Creditors paid)		15,000	Debtors	16,000	38,000
To Cash A/c (Dishonoured bill paid)		5,000	By Mala's Capital A/c (Investments)		2,000
To Cash A/c (Expenses)		800	....		...
		88,200			88,200

Dr **Partners' Capital Account** Cr

Particulars	Mala (₹)	Neela (₹)	Kala (₹)	Particulars	Mala (₹)	Neela (₹)	Kala (₹)
....	...	—	—	....	...	...	...
....	...	...	...	....	...	—	—
To Cash A/c	12,000	9,000	—	By Cash A/c	—	—	1,000
	23,000	15,000	3,000		23,000	15,000	3,000

Dr **Cash Account** Cr

Particulars	Amt (₹)	Particulars	Amt (₹)
To Balance b/d	2,800	By Realisation A/c (Creditors paid)	15,000
To Realisation A/c (Sale of assets)	38,000	By Dishonoured Bill A/c	5,000
To Kala's Capital A/c	1,000	....	...
		By Mala's Capital A/c	12,000
		By Neela's Capital A/c	9,000
	41,800		41,800

Answers

If your answer matches with the answer given here then put (✓) in the box otherwise put (✘). In case you did not attempt the question leave the box blank.

Multiple Choice Questions

1. A ☐ 2. C ☐
3. D ☐ 4. B ☐
5. C ☐ 6. A ☐
7. B ☐ 8. A ☐
9. B ☐ 10. D ☐
11. D ☐ 12. C ☐
13. D ☐ 14. A ☐
15. C ☐ 16. B ☐
17. D ☐ 18. C ☐
19. B ☐ 20. D ☐
21. B ☐ 22. C ☐
23. C ☐ 24. D ☐
25. D ☐ 26. D ☐
27. C ☐ 28. B ☐
29. A ☐ 30. A ☐
31. C ☐ 32. A ☐
33. B ☐ 34. C ☐
35. B ☐ 36. A ☐

Your Score__________ *(No. of Correct Answers)*

Assertion-Reason Questions

1. C ☐ 2. D ☐
3. B ☐ 4. D ☐
5. B ☐ 6. A ☐
7. B ☐ 8. A ☐

Your Score__________ *(No. of Correct Answers)*

Correct/Incorrect Statements

1. B ☐ 2. C ☐
3. A ☐ 4. C ☐
5. A ☐ 6. B ☐
7. C ☐ 8. A ☐

Your Score__________ *(No. of Correct Answers)*

Case Based Question

1. (i) B ☐
(ii) A ☐
(iii) B ☐

Your Score__________ *(No. of Correct Answers)*

Explanations

Multiple Choice Questions

1. (A) out of the capital of the partners
2. (C) When all partner become insolvent except two partners
3. (D) (ii) (i) (iii)
4. (B) partners' capital account
5. (C) Book Value of Assets = 50,000 + 48,000 − 3,000 = ₹95,000

   Loss on Assets Realised = $95,000 \times \frac{12}{100}$ = ₹ 11,400
6. (A) Amount Realised from Debtor = 50,000 − 10,000 = 40,000 − 2,000 (5% discount on ₹ 40,000) = ₹ 38,000
7. (B) Since the payment is in full and final settlement, the total amount of creditors will be deducted.
8. (A) Book Value of Assets taken over

   $= \frac{3,85,000}{110} \times 100$ = ₹ 3,50,000

   Profit on Realisation = 3,85,000 − 3,50,000 = ₹ 35,000

   Vipul's Share in Profit = $35,000 \times \frac{3}{8}$ = ₹ 13,125
9. (B) Debit realisation account and credit bank account by ₹ 10,000
10. (D) **Amount Credited to Realisation Account**

	Amt (₹)
Amount Received from Bad Debts $= 25,000 \times \frac{40}{100}$	= 10,000
(+) Remaining Debtors Realised $= 35,000 \times \frac{80}{100}$	= 28,000
	38,000

11. (D) No treatment as realised value is not given
12. (C) Remaining stock = 60,000 − 20,000 = ₹ 40,000
13. (D) Total Amount transferred to Realisation Account

    $= 35,000 + \left(50,000 \times \frac{80}{100}\right)$

    = 35,000 + 40,000 = ₹ 75,000
14. (A) Amount Debited to Realisation Account

    $= 1,00,000 \times \frac{90}{100}$ = ₹ 90,000
15. (C) Cash account by ₹ 2,500
16. (B) Partner's Opening Capitals = Closing Capitals − Realisation Profit + Assets taken over

    X's Capital= 1,20,000 − 15,000 + 10,000 = ₹ 1,15,000

    Y's Capital = 1,00,000 − 5,000 = ₹ 95,000
17. (D) Realisation Gain = $50,000 \times \frac{20}{100}$ = ₹ 10,000
18. (C)

	Amt (₹)
Debtors	34,000
(−) Bad Debts	(1,000)
	33,000

Amount realised = 33,000 × 60% = ₹ 19,800

19. (B)

	Amt (₹)
Total Value of Furniture	2,00,000
(−) Taken Over by Partner (2,00,000 × 50%)	(1,00,000)
Remaining Value	1,00,000
(−) Sold at 20% Less than Book Value (20% of 1,00,000)	(20,000)
Cash Realised	80,000

20. (D) Total Assets = 70,000 + 1,20,000 = ₹ 1,90,000

    Other Assets = 1,90,000 − 10,000 = ₹ 1,80,000

    Loss on Assets Realised = 1,80,000 − 1,50,000 = ₹ 30,000
21. (B) 50,000 + 8,000 − 10,000 = ₹ 48,000
22. (C) A's Share in Reserves = Total Workmen Reserve × A's Profit Share

    1,00,000 = Total Workmen Reserve $\times \frac{2}{3}$

    Total Workmen Reserve = $1,00,000 \times \frac{3}{2}$ = ₹ 1,50,000
23. (C) Final Payment to the Partners

    = 42,000 + 9,000 + 3,000

    = ₹ 54,000
24. (D) Since firm is not involved as partner has to pay the dissolution expenses, it will not be recorded.

25. (D) Since the remuneration and the expenses are paid by the firm, the firm will record ₹ 1,15,000 (70,000 + 45,000).

26. (D) Book Value of the Assets (except cash)

= Capital + Liabilities – Profit and Loss Account – Cash

= 1,50,000 + 35,000 – 7,000 – 8,000 = ₹ 1,70,000

Amount Realised by Sale of Assets

= 1,70,000 + 5,000 – 25,000 = ₹ 1,50,000

27. (C) Debit Realisation A/c and Credit Naresh by ₹ 14,500

28. (B)

Dr **Realisation Account** Cr

Particulars	Amt (₹)	Particulars	Amt (₹)
To Assets A/c	30,00,000	By Liabilities A/c	6,00,000
To Cash A/c (Liabilities settled)	5,70,000	By Cash A/c (Assets realised)	24,00,000
To Cash A/c (Realisation expenses)	30,000	By Realisation Loss (B/F)	6,00,000
	36,00,000		36,00,000

29. (A) The firm will record only that amount which is paid by them.

30. (A) Since loan is paid ₹ 500 less, it is a benefit to the firm and will be recorded on the credit side of realisation account.

31. (C) transferring it to the debit side of respective partner's capital account

32. (A) Bank A/c Dr
To Loan to Partner A/c

33. (B) (ii) (iii) (i) (iv)

34. (C) (iii) (i) (ii)

35. (B) (ii) (i) (iv) (iii)

36. (A) (i) (ii) (iii)

Assertion-Reason Questions

1. (C) Dissolution of partnership is reconstitution of partnership and in dissolution of partnership firm, the firm comes to an end.

2. (D) There are other modes of dissolution as well apart from intervention of court.

3. (B) Both Assertion (A) and Reason (R) are true, but Reason (R) is not the correct explanation of Assertion (A)

4. (D) Dissolution expenses paid by the firm on behalf of a partner are debited to partners capital account.

5. (B) Both Assertion (A) and Reason (R) are true, but Reason (R) is not the correct explanation of Assertion (A)

6. (A) Both Assertion (A) and Reason (R) are true and Reason (R) is the correct explanation of Assertion (A)

7. (B) Both Assertion (A) and Reason (R) are true, but Reason (R) is not the correct explanation of Assertion (A)

8. (A) Both Assertion (A) and Reason (R) are true and Reason (R) is the correct explanation of Assertion (A)

Correct/Incorrect Statements

1. (B) The continuity of the firm is not impacted by retirement of a partner.

2. (C) Realisation account is a nominal account.

3. (A) Both statements are correct

4. (C) On dissolution of firm, all assets (except cash and fictitious assets) are transferred to the debit of realisation account.

5. (A) Both statements are correct

6. (B) Loan by a partner to the firm is transferred to credit side of cash account.

7. (C) Loan provided by the firm to the partner is transferred to the debit side of partners' capital account.

8. (A) Both statements are correct

Case Based Question

1. (i) (B) Amount paid to Creditors

$$= 2,00,000 - \left(2,00,000 \times \frac{3}{100} \times \frac{2}{12}\right)$$

$$= ₹\ 1,99,000$$

(ii) (A) Amount Credited to Angel

$$= (1,00,000 - 40,000) \times \frac{2}{5}$$

$$= 60,000 \times \frac{2}{5}$$

$$= ₹\ 24,000$$

(iii) (B) Realisation A/c Dr 30,000
To Cash A/c 30,000

Subjective Questions

1. **JOURNAL**

Date	Particulars		LF	Amt (Dr)	Amt (Cr)
(i)	Arun's Capital A/c	Dr		4,200	
	To Realisation A/c				4,200
	(Being stock took over by Arun)				
(ii)	No entry				
(iii)	Cash A/c	Dr		7,200	
	To Realisation A/c				7200
	(Being stock realised)				
(iv)	Realisation A/c	Dr		6,300	
	To Cash A/c				6,300
	(Being creditors paid)				

2. **JOURNAL**

Date	Particulars		LF	Amt (Dr)	Amt (Cr)
(i)	Bank/Cash A/c	Dr		80,000	
	To Realisation A/c				80,000
	(Being creditor accepted furniture and paid the remaining cash to the firm)				
(ii)	Realisation A/c	Dr		99,000	
	To Bank/Cash A/c				99,000
	(Being bank loan settled along with interest)				
(iii)	Realisation A/c	Dr		8,000	
	To Mudit's Capital A/c				8,000
	(Being dissolution expenses paid by Mudit)				
(iv)	Radha's Capital A/c	Dr		12,000	
	Mudit's Capital A/c	Dr		8,000	
	To Realisation A/c				20,000
	(Being loss on realisation divided between the partners)				

3. **JOURNAL**

Date	Particulars		LF	Amt (Dr)	Amt (Cr)
(i)	Realisation A/c	Dr		800	
	To Cash A/c				800
	(Being realisation expenses paid)				
(ii)	Realisation A/c	Dr		800	
	To Prem's Capital A/c				800
	(Being expenses paid by Prem)				
(iii)	Realisation A/c	Dr		10,000	
	To Geetu's Capital A/c				10,000
	(Being expenses paid by Geetu)				
(iv)	Realisation A/c	Dr		5,000	
	To Jaskirat's Capital A/c				5,000
	(Being dissolution expense paid by Jaskirat)				
	Jaskirat's Capital A/c	Dr		5,500	
	To Amar's Capital A/c				5,500
	(Being Amar paid expenses on behalf of Jaskirat)				
(v)	No entry				

4. **JOURNAL**

Date	Particulars		LF	Amt (Dr)	Amt (Cr)
(i)	Realisation A/c	Dr		20,000	
	To Bank A/c				20,000
	(Being payment of outstanding bills for repairs)				
(ii)	Tina's Capital A/c (80,000 × 50% × 80%)	Dr		32,000	
	To Realisation A/c				32,000
	(Being stock taken over by Tina)				
	Cash A/c	Dr		52,000	
	To Realisation A/c				52,000
	(Being the remaining stock sold for cash)				
(iii)	Tina's Capital A/c	Dr		1,200	
	Rina's Capital A/c	Dr		800	
	To Realisation A/c				2,000
	(Being 100 shares of ₹ 20 each transferred to Tina and Rina in 3 : 2)				
(iv)	Realisation A/c	Dr		4,000	
	To Rina's Capital A/c				4,000
	(Being realisation expenses paid by Rina)				
(v)	Tina's Loan A/c	Dr		40,000	
	To Bank A/c				40,000
	(Being Tina's loan paid-off)				
(vi)	Realisation A/c	Dr		9,000	
	To Rina's Capital A/c				9,000
	(Being Rina's husband loan taken over by Rina)				

5. Dr **Realisation Account** Cr

Particulars	Amt (₹)	Particulars		Amt (₹)
To Debtors A/c	3,40,000	By Creditors A/c		1,50,000
To Stock A/c	1,50,000	By Bank A/c (Assets realised)		
To Furniture A/c	4,60,000	Debtors	3,23,000	
To Machinery A/c	8,20,000	Stock	65,000	
To Bank A/c (Creditors)	1,50,000	Machinery	74,000	4,62,000
To Hanif's Capital A/c (Expenses)	8,000	By Hanif's Capital A/c (Stock)		67,500
		By Jubed's Capital A/c (Furniture)		1,35,000
		By Loss transferred to		
		Hanif's Capital A/c	7,42,333	
		Jubed Capital A/c	3,71,167	11,13,500
	19,28,000			19,28,000

6. **JOURNAL**

Date	Particulars		LF	Amt (Dr)	Amt (Cr)
2023					
Apr 1	Realisation A/c	Dr		2,10,000	
	To Land and Building A/c				70,000
	To Machinery A/c				60,000
	To Debtors A/c				80,000
	(Being assets transferred to realisation account)				

Date	Particulars		LF	Amt (Dr)	Amt (Cr)
	Creditors A/c	Dr		70,000	
	To Realisation A/c				70,000
	(Being creditors transferred to realisation account)				
	Realisation A/c	Dr		20,000	
	To Bank A/c (70,000 – 50,000)				20,000
	(Being remaining creditors paid-off)				
	Bank A/c (42,000 + 79,500)	Dr		1,21,500	
	To Realisation A/c				1,21,500
	(Being machinery of ₹ 42,000 and debtors at ₹ 79,500 realised)				
	Realisation A/c	Dr		1,700	
	To Bank A/c				1,700
	(Being realisation expenses paid)				
	Verma's Capital A/c (40,200 × 3/4)	Dr		30,150	
	Sharma's Capital A/c (40,200 × 1/4)	Dr		10,050	
	To Realisation A/c				40,200
	(Being realisation loss transferred to Partners' capital account)				
	Verma's Capital A/c	Dr		89,850	
	Sharma's Capital A/c	Dr		69,950	
	To Bank A/c				1,59,800
	(Being final payment made to partners)				

Working Notes

1. Dr **Realisation Account** Cr

Particulars		Amt (₹)	Particulars		Amt (₹)
To Sundry Assets A/c			By Creditors A/c		70,000
Land and Building	70,000		By Bank A/c		
Machinery	60,000		Machinery	42,000	
Debtors	80,000	2,10,000	Debtors	79,500	1,21,500
To Bank A/c (Creditors)		20,000	By Loss transferred to		
To Bank A/c (Expenses)		1,700	Verma's Capital A/c	30,150	
			Sharma's Capital A/c	10,050	40,200
		2,31,700			2,31,700

2. Dr **Partners' Capital Account** Cr

Particulars	Verma (₹)	Sharma (₹)	Particulars	Verma (₹)	Sharma (₹)
To Realisation A/c (Loss)	30,150	10,050	By Balance b/d	1,20,000	80,000
To Bank A/c (Final payment)	89,850	69,950			
	1,20,000	80,000		1,20,000	80,000

3. No entry is required for adjustment (i), since creditors have accepted the asset (land and building) in full and final settlement.

7. Dr **Realisation Account** Cr

Particulars	Amt (₹)	Particulars		Amt (₹)
To Sundry Assets A/c	1,17,000	By Loan A/c		11,500
To Furniture A/c	11,000	By Creditors A/c		16,000
To Debtors A/c	1,24,200	By Provision for Doubtful Debts		1,200
To Stock A/c	17,800	By X's Capital A/c		
To X's Capital A/c (Creditors)	16,000	Furniture	8,000	
To Z's Capital A/c (Loan)	13,800	Debtors	1,17,200	1,25,200
To Cash A/c (Expense)	2,700	By Y's Capital A/c		
		Stock	17,000	
		Sundry Assets	72,000	89,000
		By Z's Capital A/c (Sundry Assets)		29,600
		By Cash A/c (Debtors)		2,100
		By Loss transferred to		
		X's Capital A/c	11,160	
		Y's Capital A/c	11,160	
		Z's Capital A/c	5,580	27,900
	3,02,500			3,02,500

Dr **Partners' Capital Account** Cr

Particulars	X (₹)	Y (₹)	Z (₹)	Particulars	X (₹)	Y (₹)	Z (₹)
To Realisation A/c	1,25,200	89,000	29,600	By Balance b/d	1,27,500	1,10,000	17,000
To Realisation A/c	11,160	11,160	5,580	By Realisation A/c	16,000	—	13,800
To Cash A/c (Final payment)	7,140	9,840	—	By Cash A/c (Balancing figure)	—	—	4,380
	1,43,500	1,10,000	35,180		1,43,500	1,10,000	35,180

8. Dr **Realisation Account** Cr

Particulars	Amt (₹)	Particulars		Amt (₹)
To Stock A/c	24,000	By Provision for Doubtful Debts		2,000
To Investment A/c	30,000	By Creditors A/c		90,000
To Debtors A/c	20,000	By Mrs. Aadish's Loan		30,000
To Plant A/c	1,00,000	By Bank A/c (Debtors realised)		17,000
To Aadish' Capital A/c	30,000	By Bank A/c (Plant realised)		1,10,000
To Bank A/c (Creditors paid)	81,000	By Aadish's Capital A/c		20,000
To Bank A/c (Realisation expenses)	7,000	By Shreyansh's Capital A/c		13,500
		By Bank A/c (Investment realised)		4,500
		By Realisation Loss transferred to		
		Aadish	3,000	
		Shreyansh	2,000	5,000
	2,92,000			2,92,000

Working Note

Investments $= 30{,}000 \times \frac{1}{2} =$ ₹ 15,000 ; Taken over by Shreyansh $= 15{,}000 - \left(15{,}000 \times \frac{10}{100}\right) =$ ₹ 13,500

9. Dr **Realisation Account** Cr

Particulars		Amt (₹)	Particulars		Amt (₹)
To Sundry Assets A/c			By Provision for Doubtful Debts A/c		1,000
Machinery	10,000		By Sundry Creditors A/c		15,000
Stock	21,000		By Sheela' Loan A/c		13,000
Debtors	20,000		By Repairs and Renewals Reserve A/c		1,200
Prepaid Insurance	400		By Cash A/c (Assets sold)		
Investments	3,000	54,400	Machinery	8,000	
To Mala's Capital A/c (Sheela's loan)		13,000	Stock	14,000	
To Cash A/c (Creditors paid)		15,000	Debtors	16,000	38,000
To Cash A/c (Dishonoured bill paid)		5,000	By Mala's Capital A/c (Investments)		2,000
To Cash A/c (Expenses)		800	**By Loss transferred to Capital A/cs**		
			Mala	**9,000**	
			Neela	**6,000**	
			Kala	**3,000**	**18,000**
		88,200			88,200

Dr **Partners' Capital Account** Cr

Particulars	Mala (₹)	Neela (₹)	Kala (₹)	Particulars	Mala (₹)	Neela (₹)	Kala (₹)
To Realisation A/c (Investment)	**2,000**	—	—	By **Balance b/d**	**10,000**	**15,000**	**2,000**
				By **Realisation A/c** (Sheela's loan)	**13,000**	—	—
To Realisation A/c (Loss)	**9,000**	**6,000**	**3,000**	By Cash A/c	—	—	1,000
To Cash A/c	12,000	9,000	—				
	23,000	15,000	3,000		23,000	15,000	3,000

Dr **Cash Account** Cr

Particulars	Amt (₹)	Particulars	Amt (₹)
To Balance b/d	2,800	By Realisation A/c (Creditors paid)	15,000
To Realisation A/c (Sale of assets)	38,000	By Dishonoured Bill A/c	5,000
To Kala's Capital A/c	1,000	**By Realisation A/c** (Expenses)	**800**
		By Mala's Capital A/c	12,000
		By Neela' Capital A/c	9,000
	41,800		41,800

CHAPTER -6

Accounting for Share Capital

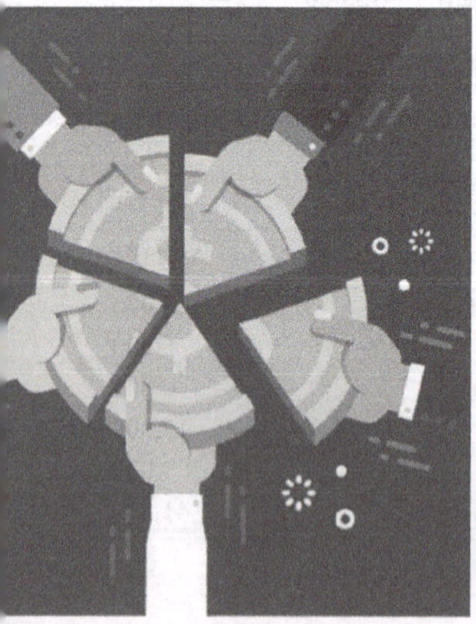

Types & Nos. of Questions

Multiple Choice Questions - 34
Assertion-Reason Questions - 8
Correct/Incorrect Statements - 9
Case Based Questions - 2 Cases, *with 3/4 Questions*
Subjective Questions - 8

Trend Analysis

On the basis of analysis of last 2 years' papers, it is found that on an average 3 Multiple Choice Questions, 1 Short Answer Type Question and 1 Long Answer Type Question are asked from this chapter.

Focus Topics of the Chapter

- Meaning of a Company and Share
- Issue of Shares
- Issue of Shares for Consideration other than Cash
- Forfeiture and Re-issue of Shares

Multiple Choice Questions

No. of Questions : **34** Suggested Time : **50 Minutes**

Direction Each of the question given below is Multiple Choice Question (MCQ) i.e. there are Four Options/Choices for answer, out of which ONLY ONE is correct. You have to select the correct option. A response box is given with each option, mark (✓) in the box of the correct option. For each correct answer you will get 1 mark, while there is no penalty for incorrect answer or missed out questions.

1. Nominal share capital is

(A) that part of authorised capital which is issued by the company ☐

(B) the amount of capital which is actually applied for by the prospective shareholders ☐

(C) the maximum amount of share capital which a company is authorised to issue ☐

(D) the amount actually paid by the shareholders ☐

2. Uncalled capital is that portion of the ...... which has not yet been called-up and the portion of such uncalled capital to be called only in the event of winding up of the company is called ....

(A) subscribed capital; reserve capital ☐

(B) issued capital; reserve capital ☐

(C) authorised capital; capital reserve ☐

(D) registered capital; capital reserve ☐

3. Which of the following statement is/are true?

(i) Authorised Capital < Issued Capital

(ii) Authorised Capital ≥ Issued Capital

(iii) Subscribed Capital ≤ Issued Capital

(iv) Subscribed Capital > Issued Capital

Codes

(A) Only (i) ☐

(B) Both (i) and (iv) ☐

(C) Both (ii) and (iii) ☐

(D) Only (ii) ☐

4. Which of the following does not relate to reserve capital?

(A) It is a part of subscribed capital ☐

(B) It can be used for writing-off capital losses ☐

(C) It is part of uncalled capital of the company ☐

(D) It cannot be used during the lifetime of the company ☐

5. Securities premium reserve cannot be utilised for

(A) issuing fully paid bonus shares ☐

(B) in writing-off the preliminary expenses of the company ☐

(C) creating general reserves ☐

(D) buy-back of its own shares ☐

6. Alpha Ltd. issued a prospectus inviting application for 12,000 shares of ₹ 10 each payable ₹ 3 on application, ₹ 5 on allotment and balance on call. Public had applied for certain number of shares and application money was received.

Which of the following application money, if received restricts the company to proceed with the allotment of shares, as per SEBI guidelines?

(A) ₹ 30,000 ☐ (B) ₹ 32,400 ☐

(C) ₹ 36,000 ☐ (D) ₹ 45,000 ☐

7. Zeehan Ltd., invited application for issuing 20,000 shares of ₹ 10 each and received applications for 25,000 shares. Which of the following can be followed for the allotment of shares?

(i) Refund the excess application money and allot full shares to rest.

(ii) Not to allot any share to some applicants, allot full to some applicants and allot remaining on pro-rata basis.

(iii) Not to allot any share and refund the total application money to the applicants.

Codes

(A) Only (i) ☐
(B) Only (ii) ☐
(C) Only (iii) ☐
(D) Any one of (i) and (ii) ☐

8. The subscribed capital of a company is ₹ 4,00,000 and nominal value is ₹ 10 each. There is no arrear till first call but final call was paid on 36,000 shares. The balance in the calls-in-arrears amounted to ₹ 12,000. Calculate the amount of final call.

(A) 2 ☐ (B) 3 ☐
(C) 4 ☐ (D) 5 ☐

9. If vendors are issued fully paid shares of ₹1,25,000 in purchase consideration of net assets of ₹ 1,50,000, the balance of ₹ 25,000 will be credited to *[CBSE 2024]*

(A) statement of profit and loss ☐
(B) goodwill account ☐
(C) capital reserve account ☐
(D) profit and loss adjustment account ☐

10. Akshita Ltd. issued fully paid shares of ₹ 5,00,000 in purchase consideration of net assets of ₹ 4,70,000. The balance of ₹ 30,000 will be ..... to ..... account. *[CBSE 2023]*

(A) debited, goodwill ☐
(B) debited, capital reserve ☐
(C) credited, capital reserve ☐
(D) credited, general reserve ☐

11. M Ltd. forfeited 5,000 equity shares of ₹ 10 each issued at a premium of 10% for non-payment of final call of ₹ 2 per share.

The minimum amount at which these shares can be re-issued as fully paid-up will be *[CBSE 2024]*

(A) ₹ 5,000 ☐ (B) ₹ 10,000 ☐
(C) ₹ 12,000 ☐ (D) ₹ 50,000 ☐

12. Rancho Ltd. took over assets worth ₹ 20,00,000 from PK Ltd. by paying 30% through bank draft and balance by issue of shares of ₹ 100 each at a premium of 10%.

The entry to be passed by Rancho Ltd. for settlement will be

(A)

PK Ltd. Dr	20,00,000	
To Share Capital A/c		12,72,700
To Securities Premium A/c		1,27,270
To Bank A/c		6,00,000
To Statement of Profit and Loss		30
(Being settlement of amount due to vendors)		

☐

(B)

PK Ltd. Dr	20,00,000	
To Share Capital A/c		12,72,700
To Securities Premium A/c		1,27,270
To Bank A/c		6,00,030
(Being settlement of amount due to vendors)		

☐

(C)

PK Ltd. Dr	20,00,000	
To Share Capital A/c		12,72,700
To Securities Premium A/c		1,27,300
To Bank A/c		6,00,000
(Being settlement of amount due to vendors)		

☐

(D)

PK Ltd. Dr	20,00,000	
To Share Capital A/c		12,73,000
To Securities Premium A/c		1,27,300
To Bank A/c		5,99,700
(Being settlement of amount due to vendors)		

☐

13. A company issued a prospectus inviting applications for 6,000 shares. Application were received for 9,000 shares. Company rejected 1,800 shares and remaining adjusted on pro-rata basis.

If Raju has been allotted 80 shares, how many shares he applied for?

(A) 80 ☐ (B) 53 ☐
(C) 96 ☐ (D) 120 ☐

14. Aman Ltd., invited application for issuing 30,000 shares of ₹ 10 each at par. The amount was payable as follows

On application ₹ 4 per share, on allotment ₹ 2 per share, on first and final call ₹ 4 per share.

Application were received for 70,000 shares and allotment was made on pro-rata basis and excess money to be adjusted on allotment and first call. Amount refunded to applicants will be

(A) ₹ 60,000 ☐
(B) ₹ 1,00,000 ☐
(C) ₹ 1,20,000 ☐
(D) Nil ☐

15. If a share of ₹ 10 issued at a premium of ₹ 1 on which ₹ 9 (including premium) have been called and ₹ 7 including premium is paid is forfeited. The amount to be credited in share forfeiture account will be

(A) 6 ☐ (B) 7 ☐
(C) 8 ☐ (D) 9 ☐

16. Tina Ltd. issued 10,000 shares of ₹ 10 each payable as ₹ 3 on application, ₹ 2 on allotment, ₹ 3 on first call and balance on final call.

All the shares were subscribed and all the money was duly received but one shareholder holding 1,000 shares failed to pay first call money and his shares were forfeited. Amount to be debited to share capital will be

(A) ₹ 8,000 ☐ (B) ₹ 10,000 ☐
(C) ₹ 2,000 ☐ (D) ₹ 20,000 ☐

17. As per the provisions of Companies Act, 2013 securities premium cannot be utilised for *[CBSE 2024]*

(A) buy-back of shares ☐
(B) issue of partly paid bonus shares ☐
(C) writing-off discount on issue of debentures ☐
(D) writing-off preliminary expenses ☐

18. If 10,000 shares of ₹ 10 each were forfeited for non-payment of final call money of ₹ 3 per share and only 7,000 shares were re-issued @ ₹ 11 per share as fully paid-up, then what is the amount of maximum possible discount that company can allow at the time of reissue of the remaining 3,000 shares?

(A) ₹ 9,000 ☐
(B) ₹ 16,000 ☐
(C) ₹ 21,000 ☐
(D) ₹ 28,000 ☐

19. The directors of a company forfeited 800 shares of ₹ 10 each at a premium of 3 per share (payable with allotment) for non-payment of first call money of ₹ 2 per share. The final call of ₹ 2 per share has not yet been made.

While recording the forfeiture of such shares, share capital and securities premium reserve account will be debited respectively by

(A) ₹ 8,000 and ₹ 2,400 ☐
(B) ₹ 6,400 and Nil ☐
(C) ₹ 6,400 and ₹ 2,400 ☐
(D) ₹ 8,000 and Nil ☐

20. A share of ₹ 10 each, issued at ₹ 4 premium out of which ₹ 7 (including ₹ 1 premium) was called-up and paid-up. The uncalled capital will be

(A) ₹ 3 ☐ (B) ₹ 4 ☐
(C) ₹ 7 ☐ (D) ₹ 8 ☐

21. Vishnu Ltd. forfeited 20 shares of ₹ 10 each, ₹ 8 called-up, on which John had paid application and allotment money of ₹ 5 per share. Of these, 15 shares were reissued to Parker as fully paid-up ₹ 6 per share.

What is the balance in the share forfeiture account after the relevant amount has been transferred to capital reserve account?

(A) Nil ☐ (B) ₹ 5 ☐
(C) ₹ 25 ☐ (D) ₹ 100 ☐

22. What will be the correct sequence of events?
(i) Forfeiture of shares
(ii) Defaults on calls
(iii) Reissue of shares
(iv) Amount transferred to capital reserve

Codes

(A) (i), (iv), (ii), (iii) ☐
(B) (ii), (iv), (i), (iii) ☐
(C) (ii), (i), (iii), (iv) ☐
(D) (iii), (iv), (i), (ii) ☐

23. Prachi Ltd., forfeited 4,000 shares of ₹ 10 each issued at premium of 10% for non-payment of first and final call of ₹ 3 per share. The maximum amount of discount at which shares can be reissued will be

(A) ₹ 12,000 ☐ (B) ₹ 28,000 ☐
(C) ₹ 40,000 ☐ (D) ₹ 32,000 ☐

24. A Co., forfeited 1,000 shares of ₹ 10 each fully called, on which ₹ 6,000 has been paid. Out of these, 800 shares were reissued upon payment of ₹ 6,600. What is the amount of capital reserve?

(A) ₹ 4,800 ☐ (B) ₹ 4,600 ☐
(C) ₹ 6,000 ☐ (D) ₹ 3,400 ☐

25. Manmohan Ltd. invited applications for issuing 50,000 equity shares of ₹ 10 each at par. The amount payable per share was as follows

On application ₹ 3, on allotment ₹ 4 and on first and final call ₹ 3. Applications were received for 1,45,000 equity shares. Applications for 20,000 equity shares were rejected and remaining applicants were allotted shares on a pro-rata basis.

Excess application money received with application was adjusted towards sums due on allotment and first and final call. Amount credited to calls-in-advance account was

[CBSE 2023]

(A) ₹ 2,25,000 ☐ (B) ₹ 25,000 ☐
(C) ₹ 1,75,000 ☐ (D) Nil ☐

26. APJ Ltd., forfeited 300 shares of ₹ 100 each, ₹ 75 called-up, for non-payment of first call of ₹ 20 per share.

All these shares were reissued at ₹ 75 paid-up. If amount transferred to capital reserve is ₹ 40 per share, than what is the reissue price?

(A) ₹ 55 per share ☐
(B) ₹ 45 per share ☐
(C) ₹ 60 per share ☐
(D) ₹ 40 per share ☐

27. A share of ₹ 10 each, issued at ₹ 4 premium out of which ₹ 7 (including ₹ 1 premium) was called-up and paid-up. The uncalled capital will be ....

(A) ₹ 7 per share ☐
(B) ₹ 4 per share ☐
(C) ₹ 8 per share ☐
(D) ₹ 3 per share ☐

28. Sara Ltd., issue 3,000 shares of ₹ 10 each. The amount payable as ₹ 3 on application, ₹ 5 on allotment, ₹ 2 on first and final call. All the shares were subscribed.

Sonu applied for 500 shares, paid entire money with application and another with 300 shares paid allotment money with application.

The amount received on application will be

(A) ₹ 13,000 ☐ (B) ₹ 14,000 ☐
(C) ₹ 30,000 ☐ (D) ₹ 10,600 ☐

29. Attire Ltd. issued a prospectus inviting applications for 12,000 shares of ₹ 10 each payable ₹ 3 on application, ₹ 5 on allotment and balance on call. Public had applied for certain number of shares and application money was received.

Which of the following application money, if received restricts the company to proceed with the allotment of shares, as per SEBI guidelines?

(A) ₹ 36,000 ☐ (B) ₹ 45,000 ☐
(C) ₹ 30,000 ☐ (D) ₹ 32,400 ☐

30. Lata Ltd. forfeited Maya's shares. Maya who had applied for 600 shares of ₹ 10 each and was allotted 400 shares failed to pay allotment money of ₹ 4 per share including premium of ₹ 2. She had paid only the application money of ₹ 2 per share.

The first and final call was not yet called. The journal entry for forfeiture of shares by opening calls in arrears account will be

(A) Share Capital A/c Dr 1,600
 To Share Forfeited A/c 800
 To Calls-in-arrears A/c 800 ☐

(B) Share Capital A/c Dr 1,600
 Securities Premium Reserve A/c Dr 800
 To Share Forfeited A/c 1,200
 To Calls-in-arrears A/c 1,200 ☐

(C) Share Capital A/c Dr 1,600
 Securities Premium Reserve A/c Dr 800
 To Share Forfeited A/c 1,600
 To Calls-in-arrears A/c 800 ☐

(D) Share Capital A/c Dr 2,000
 To Share Forfeited A/c 1,200
 To Calls-in-arrears A/c 800 ☐

31. Vishant Ltd. invited applications for issuing 6,000 equity shares of ₹ 10 each at 10% premium. The issue was fully subscribed. The amount per share was payable as follows

On application ₹ 3, on allotment ₹ 3 (including premium), on first call ₹ 3 and on final call ₹ 2. Ashish the holder of 200 shares paid the entire money along with allotment. The total amount received on allotment was *[CBSE 2024]*

(A) ₹ 18,000 ☐ (B) ₹ 19,000 ☐

(C) ₹ 25,000 ☐ (D) ₹ 21,000 ☐

32. Match the following

Column I	Column II
A. Share application	(i) Personal account
B. Securities premium	(ii) Real account
C. Cash	(iii) Nominal account

Codes

	A	B	C	
(A)	(iii)	(ii)	(i)	☐
(B)	(iii)	(i)	(ii)	☐
(C)	(i)	(iii)	(ii)	☐
(D)	(i)	(ii)	(iii)	☐

33. Match the following

Column I	Column II
A. Interest on calls-in-arrears	(i) 6% p.a.
B. Interest on calls-in-advance	(ii) 10% p.a.
	(iii) 12% p.a.

Codes

	A	B			A	B	
(A)	(iii)	(ii)	☐	(B)	(ii)	(i)	☐
(C)	(ii)	(iii)	☐	(D)	(i)	(ii)	☐

34. Match the following

Column I	Column II
A. Capital reserve	(i) Can be used for specific purposes
B. Reserve capital	(ii) Can be used only at the time of winding-up
C. Securities premium	(iii) No resolution required to create capital reserve

Codes

	A	B	C	
(A)	(iii)	(ii)	(i)	☐
(B)	(iii)	(i)	(ii)	☐
(C)	(i)	(iii)	(ii)	☐
(D)	(i)	(ii)	(iii)	☐

Assertion-Reason Questions

No. of Questions : **8**

Suggested Time : **15 Minutes**

Direction Each of the question given below consist of the two statements; one labelled as **Assertion** (A) and other as **Reason** (R). List of common options applicable for each question is given below

(A) Both Assertion (A) and Reason (R) are true and Reason (R) is the correct explanation of Assertion (A)

(B) Both Assertion (A) and Reason (R) are true, but Reason (R) is not the correct explanation of Assertion (A)

(C) Assertion (A) is true, but Reason (R) is false

(D) Assertion (A) is false, but Reason (R) is true

You have to select the codes as *A, B, C* or *D* as your answer to the question by marking (✓) in the response box given against each option.

1. **Assertion** (A) A company is registered with an authorised capital of 5,00,000 equity shares of ₹ 10 each of which 2,00,000 equity shares were issued and subscribed. All the money had been called-up except ₹ 2 per share which was declared as 'reserve capital'. The share capital reflected in balance sheet as 'subscribed and fully paid-up' will be zero.

   Reason (R) Reserve capital can be called-up only at the time of winding up of the company.

   (A) ☐ (B) ☐ (C) ☐ (D) ☐

2. **Assertion** (A) Incorporation account is to be opened when shares are issued to promoters.

   Reason (R) A company may issue shares to its promoters for their services rendered to the company.

   (A) ☐ (B) ☐ (C) ☐ (D) ☐

3. **Assertion** (A) A company is authorised to charge interest on calls-in-arrears at any rate, even if it is specified in article of association or not.

   Reason (R) Interest on calls-in-arrears shall be charged at rate not exceeding 10% p.a.

   (A) ☐ (B) ☐ (C) ☐ (D) ☐

4. **Assertion** (A) Maximum amount of discount allowed at the time of reissue of forfeited shares should not exceed the forfeited amount.

   Reason (R) The excess amount of forfeited shares account is transferred to capital reserve account.

   (A) ☐ (B) ☐ (C) ☐ (D) ☐

5. **Assertion** (A) In case of shares issued on pro-rata basis, excess money received at the time of application can be utilised till allotment only.

   Reason (R) Company has to pay interest on calls-in- advance @ 12% p.a. for amount adjusted towards calls (if any).

   (A) ☐ (B) ☐ (C) ☐ (D) ☐

6. **Assertion** (A) Forfeited shares may be issued at a discount also.

   Reason (R) Amount of discount on reissue of forfeited shares cannot exceed the amount forfeited on reissued shares.

   (A) ☐ (B) ☐
   (C) ☐ (D) ☐

7. **Assertion** (A) A company forfeited 400 shares of ₹ 10 each for non-payment of first call of ₹ 2 per share.

Final call of ₹ 3 per share is not yet called. The amount transferred to share forfeiture account will be ₹ 2,000.

Reason (R) Share forfeiture account is credited with the amount not yet paid by the defaulter.

(A) ☐ (B) ☐ (C) ☐ (D) ☐

8. **Assertion** (A) Shares can be forfeited only if the articles of association of the company allow them.

Reason (R) Forfeiture can be done after giving 14 days notice to the defaulter.

(A) ☐ (B) ☐
(C) ☐ (D) ☐

Correct/Incorrect Statements

No. of Questions : **9** Suggested Time : **15 Minutes**

Direction Each of the question given below consist of the two statements. List of common options applicable for each question is given below

(A) Both statements are correct
(B) Statement I is correct and Statement II is incorrect
(C) Statement I is incorrect and Statement II is correct
(D) Both statements are incorrect

You have to select the codes as *A*, *B*, *C* or *D* as your answer to the question by marking (✓) in the response box given against each option.

1. **Statement I** Capital reserves are created out of capital profits.

Statement II The subscribed capital which has not yet been called is known as reserve capital.

(A) ☐ (B) ☐ (C) ☐ (D) ☐

2. **Statement I** Authorised capital can be increased or decreased as per the procedure laid down in the Companies Act.

Statement II The authorised capital which is not offered for public subscription is known as reserve capital.

(A) ☐ (B) ☐ (C) ☐ (D) ☐

3. **Statement I** Securities premium can be utilised to pay interest to shareholders.

Statement II Securities premium can be used to issue fully paid bonus shares to members of the company.

(A) ☐ (B) ☐ (C) ☐ (D) ☐

4. **Statement I** Share application account is a personal account.

Statement II Shares issued to employees can be issued at discount.

(A) ☐ (B) ☐ (C) ☐ (D) ☐

5. **Statement I** Minimum subscription cannot be less than 90% of the issued amount.

Statement II The company has to get minimum subscription within 90 days from the date of issue of the prospectus.

(A) ☐ (B) ☐ (C) ☐ (D) ☐

6. **Statement I** A company cannot issue shares at discount.

Statement II A company can issued shares at discount in case of reissue of forfeited shares or issue of sweat equity shares.

(A) ☐ (B) ☐
(C) ☐ (D) ☐

7. **Statement I** Calls-in-arrears are deducted from subscribed capital.

Statement II Calls-in-advance are added to subscribed capital.

(A) ☐ (B) ☐ (C) ☐ (D) ☐

8. **Statement I** The balance of share forfeiture account after reissue of shares will be transferred to capital reserve account.

Statement II Capital reserve is not treated as capital profit for the company.

(A) ☐ (B) ☐ (C) ☐ (D) ☐

9. **Statement I** Maximum amount of discount allowed at the time of reissue of forfeited shares should not exceed the forfeited amount.

Statement II The excess of forfeited shares account is transferred to capital reserve account.

(A) ☐ (B) ☐
(C) ☐ (D) ☐

Case Based Questions

No. of Questions : **2** Suggested Time : **10 Minutes**

Direction This section contains 2 cases having 3/4 Questions of 1 mark each. You have to write the answer of each question based on the context of the related case.

Case 1 Zee Ltd., invited application for 40,000 shares. Applications were received in excess of 50% of the shares offered for subscription and pro-rata allotment was made to the applicants of 48,000 shares and a letter of regret was sent to the remaining. Raghu was allotted 1,600 shares and Mohan applied for 2,400 shares.

Questions

(i) How many applications have been rejected?

(A) 8,000 shares ☐
(B) 9,000 shares ☐
(C) 10,000 shares ☐
(D) 12,000 shares ☐

(ii) What will be the pro-rata ratio adopted by the company?

(A) 3 : 2 ☐ (B) 4 : 3 ☐
(C) 5 : 6 ☐ (D) 6 : 5 ☐

(iii) Number of shares applied by Raghu will be

(A) 1,800 ☐ (B) 1,850 ☐
(C) 1,920 ☐ (D) 2,000 ☐

Case 2 Nidiya Limited was incorporated on 1st April, 2017 with registered office in Mumbai. The capital clause of Memorandum of Association reflected a registered capital of 8,00,000 equity shares of ₹ 10 each and 1,00,000 preference shares of ₹ 50 each.

Since some large investments were required for building and machinery the company in consultation with vendors, Ms.VPS Enterprises, issued 1,00,000 equity shares and 20,000 preference shares at par to them in full consideration of assets acquired. Besides this the company issued 2,00,000 equity shares for cash at par payable as ₹ 3 on application, ₹ 2 on allotment, ₹ 3 on first call and ₹ 2 on second call. Till date second call has not yet been made and all the shareholders have paid except Mr. Ajay who did not pay allotment and calls on his 300 shares and Mr. Vipul who did not pay first call on his 200 shares. Shares of Mr. Ajay were then forfeited and out of them 100 shares were reissued at ₹ 12 per share.
Based on above information you are required to answer the following questions. *[CBSE QB]*

Questions

(i) Shares issue to vendors of building and machinery, Ms.VPS Enterprises, would be classified as

(A) preferential allotment ☐
(B) employee stock option plan ☐
(C) issue for consideration other than cash ☐
(D) right issue of shares ☐

(ii) How many equity shares of the company have been subscribed?

(A) 3,00,000 ☐
(B) 2,99,500 ☐
(C) 2,99,800 ☐
(D) None of the above ☐

(iii) What is the amount of security premium reflected in the balance sheet at the end of the year?

(A) ₹ 200 ☐ (B) ₹ 600 ☐
(C) ₹ 400 ☐ (D) ₹ 1,000 ☐

(iv) What amount of share forfeiture would be reflected in the balance sheet?

(A) ₹ 600 ☐
(B) ₹ 900 ☐
(C) ₹ 200 ☐
(D) ₹ 300 ☐

Subjective Questions

Free Response Questions, Open-ended Questions etc.

No. of Questions : **8** Suggested Time : **65 Minutes**

1. Complete the journal entries.

JOURNAL

Date	Particulars		LF	Amt (Dr)	Amt (Cr)
	Share Capital A/c	Dr		2,25,000	
	Securities Premium Reserve A/c	Dr		...	
	To Share Forfeiture A/c				...
	To Calls-in-arrears A/c				...
	(Being 3,000 shares of ₹ 100 each, ₹ 75 called, forfeited for non-payment of allotment of ₹ 45 each including premium of ₹ 5 per share)				
	....	Dr		...	
	....	Dr		...	
	To				...
	(Being reissue of 2,000 shares at ₹ 60 per share, ₹ 75 paid-up)				
	....	Dr		...	
	To Capital Reserve A/c				...
	(...)				

2. Complete the following journal entries.

JOURNAL

Date	Particulars		LF	Amt (Dr)	Amt (Cr)
	Building A/c	Dr		7,00,000	
	Debtors A/c	Dr		5,00,000	
	Stock A/	Dr		4,00,000	
	To Creditors A/c				3,20,000
	To Bills Payable A/c				20,000
	To Vishesh Ltd.				12,60,000
	(...)				
	....	Dr		....	
	To				....
	To				....
	(Being payment made by issue of 12,000 equity shares of ₹ 100 each at 5 premium)				

3. Yash Ltd. invited applications for 50,000 equity shares of ₹ 10 each at a premium of 10%. The amount was payable as follows

On application ₹ 3 per share, on allotment (including premium) ₹ 3 per share and on first and final call the balance amount.

Applications were received for 1,20,000 shares and shares were allotted on pro-rata basis to all applicants. The excess money received on application as to be adjusted towards sums due on allotment.

Application money in excess of sums due on allotment was refunded. A shareholder who applied for 6,000 shares could not pay the first and final call money and his shares were forfeited. The forfeited shares were reissued for ₹ 60,000 fully paid-up.

Pass necessary journal entries for the above transactions in the books of Yash Ltd. *[CBSE 2023]*

4. Karan Ltd., issued a prospectus inviting applications for 80,000 equity shares of 10 each payable as follows

₹ 2 on application

₹ 3 on allotment

₹ 2 on first call

₹ 3 on final call

Applications were received for 1,20,000 equity shares. It was decided to adjust the excess amount received on account of over subscription till allotment only. Hence allotment was made as under

(i) To applicants for 20,000 shares – full

(ii) To applicants for 40,000 shares – 10,000 shares

(iii) To applicants for 60,000 shares – 50,000 shares

Allotment was made and all shareholders except Tammana, who had applied for 2,400 shares out of the group (iii), could not pay allotment money. Her shares were forfeited immediately after allotment. Another shareholder Chhaya, who was allotted 500 shares out of group (ii), failed to pay first call. 50% of Tamanna's shares were reissued to Satnaam as ₹ 7 paid-up for payment of ₹ 9 per share.

Pass necessary journal entries in the books of Karan Ltd.

5. Lazal Ltd. invited applications for issuing 2,00,000 equity shares of ₹ 10 each, at 20% premium. Amount per share was payable as follows

₹ 5 on application, ₹ 4 (including premium) on allotment and balance on first and final call.

Public applied for 3,20,000 shares, out of which applications for 20,000 shares were rejected and shares were allotted on pro-rata basis to the remaining applications. Kavita, an applicant of 15,000 shares failed to pay allotment and call money. Her shares were forfeited.

Pass necessary journal entries for the above transactions in the books of the company. [CBSE 2024]

6. X Ltd., has offered 50,000 equity shares of ₹ 100 each at a premium of ₹ 20 payable as follows

Application ₹ 50

Allotment ₹ 40 (including premium) and balance on first and final call

The bank account of the company has received ₹ 35,00,000 on account of share application money. X Ltd. decided to allot shares to all the applicants on pro-rata basis.

The balance in calls-in-arrears account at the time of allotment and first and final call amounted to ₹ 1,00,000 and ₹ 1,50,000 respectively. These shares were forfeited and reissued at 90 per share as fully paid-up. Journalise.

7. Sandesh Ltd. has an authorised capital of ₹ 30,00,000 divided into equity shares of ₹ 10 each. The company invited application for issuing 70,000 shares.

Applications for 69,000 shares were received. All calls were made and duly received except the first and final call of ₹ 2 per share on 3,000 shares.

These shares were forfeited.

(i) Present the 'share capital in the balance sheet of the company as per Schedule III, Part I of the Companies Act, 2013.

(ii) Also prepare 'notes to accounts' for the same. [CBSE 2023]

8. Ronit Ltd. was registered with an authorised capital of ₹ 75,00,000 divided into 75,000 equity shares of ₹ 100 each.

The company invited applications for issuing 45,000 shares.

The amount was payable as follows

₹ 30 per share on application, ₹ 30 per share on allotment, ₹ 25 per share on first call and balance on final call.

Applications were received for 42,000 shares and allotment was made to all the applicants. Charvi, to whom 3,300 shares were allotted, failed to pay both the calls.

Her shares were forfeited. Present the share capital in the balance sheet of the company as per Schedule III, Part I of the Companies Act, 2013. Also prepare notes to accounts. [CBSE 2024]

Answers

If your answer matches with the answer given here then put (✓) in the box otherwise put (✗). In case you did not attempt the question leave the box blank.

Multiple Choice Questions

1. C ☐
2. A ☐
3. C ☐
4. B ☐
5. C ☐
6. A ☐
7. D ☐
8. B ☐
9. C ☐
10. A ☐
11. B ☐
12. B ☐
13. C ☐
14. D ☐
15. A ☐
16. A ☐
17. B ☐
18. C ☐
19. B ☐
20. B ☐
21. C ☐
22. C ☐
23. B ☐
24. D ☐
25. A ☐
26. C ☐
27. B ☐
28. B ☐
29. C ☐
30. B ☐
31. B ☐
32. C ☐
33. C ☐
34. A ☐

Your Score__________ *(No. of Correct Answers)*

Assertion-Reason Questions

1. A ☐ 2. A ☐
3. D ☐ 4. B ☐
5. D ☐ 6. B ☐
7. C ☐ 8. B ☐

Your Score__________ *(No. of Correct Answers)*

Correct/Incorrect Statements

1. B ☐ 2. B ☐
3. C ☐ 4. A ☐
5. B ☐ 6. A ☐
7. B ☐ 8. B ☐
9. A ☐

Your Score__________ *(No. of Correct Answers)*

Case Based Questions

1. (i) D ☐ (ii) D ☐
(iii) C ☐
2. (i) C ☐ (ii) C ☐
(iii) C ☐ (iv) A ☐

Your Score__________ *(No. of Correct Answers)*

Explanations

Multiple Choice Questions

1. (C) the maximum amount of share capital which a company is authorised to issue
2. (A) subscribed capital; reserve capital
3. (C) Both (ii) and (iii)
4. (B) it can be used for writing-off capital losses
5. (C) creating general reserves
6. (A) As per SEBI, minimum 90% shares must be applied for. So 90% of 12,000 i.e. 10,800 shares must pay application of ₹ 3. So, minimum amount to be received is ₹ 32,400. Any amount less than ₹ 32,400 restricts to proceed with allotment.
7. (D) Any one of (i) and (ii)
8. (B) Final Call $= \frac{12,000}{4,000} = 3$ per share
9. (C) capital reserve account
10. (A) debited, goodwill
11. (B) (5,000 × 2) = ₹ 10,000
12. (B) Issue Price of Shares = ₹ 110

    Number of Shares Issued $= \frac{(20,00,000 - 6,00,000)}{110}$

    = 12,727.27 shares

    Since the company cannot issue shares in fractions, 0.27 shares will be paid through the bank. 0.27 × 110 = ₹ 30 (approx).

    Payment through bank = 6,00,000 + 30

    = ₹ 6,00,030
13. (C) Shares Applied $= \frac{7,200}{6,000} \times 80 = 96$ shares
14. (D) Share Applied : Share Allotted

    70,000 : 30,000

    Excess application money

    = 40,000 × 4 = ₹ 1,60,000

    Sum due on allotment = 30,000 × 2 = ₹ 60,000

    Adjusted on allotment = ₹ 60,000, remaining to be adjusted on call = 1,60,000 – 60,000

    = ₹ 1,00,000

    Sum due on first call = 30,000 × 4 = ₹ 1,20,000

    Adjusted on Ist call = ₹ 1,00,000

    ∴ Amount refunded = Nil
15. (A) Share forfeiture account

    = 8 (Called) –2 (Unpaid) = 6 (Paid)
16. (A) Called-up = 1,000 × 8 = ₹ 8,000
17. (B) issue of partly paid bonus shares
18. (C) Maximum discount at the time of reissue

    = 3,000 × 7 = ₹ 21,000
19. (B)

Date	Particulars		Amt (Dr)	Amt (Cr)
	Share Capital A/c (800 × 8)	Dr	6,400	
	Securities Premium Reserve A/c	Dr	—	
	To Share Forfeiture A/c			4,800
	To Calls-in-arrears A/c (800 × 2)			1,600

20. (B) Uncalled Capital = 10 – 6 = 4
21. (C) Balance in forfeiture $= \left(\frac{100}{20} \times 5\right) = 25$
22. (C) (ii), (i), (iii), (iv)

23. (B) Maximum discount at forfeiture
= Forfeiture credit balance
= 4,000 × 7 = ₹ 28,000

24. (D) Capital Reserve =

$$\left(\frac{\text{Profit on Forfeiture}}{\text{Forfeited Shares}} \times \text{Re-issued Shares}\right) - \text{Loss on Re-issue}$$

$$= \left(\frac{6,000}{1,000} \times 800\right) - 1,400$$

= ₹ 3,400

25. (A)

	Amt (₹)
Total applications received	1,45,000
(–) Rejected	(20,000)
	1,25,000
(–) Issued	(50,000)
Excess application	75,000

Excess money received = 75,000 × 3 = ₹ 2,25,000

26. (C) Capital Reserve = Profit on Forfeiture – Loss on Re-issue

40 = 55 (75 – 20) – Loss on Re-issue

Loss on Re-issue = 55 – 40 = ₹ 15

Re-issue Price = 75 – 15 = 60 per share

27. (B)

Face Value per Share	₹ 10
(–) Called-up Amount per Share (7 – 1)	(₹ 6)
Uncalled Amount	₹ 4

28. (B) Amount recieved on application
= 3,000 × 3 + 500 × 7 + 300 × 5 = ₹ 14,000

29. (C) Minimum application received should be 90% of the issued shares.

Minimum shares subscribed (12,000 × 90%) = 10,800 shares

Minimum application money should be received = 10,800 × 3 = ₹ 32,400

In case of less than ₹ 32,400, SEBI restricts company to proceed with allotment.

30. (B)

Share Capital A/c	Dr	1,600	
Securities Premium Reserve A/c	Dr	800	
To Share Forfeited A/c			1,200
To Calls-in-arrears A/c			1,200

31. (B) Amount received on allotment

	Amt (₹)
(6,000 × 3) =	18,000
(200 × 5) =	1,000
	19,000

32. (C) (i) (iii) (ii)

33. (C) (ii) (iii)

34. (A) (iii) (ii) (i)

Assertion-Reason Questions

1. (A) Both Assertion (A) and Reason (R) are true and Reason (R) is the correct explanation of Assertion (A)
2. (A) Both Assertion (A) and Reason (R) are true and Reason (R) is the correct explanation of Assertion (A)
3. (D) If interest is not mentioned, it will be charged at 10% p.a.
4. (B) Both Assertion (A) and Reason (R) are true, but Reason (R) is not the correct explanation of Assertion (A)
5. (D) Assertion (A) is false, but Reason (R) is true
6. (B) Both Assertion (A) and Reason (R) are true, but Reason (R) is not the correct explanation of Assertion (A)
7. (C) Share forfeiture account is credited with the amount paid by the defaulter.
8. (B) Both Assertion (A) and Reason (R) are true, but Reason (R) is not the correct explanation of Assertion (A)

Correct/Incorrect Statements

1. (B) The subscribed share capital that has not been called is known as uncalled capital.
2. (B) Authorised capital which is not offered to public for subscription is known as unissued share capital.
3. (C) Indian Companies Act, 2013 restricts the usage of securities premium. It cannot be used to issue interest.
4. (A) Both statements are correct
5. (B) The company has to get minimum subscription within 120 days from the date of issue of prospectus.
6. (A) Both statements are correct
7. (B) Calls-in-advance is shown under current liabilities as other current liabilities.
8. (B) Capital reserves are made from capital profits.
9. (A) Both statements are correct

Case Based Questions

1. (i) (D) Application rejected = 60,000 – 48,000 = 12,000 shares

   (ii) (D) Pro-rata ratio will be = 48,000 : 40,000 *or* 6 : 5 (iii) (C) Share Applied = $\frac{48,000}{40,000} \times 1,600 = 1,920$ shares

2. (i) (C) issue for consideration other than cash

   (ii) (C)

		Amt (₹)
Shares subscribed	=	1,00,000
	=	2,00,000
	=	3,00,000
	=	(200)
	=	2,99,800
(–) Calls in arrears (200 × 3)	=	(600)
(+) Share forfeited account (200 × 3)	=	600
		2,99,800

   (iii) (C) Security premium reflected in the balance sheet at the end of year would be ₹ 400 (100 × 4).

   (iv) (A) Share forfeiture reflected in balance would be ₹ 600 (200 × 3).

Subjective Questions

1. **JOURNAL**

Date	Particulars		Amt (Dr)	Amt (Cr)
	Share Capital A/c	Dr	2,25,000	
	Securities Premium A/c (3,000 × 5)	Dr	**15,000**	
	To Share Forfeiture A/c			**1,05,000**
	To Calls-in-arrears A/c			**1,35,000**
	(Being 3,000 shares of ₹ 100 each, ₹ 75 called, forfeited for non-payment of allotment of ₹ 45 each including premium of ₹ 5 per share)			
	Bank A/c (2,000 × 60)	Dr	**1,20,000**	
	Share Forfeiture A/c	Dr	**30,000**	
	To **Share Capital A/c (2,000 × 75)**			**1,50,000**
	(Being reissue of 2,000 shares at ₹ 60 per share, ₹ 75 paid-up)			
	Share Forfeiture A/c	Dr	**40,000**	
	To Capital Reserve A/c			**40,000**
	(Being balance of share forfeiture transferred to capital reserve)			

Working Note

$$\text{Capital Reserve} = \left(\frac{\text{Share Forfeiture Credit}}{\text{Forfeit Shares}} \times \text{Reissue Share}\right) - \text{Share Forfeiture Debit}$$

$$= \left(\frac{1,05,000}{3,000} \times 2,000\right) - 30,000 = ₹\ 40,000$$

2. **JOURNAL**

Date	Particulars		Amt (Dr)	Amt (Cr)
	Building A/c	Dr	7,00,000	
	Debtors A/c	Dr	5,00,000	
	Stock A/c	Dr	4,00,000	
	To Creditors A/c			3,20,000
	To Bills Payable A/c			20,000
	To Vishesh Ltd.			12,60,000
	(Being assets and liabilities taken over of Vishesh Ltd.)			

Date	Particulars	Amt (Dr)	Amt (Cr)
	Vishesh Ltd. A/c Dr	**12,60,000**	
	To **Equity Share Capital A/c (12,000 × 100)**		**12,00,000**
	To **Securities Premium A/c (12,000 × 5)**		**60,000**
	(Being payment made by issue of 12,000 equity shares of ₹ 100 each at 5 premium)		

3\. **JOURNAL of Yash Ltd.**

Date	Particulars	LF	Amt (Dr)	Amt (Cr)
	Bank A/c Dr		3,60,000	
	To Share Application A/c			3,60,000
	(Being application money received on 1,20,000 shares @ 3 each)			
	Share Application A/c Dr		3,60,000	
	To Share Capital A/c (50,000 × 3)			1,50,000
	To Share Allotment A/c (50,000 × 3)			1,50,000
	To Bank A/c			60,000
	(Being application money adjusted and excess money refunded)			
	Share Allotment A/c (50,000 × 3) Dr		1,50,000	
	To Share Capital A/c			1,00,000
	To Securities Premium A/c			50,000
	(Being allotment money due)			
	Share First and Final Call A/c (50,000 × 5) Dr		2,50,000	
	To Share Capital A/c			2,50,000
	(Being first and final call money due)			
	Bank A/c Dr		2,37,500	
	To Share First and Final Call A/c			2,37,500
	(Being money received for first and final call on 47,500 shares @ ₹ 5 each)			
	(Alloted shares on application of 6,000 shares = 50,000/1,20,000 × 6,000 = 2,500 shares)			
	Share Capital A/c (2,500 × 10) Dr		25,000	
	To Share First and Final Call A/c (2,500 × 5)			12,500
	To Share Forfeiture A/c			12,500
	(Being 2,500 shares forfeited for non-payment of first and final call)			
	Bank A/c Dr		60,000	
	To Share Capital A/c (2,500 × 10)			25,000
	To Securities Premium A/c			35,000
	(Being reissue of forfeited shares @ ₹ 10 each plus premium @ ₹ 14 per share)			
	Share Forfeiture A/c Dr		12,500	
	To Capital Reserve A/c			12,500
	(Being balance of share forfeiture account transfer to capital reserve account)			

Working Note

Calculation for the amount refunded excess to allotment money adjusted

	Amt (₹)
Application money received (1,20,000 × 3)	3,60,000
Application money received on alloted shares (50,000 × 3)	(1,50,000)
	2,10,000
(–) Amount due on allotment including premium (50,000 × 3)	(1,50,000)
Excess money after adjustment of allotment	60,000

4. **JOURNAL**

Date	Particulars		Amt (Dr)	Amt (Cr)
	Bank A/c (1,20,000 × 2)	Dr	2,40,000	
	To Equity Share Application A/c			2,40,000
	(Being application money received)			
	Equity Share Application A/c	Dr	2,40,000	
	To Equity Share Capital A/c (80,000 × 2)			1,60,000
	To Equity Share Allotment A/c			50,000
	To Bank A/c			30,000
	(Being application money due and balance adjusted)			
	Equity Share Allotment A/c	Dr	2,40,000	
	To Equity Share Capital A/c			2,40,000
	(Being allotment money due)			
	Bank A/c	Dr	1,84,800	
	Calls-in-arrears A/c	Dr	5,200	
	To Equity Share Allotment A/c			1,90,000
	(Being allotment money received)			
	Equity Share Capital A/c (2,000× 5)	Dr	10,000	
	To Share Forfeited A/c			4,800
	To Calls-in-arrears A/c			5,200
	(Being shares forfeited)			
	Equity Share First Call A/c (78,000× 2)	Dr	1,56,000	
	To Equity Share Capital A/c			1,56,000
	(Being first call due on 78,000 shares)			
	Bank A/c	Dr	1,55,000	
	Calls-in-arrears A/c	Dr	1,000	
	To Equity Share First Call A/c			1,56,000
	(Being first call money received)			
	Bank A/c (1,000 × 9)	Dr	9,000	
	To Equity Share Capital A/c			7,000
	To Securities Premium A/c			2,000
	(1,000 shares reissued at 7 paid for 9 per share)			

Date	Particulars		Amt (Dr)	Amt (Cr)
	Share Forfeited A/c	Dr	2,400	
	To Capital Reserve A/c			2,400
	(Being balance of forfeiture transfer to capital reserve)			

Working Note

Excess Money in Category (ii) = 30,000 × 2 = 60,000

Amount due on Allotment = 10,000 × 3 = 30,000

∴ Money Adjusted = 30,000

Excess money in category (iii) = 10,000 × 2 = 20,000

Amount due on allotment = 50,000 × 3 = 1,50,000

∴ Money Adjusted = 20,000

$$\text{Shares Allotted} = \frac{50,000}{60,000} \times 2,400 = 2,000$$

Excess Application Money = 400 × 2 = ₹ 800

Arrear of Allotment = 6,000 – 800 = ₹ 5,200

Arrear of First call = 500 × 2 = 1,000

$$\text{Capital Reserve} = \left(\frac{4,800}{2,000} \times 1,000\right) - 0 = ₹\ 2,400$$

5. **JOURNAL**

Date	Particulars		LF	Amt (Dr)	Amt (Cr)
	Bank A/c (3,20,000 × 5)	Dr		16,00,000	
	To Equity Share Application A/c				16,00,000
	(Being application money received)				
	Equity Share Application A/c	Dr		16,00,000	
	To Share Capital A/c (2,00,000 × 5)				10,00,000
	To Share Allotment A/c				5,00,000
	To Bank A/c (20,000 × 5)				1,00,000
	(Being application money adjusted)				
	Equity Share Allotment A/c	Dr		8,00,000	
	To Share Capital A/c (2,00,000 × 2)				4,00,000
	To Securities Premium Reserve A/c (2,00,000 × 2)				4,00,000
	(Being allotment money due)				
	Bank A/c (WN 3)	Dr		2,85,000	
	To Share Allotment A/c				2,85,000
	(Being amount received on allotment)				
	Equity Share First and Final Call A/c	Dr		6,00,000	
	To Share Capital A/c (2,00,000 × 3)				6,00,000
	(Being first and final call due)				
	Bank A/c (1,90,000 × 3)	Dr		5,70,000	
	To Share First and Final Call A/c				5,70,000
	(Being first and final call received)				

Date	Particulars		LF	Amt (Dr)	Amt (Cr)
	Share Capital A/c	Dr		1,00,000	
	Securities Premium Reserve A/c (WN 4)	Dr		15,000	
	To Share Allotment A/c				15,000
	To Share First and Final Call A/c				30,000
	To Share Forfeiture A/c				70,000
	(Being shares forfeited)				

Working Notes

1. Shares Allotted to Kavita $= \frac{2,00,000}{3,00,000} \times 15,000 = 10,000$

   Excess application money received = 15,000 − 10,000 shares = 5,000 shares × 5 = ₹ 25,000

2. Amount due from Kavita on allotment (10,000 × 4) — 40,000
   (–) Excess received on application — (25,000)
   Amount not received on allotment — ₹15,000

3. Total amount due on allotment (2,00,000 × 4) — 8,00,000
   (–) Excess amount received on application — (5,00,000)
   3,00,000
   (–) Amount not received on allotment — (15,000)
   ₹ 2,85,000

4. Out of excess application money of ₹ 25,000, ₹ 20,000 are adjusted against face value of allotment money and ₹ 5,000 against premium. So, only ₹ 15,000 premium is outstanding. As per the rule, we can only debit outstanding amount during forfeiture.

6.

JOURNAL

Date	Particulars		Amt (Dr)	Amt (Cr)
	Bank A/c	Dr	35,00,000	
	To Equity Share Application A/c			35,00,000
	(Being application money received of 70,000 shares @ 50 each)			
	Equity Share Application A/c	Dr	35,00,000	
	To Equity Share Capital A/c			25,00,000
	To Equity Share Allotment A/c			10,00,000
	(Being shares allotted on pro-rata basis)			
	Equity Share Allotment A/c	Dr	20,00,000	
	To Equity Share Capital A/c			10,00,000
	To Securities Premium Reserve A/c			10,00,000
	(Being shares allotment money including premium)			
	Bank A/c	Dr	9,00,000	
	Calls-in-arrears A/c	Dr	1,00,000	
	To Equity Share Allotment A/c			10,00,000
	(Being allotment money received)			
	Equity Share First and Final Call A/c	Dr	15,00,000	
	To Equity Share Capital A/c			15,00,000
	(Being share first and final call due)			

Date	Particulars		Amt (Dr)	Amt (Cr)
	Bank A/c	Dr	13,50,000	
	Calls-in-arrears A/c		1,50,000	
	To Equity Share First and Final Call A/c			15,00,000
	(Being first and final call received)			
	Equity Share Capital A/c	Dr	5,00,000	
	Securities Premium Reserve A/c	Dr	1,00,000	
	To Share Forfeited A/c			3,50,000
	To Calls-in-arrears A/c			2,50,000
	(Being 5,000 shares were forfeited)			
	Bank A/c	Dr	4,50,000	
	Share Forfeiture A/c		50,000	
	To Share Capital A/c			5,00,000
	(Being 5,000 shares reissued)			
	Share Forfeiture A/c	Dr	3,00,000	
	To Capital Reserve A/c			3,00,000
	(Being forfeiture balance transfer) (Forfeiture Credit – Forfeiture Debit)			

7. (i)

Extract of Balance Sheet

as at ......

Particulars	Note No.	Amt (₹)
I. **EQUITY AND LIABILITIES**		
1. **Shareholders' Funds**		
Share Capital	1	6,84,000
		6,84,000

(ii) **Notes to Accounts**

Particulars	Amt (₹)
1. **Share Capital**	
Authorised Capital	
3,00,000 Equity Shares of ₹ 10 each	30,00,000
Issued Capital	
70,000 Equity Shares of ₹ 10 each	7,00,000
Subscribed Capital	
Subscribed and Fully Paid-up	
66,000 Equity Shares of ₹ 10 each	6,60,000
(+) Shares Forfeited Account (3,000 × 8)	24,000
	6,84,000

8.

Extract of Balance Sheet
as at

Particulars	Note No.	Amt (₹)
I. **EQUITY AND LIABILITIES**		
1. **Shareholders' Funds**		
Share Capital	1	40,68,000

Notes to Accounts

Particulars		Amt (₹)
1. **Share Capital**		
Authorised Capital		
75,000 Equity Shares of ₹ 100 each		75,00,000
Issued Capital		
45,000 Equity Shares of ₹ 100 each		45,00,000
Subscribed Share Capital		
Subscribed and Fully Paid-up		
38,700 Equity Shares of ₹ 100 each Fully Paid-up		38,70,000
Subscribed but not Fully Paid-up		
3,300 Equity Shares of ₹ 100 each Fully Called-up	3,30,000	
(−) Calls-in-arrears (3,300 × 40)	(1,32,000)	1,98,000
		40,68,000

CHAPTER -7

Accounting for Debentures

Types & Nos. of Questions

Multiple Choice Questions	-	30
Assertion-Reason Questions	-	5
Correct/Incorrect Statements	-	5
Case Based Questions	-	2 Cases, *each with 3 Questions*
Subjective Questions	-	8

Trend Analysis

On the basis of analysis of last 2 years' papers, it is found that on an average 3 Multiple Choice Questions, 1 Short Answer Type Question and 1 Long Answer Type Question are asked from this chapter.

Focus Topics of the Chapter

- Issue of Debentures for Cash
- Issue of Debentures for Consideration Other than Cash
- Issues of Debentures as Collateral Security
- Various Cases from the Point of view of Redemption
- Interest on Debentures

Multiple Choice Questions

No. of Questions : **30**

Suggested Time : **45 Minutes**

Direction Each of the question given below is Multiple Choice Question (MCQ) i.e. there are Four Options/Choices for answer, out of which ONLY ONE is correct. You have to select the correct option.
A response box is given with each option, mark (✓) in the box of the correct option. For each correct answer you will get 1 mark, while there is no penalty for incorrect answer or missed out questions.

1. What is the maximum rate of discount for issue of debentures by company?
   (A) 6% ☐
   (B) 9% ☐
   (C) 10% ☐
   (D) No restriction (decided by the directors) ☐

2. Premium received on issue of debentures may be utilised for
   I. Writing-off preliminary expenses
   II. Writing-off underwriting commission
   III. Writing-off discount allowed on issue of debentures

   Which of the following statement(s) are correct?
   (A) Only I ☐ (B) I and II ☐
   (C) I, II and III ☐ (D) I and III ☐

3. Which of the following statements is incorrect? *[CBSE 2023]*
   (A) Interest on debentures is a charge and not an appropriation ☐
   (B) Debentures can be issued at discount ☐
   (C) Debentureholders do not have voting rights ☐
   (D) Debentures cannot be converted into shares ☐

4. Which of the following statements is incorrect about debentures?
   (A) Interest on debentures is an appropriation of profits ☐
   (B) Debentureholders are the creditors of a company ☐
   (C) Debentures can be issued to vendors at discount ☐
   (D) Interest is not paid on debentures issued as collateral security ☐

5. K Ltd. issued 20,000, 10% debentures of ₹ 10 each at a premium of 20%. The whole amount was payable on application. On the date of transfer of application money, following entry was passed.

Debenture Application A/c Dr	3,60,000	
To 10% Debentures A/c		2,00,000
To Securities Premium Reserve A/c		40,000
To Bank A/c		1,20,000

   Number of applications received by the company is
   (A) 36,000 ☐ (B) 20,000 ☐
   (C) 30,000 ☐ (D) 10,000 ☐

6. Discount on issue of debentures is in the nature of
   (A) revenue loss ☐
   (B) capital loss ☐
   (C) deferred revenue expenditure ☐
   (D) None of the above ☐

7. A Ltd. issued 60,000, 12% debentures of ₹ 100 each at a premium of 20%. The whole amount was payable on application. Application for 1,00,000 debentures were received. Amount refunded by the company will be
   (A) ₹ 40,00,000 ☐ (B) ₹ 48,00,000 ☐
   (C) ₹ 60,00,000 ☐ (D) Nil ☐

8. Debentures of ₹ 80,000 were issued by MBC Ltd. in consideration of net assets of ₹ 1,00,000. Here, the balance of ₹ 20,000 will be credited to

(A) statement of profit and loss ☐
(B) goodwill account ☐
(C) general reserve account ☐
(D) capital reserve account ☐

9. ABC Ltd. purchased a machine from Y Ltd. payable ₹ 55,000 in cash and balance by issue of ₹ 50,000, 12% debentures of ₹ 10 each issued at a discount of 10%. Value of machine will be

(A) ₹ 4,50,000 ☐ (B) ₹ 4,95,000 ☐
(C) ₹ 5,55,000 ☐ (D) ₹ 5,05,000 ☐

10. Arnav Ltd. purchased assets worth ₹ 24,00,000. It issued 9% debentures of ₹ 100 each at a discount of 4% for payment of the purchase consideration. The number of debentures issued to vendor were *[CBSE 2024]*

(A) 24,000 ☐ (B) 25,000 ☐
(C) 30,000 ☐ (D) 28,000 ☐

11. Alexa Ltd. purchased building from Siri Ltd. for ₹ 8,00,000. The consideration was paid by issue of 6% debentures of ₹ 100 each at a discount of 20%.

The 6% debentures account is credited with

(A) ₹ 10,40,000 ☐ (B) ₹ 10,00,000 ☐
(C) ₹ 9,60,000 ☐ (D) ₹ 6,40,000 ☐

12. Maira Ltd. took over assets of ₹ 12,00,000 and liabilities of ₹ 4,00,000 of Subav Ltd. for an agreed purchase consideration of ₹ 9,00,000.

The amount was payable by issue of 11% debentures of ₹ 100 each at 10% discount. The number of debentures issued will be *[CBSE 2023]*

(A) 9,000 ☐ (B) 10,000 ☐
(C) 8,000 ☐ (D) 11,000 ☐

13. Daman Ltd. made the following issue of debentures

(i) for cash at 95%, 500 debentures of ₹ 100 each
(ii) to a creditor who supplied machinery costing ₹ 16,000, 170 debentures of ₹ 100 each
(iii) to a bank for loan of ₹ 80,000 as a collateral security

In which of the above issue, debenture suspense account will be opened

(A) (i) and (ii) ☐ (B) (ii) and (iii) ☐
(C) Only (iii) ☐ (D) (i), (ii) and (iii) ☐

14. On 1st May, 2023, Amrit Ltd. issued 10,000, 10% debentures of ₹ 100 each at a premium of 10% redeemable at a premium of 10%. Loss on issue of debentures will be *[CBSE 2024]*

(A) ₹ 2,00,000 ☐ (B) ₹ 1,30,000 ☐
(C) ₹ 1,00,000 ☐ (D) ₹ 80,000 ☐

15. Raman Ltd., issued 50,000, 8% debentures of ₹ 100 each at certain rate of premium and to be redeemed at 10% premium. At the time of writing-off loss on issue of debentures, statement of profit and loss was debited with ₹ 2,00,000. At what rate of premium, these debentures were issued?

(A) 10% ☐ (B) 16% ☐
(C) 6% ☐ (D) 4% ☐

16. Durga Ltd., issued 80,000, 10% debentures of ₹ 100 each at certain rate of discount and was to be redeemed at 20% premium.

Existing balance of securities premium before issuing of these debentures was ₹ 25,00,000 and after writing-off loss on issue of debentures, the balance of securities premium was ₹ 5,00,000. At what rate of discount, these debentures were issued?

(A) 10% ☐ (B) 5% ☐
(C) 25% ☐ (D) 15% ☐

17. Rahul Ltd. issued 11% debentures of ₹ 10 each at a premium of 20%. The whole amount was payable on application. On transfer of application money, securities premium account is credited with ₹ 1,20,000. Application money received by the company will be

(A) ₹ 10,000 ☐
(B) ₹ 1,00,000 ☐
(C) ₹ 7,20,000 ☐
(D) ₹ 6,00,000 ☐

18. Premium on redemption of debentures is shown under

(A) share capital ☐
(B) reserves and surplus ☐
(C) non-current liabilities ☐
(D) current liabilities ☐

19. Holder of debentures as a collateral security is entitled to

(A) interest on debentures ☐
(B) dividend ☐
(C) commission ☐
(D) None of the above ☐

20. Rohit Ltd. issued 2,000, 9% debentures of ₹ 100 each at ₹ 95 per debenture. 9% debentures account will be credited by *[CBSE 2023]*

(A) ₹ 1,90,000 ☐ (B) ₹ 1,10,000 ☐
(C) ₹ 2,00,000 ☐ (D) ₹ 10,000 ☐

21. Ashika Ltd. issued 2,00,000, 7% debentures of ₹ 100 each at a discount of 5% redeemable at a premium of 5%. Discount on issue and premium on redemption were accounted for through 'loss on issue of debentures account'.

On issue of debentures, 'loss on issue of debentures account' will be

(A) credited by ₹ 10,00,000 ☐
(B) debited by ₹ 10,00,000 ☐
(C) debited by ₹ 20,00,000 ☐
(D) credited by ₹ 20,00,000 ☐

22. Dumo Ltd. issued 4,000, 9% debentures of ₹ 100 each at a discount of 10%, redeemable at a premium. 'Discount on issue of debentures' and 'premium on redemption of debentures' were accounted for through 'loss on issue of debentures account'.

If the amount of 'loss on issue of debentures account' was ₹ 60,000, then the amount of premium on redemption was

(A) ₹ 60,000 ☐
(B) ₹ 40,000 ☐
(C) ₹ 20,000 ☐
(D) ₹ 80,000 ☐

23. Sinco Ltd. issued 20,000, 9% debentures of ₹ 100 each at a discount of 10%, redeemable at a premium. On issue of these debentures, 'loss on issue of debentures account' was debited with ₹ 4,00,000. The premium on redemption of debentures is

(A) ₹ 4,00,000 ☐ (B) ₹ 2,00,000 ☐
(C) ₹ 6,00,000 ☐ (D) ₹ 10,00,000 ☐

24. The following journal entry appears in the books of X Co. Ltd.

Bank A/c	Dr	4,75,000	
Loss on Issue of Debentures A/c	Dr	75,000	
To 12% Debentures A/c			5,00,000
To Premium on Redemption of Debentures A/c			50,000

Debentures have been issued at a discount of

(A) 5% ☐ (B) 10% ☐
(C) 12% ☐ (D) 15% ☐

25. Mahajan Ltd. issued 3,000, 15% debentures of ₹ 100 each at a discount of 5%, redeemable at a premium of 10% after 5 years. Which of the following statements is correct?

(A) Loss on issue of debentures will be debited by ₹ 45,000 ☐
(B) Loss on issue of debentures will be credited by ₹ 40,000 ☐

(C) Premium on redemption of debenture will be debited by ₹ 45,000 ☐

(D) Premium on redemption of debenture will be credited by ₹ 40,000 ☐

26. When debentures are issued at lumpsum, journalise the acceptance of application of debentures from public.

(A) Bank A/c Dr
To Debenture Application A/c ☐

(B) Debenture Application A/c Dr
To X% Debentures A/c ☐

(C) Debenture Application and Allotment A/c Dr
To X% Debentures A/c ☐

(D) None of the above ☐

27. Journalise the writing-off discount on issue of debentures, when company has all reserves and profits required to cover this loss.

(A) General Reserve A/c Dr
To Statement of Profit and Loss
To Discount on Issue of Debentures A/c ☐

(B) Discount on Issue of Debentures A/c Dr
To General Reserve A/c
To Statement of Profit and Loss ☐

(C) Loss on Issue of Debentures A/c Dr
To Statement of Profit and Loss ☐

(D) None of the above ☐

28. Match the Column I with Column II in the following information

Column I	Column II
A. Loss on issue of debentures	(i) Real account
B. Premium on redemption of debentures	(ii) Nominal account
C. Machinery	(iii) Personal account

Codes

	A	B	C	
(A)	(i)	(ii)	(iii)	☐
(B)	(i)	(iii)	(ii)	☐
(C)	(ii)	(i)	(iii)	☐
(D)	(ii)	(iii)	(i)	☐

29. Match the Column I with Column II in the following information

Column I	Column II
A. Company issued 1,000, 10% debentures of ₹ 100 each at 4% premium and redeemable at 10% premium.	(i) 4,000
B. Company issued 1,000, 10% debentures of ₹ 100 each at 4% discount and redeemable at 10% premium.	(ii) 10,000
C. Company issued 1,000, 10% debentures of ₹ 100 each at 4% discount and redeemable at par.	(iii) 14,000

Codes

	A	B	C	
(A)	(i)	(ii)	(iii)	☐
(B)	(i)	(iii)	(ii)	☐
(C)	(ii)	(iii)	(i)	☐
(D)	(ii)	(i)	(iii)	☐

30. Match the Column I with Column II in the following information

Column I	Column II
A. Co. purchased building of ₹ 4,00,000 for purchase consideration of ₹ 4,50,000. ₹ 50,000 will be transferred to	(i) Capital reserve
B. Co. purchased building of ₹ 4,00,000 for purchase consideration of ₹ 4,50,000. Amount of ₹ 4,50,000 will be transferred to	(ii) Goodwill account
C. Co. purchased building of ₹ 4,00,000 for purchase consideration of ₹ 3,50,000. ₹ 50,000 will be transferred to	(iii) Vendor's account

Codes

	A	B	C	
(A)	(i)	(ii)	(iii)	☐
(B)	(i)	(iii)	(ii)	☐
(C)	(ii)	(iii)	(i)	☐
(D)	(ii)	(i)	(iii)	☐

Assertion-Reason Questions

No. of Questions : **5** Suggested Time : **10 Minutes**

Direction Each of the question given below consist of the two statements; one labelled as **Assertion** (A) and other as **Reason** (R). List of common options applicable for each question is given below

(A) Both Assertion (A) and Reason (R) are true and Reason (R) is the correct explanation of Assertion (A)

(B) Both Assertion (A) and Reason (R) are true, but Reason (R) is not the correct explanation of Assertion (A)

(C) Assertion (A) is true, but Reason (R) is false

(D) Assertion (A) is false, but Reason (R) is true

You have to select the codes as *A, B, C* or *D* as your answer to the question by marking (✓) in the response box given against each option.

1. **Assertion** (A) Loss/Discount on issue of debentures is written-off in the same year in which debentures are issued.

   Reason (R) Loss/Discount of debentures is written-off from securities premium if it exists and thereafter from statement of profit and loss.

   (A) ☐ (B) ☐ (C) ☐ (D) ☐

2. **Assertion** (A) Debentures are shown under the sub-head long-term borrowings and main head non-current liabilities.

   Reason (R) Non-current liabilities are those obligations which are due for settlement within one year.

   (A) ☐ (B) ☐ (C) ☐ (D) ☐

3. **Assertion** (A) Zero coupon bonds are issued without specified rate of interest.

   Reason (R) Bonds are similar to debentures since both are debt instruments.

   (A) ☐ (B) ☐ (C) ☐ (D) ☐

4. **Assertion** (A) Interest on bearer debentures is paid to a person who produces the interest coupon attached to such debentures.

   Reason (R) Bearer debentures are transferred by way of delivery and the company does not keep any record of these debentureholders. *[CBSE 2024]*

   (A) ☐ (B) ☐
   (C) ☐ (D) ☐

5. **Assertion** (A) Sarita Private Limited issued 10,000, 15% debentures at par @ ₹ 100 per debenture. The company suffered a loss but still the director of the company paid interest on debentures.

   Reason (R) Interest on debentures is an appropriation of profit and therefore its payment is not subject to earning of profit.

   (A) ☐
   (B) ☐
   (C) ☐
   (D) ☐

Correct/Incorrect Statements

No. of Questions : **5**

Suggested Time : **10 Minutes**

Direction Each of the question given below consist of the two statements. List of common options applicable for each question is given below

(A) Both statements are correct

(B) Statement I is correct and Statement II is incorrect

(C) Statement I is incorrect and Statement II is correct

(D) Both statements are incorrect

You have to select the codes as *A, B, C* or *D* as your answer to the question by marking (✓) in the response box given against each option.

1. Statement I Debentures cannot be redeemed at discount.

Statement II Debentures can be redeemed either at par or at premium.

(A) ☐ (B) ☐ (C) ☐ (D) ☐

2. Statement I Debentures includes stock, bonds and any other securities of a company.

Statement II Zero coupon bond is one which is issued without prefixed rate of interest.

(A) ☐ (B) ☐ (C) ☐ (D) ☐

3. Statement I Securities premium account will be debited at the time of redemption of debentures at a premium.

Statement II Loss on issue of debentures account will be debited at the time of redemption of debentures at a premium.

(A) ☐ (B) ☐ (C) ☐ (D) ☐

4. Statement I Debentures can be issued as secondary securities in addition to primary security.

Statement II Debentures issued as collateral security are entitled to interest as other debentures.

(A) ☐ (B) ☐ (C) ☐ (D) ☐

5. Statement I Loss on issue of debentures is to be written-off from securities premium reserve only.

Statement II Loss on issue of debentures is to be written-off from statement of profit and loss after utilising amount of securities premium.

(A) ☐ (B) ☐

(C) ☐ (D) ☐

Case Based Questions

No. of Questions : **2** Suggested Time : **10 Minutes**

Direction This section contains 2 cases having 3 Questions of 1 mark each. You have to write the answer of each question based on the context of the related case.

Case 1 Yashi Auto Ltd. is an automobile company. They are trying to expand their business for which they require additional funds of ₹ 24,00,000. Company's existing structure include 1,00,000 equity shares of ₹ 10 each and 10,000, 9% debentures of ₹ 100 each.

Now they decided to raise additional funds with issue of 9% debentures of ₹ 100 each at 20% premium and redeemable at 10% premium. You are required to answer the following

Questions

(i) Calculate the number of debentures to be issued to raise additional funds.

(A) 24,000 ☐
(B) 20,000 ☐
(C) 30,000 ☐
(D) 34,000 ☐

(ii) Calculate the amount of total fixed obligation which company has to bear during the year.

(A) ₹ 90,000 ☐
(B) ₹ 1,80,000 ☐
(C) ₹ 2,70,000 ☐
(D) ₹ 2,16,000 ☐

(iii) Amount to be written-off as loss on issue of debentures account will be

(A) ₹ 2,40,000 ☐
(B) ₹ 2,00,000 ☐
(C) ₹ 1,00,000 ☐
(D) ₹ 3,00,000 ☐

Case 2 X Ltd. invited application for issuing 5,000, 10% debentures of ₹ 100 each at a premium of ₹ 5 per debenture, redeemable at 20% premium. Applications were received for 7,000 debentures. Application for 500 debentures were rejected and remaining were allotted on pro-rata basis.

X Ltd. also took over assets of ₹ 10,00,000 and liabilities of ₹ 2,00,000 of Y Ltd. for ₹ 7,50,000. X Ltd. issued 10% debentures of ₹ 100 each at a premium of 25% in full consideration. X Ltd. also took a loan of ₹ 1,00,000 from bank and issued 1,200, 10% debentures as collateral security.

Questions

(i) Number of debentures issued to Y Ltd. for purchase consideration are

(A) 6,000 ☐
(B) 6,400 ☐
(C) 7,500 ☐
(D) 8,000 ☐

(ii) Amount of loss on issue of debentures account will be

(A) ₹ 1,50,000 ☐
(B) ₹ 1,00,000 ☐
(C) ₹ 2,50,000 ☐
(D) Nil ☐

(iii) Total amount of interest payable at the end of year

(A) ₹ 50,000 ☐ (B) ₹ 60,000 ☐
(C) ₹ 1,10,000 ☐ (D) ₹ 1,22,000 ☐

Subjective Questions

Free Response Questions, Open-ended Questions etc.

No. of Questions : **8** Suggested Time : **65 Minutes**

1. Mahesh Ltd. purchased plant and machinery from Ish Ltd. for ₹ 4,50,000. ₹ 50,000 was paid by cheque to Ish Ltd. and the balance by issuing 6% debentures of ₹ 100 each at a discount of 20%.

   Pass the necessary journal entries for the above transactions in the books of Mahesh Ltd. *[CBSE 2024]*

2. Neeraj Ltd. took over business of Ajay Enterprises on 1st April, 2023.

   The details of the agreement regarding the assets and liabilities to be taken over are

Particulars	Book Value (₹)	Agreed Value (₹)
Building	20,00,000	35,00,000
Plant and Machinery	12,00,000	8,00,000
Stock	4,00,000	4,00,000
Trade Receivables	5,00,000	4,00,000
Creditors	2,00,000	3,00,000
Outstanding Expenses	50,000	1,00,000

   It was decided to pay for purchase consideration as ₹ 7,00,000 through cheque and balance by issue of 2,00,000, 9% debentures of ₹ 20 each at a premium of 25%. Journalise.

3. Fill in the blanks.

JOURNAL

Date	Particulars	LF	Amt (Dr)	Amt (Cr)
	Sundry Assets A/c Dr		15,00,000	
	To Sundry Creditors A/c			2,00,000
	To			...
	To			...
	(Being business of Rohit & Co. purchased for a consideration of ₹ 12,00,000)			

Date	Particulars	LF	Amt (Dr)	Amt (Cr)
	.... Dr		...	
	.... Dr		...	
	To 9% Debentures A/c			...
	(Being paid to Rohit & Co. by issue of ...9% debentures of ₹ 150 each at a discount of ₹ 50 per debenture)			

4. Youth Ltd. took a loan of ₹ 15,00,000 from State Bank of India against the security of tangible assets. In addition to principal security, it issued 10,000. 11% debentures of ₹ 100 each as collateral security.

   Pass necessary journal entries for the above transactions, if the company decided to record the issue of 11% debentures as collateral security and show the presentation in the balance sheet of Youth Ltd.

5. VKR Ltd. issued 975, 9% debentures of ₹ 500 each on 31st March, 2023. Pass necessary journal entries for the issue of debentures in the following situations

   (i) When debentures were issued at a premium of 10%, redeemable at a premium of 6%.

   (ii) When debentures were issued at par, redeemable at 9% premium.

6. Pass necessary journal entries relating to issue of debentures and to write-off discount/loss on issue of debentures in the books of Ajanta Ltd. in the following cases

   (i) 200, 9% debentures of ₹ 1,000 each are issued at 10% discount and redeemable at par. Balance in securities premium account is ₹ 15,000.

   (ii) 300, 11% debentures of ₹ 1,000 each are issued at 5% discount and redeemable at a premium of 10%. Balance in securities premium account is ₹ 35,000. *[CBSE 2024]*

7. Pass necessary journal entries for the following transactions relating to the issue of debentures
   (i) Gagan Limited issued ₹ 10,00,000, 9% debentures of ₹ 100 each at a premium of 5%, redeemable at par after four years.
   (ii) KS Limited issued ₹ 10,00,000, 10% debentures of ₹ 100 each at par, redeemable at 10% premium after four year.
   (iii) QR Limited issued ₹ 10,00,000, 9% debentures of ₹ 100 each at a discount of 10%, redeemable at a premium of 5% after five years. *[CBSE 2023]*

8. On April, 2023 Hindustan Ltd. issued 10,000, 9% debentures of ₹ 100 each at a discount of 10%, redeemable after 5 years.
   The issued price is payable along with application. The debentures were subscribed. It has a balance of ₹ 1,75,000 in securities premium.
   It was decided to write-off discount in the year ended on 31st March, 2024 from securities premium. Pass the journal entries for issue of debentures and writing-off the discount and prepare discount on issue of debentures account.

Answers

If your answer matches with the answer given here then put (✓) in the box otherwise put (✗). In case you did not attempt the question leave the box blank.

Multiple Choice Questions

1. D ☐ 2. C ☐
3. D ☐ 4. A ☐
5. C ☐ 6. B ☐
7. B ☐ 8. D ☐
9. D ☐ 10. B ☐
11. B ☐ 12. B ☐
13. C ☐ 14. C ☐
15. C ☐ 16. B ☐
17. C ☐ 18. C ☐
19. D ☐ 20. C ☐
21. C ☐ 22. C ☐
23. B ☐ 24. A ☐
25. A ☐ 26. C ☐
27. D ☐ 28. D ☐
29. C ☐ 30. C ☐

Your Score________ *(No. of Correct Answers)*

Assertion-Reason Questions

1. B ☐ 2. C ☐
3. B ☐ 4. A ☐
5. C ☐

Your Score________ *(No. of Correct Answers)*

Correct/Incorrect Statements

1. A ☐ 2. A ☐
3. D ☐ 4. B ☐
5. C ☐

Your Score________ *(No. of Correct Answers)*

Case Based Questions

1. (i) B ☐ (ii) C ☐
   (iii) B ☐
2. (i) A ☐ (ii) B ☐
   (iii) C ☐

Your Score________ *(No. of Correct Answers)*

Explanations

Multiple Choice Questions

1. (D) No restriction (decided by the directors)
2. (C) I, II and III
3. (D) Convertible debentures can be converted into shares
4. (A) Interest on debentures is a charge and not an appropriation of profits
5. (C) No. of Debentures $= \frac{3,60,000}{12\,(10+2)} = 30,000$
6. (B) capital loss
7. (B)

Date	Particulars	LF	Amt (Dr)	Amt (Cr)
	Debenture Application and Allotment A/c Dr		1,20,00,000	
	To 12% Debentures A/c			60,00,000
	To Securities Premium Reserve A/c			12,00,000
	To Bank A/c			48,00,000

8. (D) capital reserve account
9. (D) Value of Machine = (50,000 × 9) + 55,000

   = 4,50,000 + 55,000 = ₹ 5,05,000
10. (B) Number of Debentures Issued to Vendors

    $= \frac{24,00,000}{(100-4)} = 25,000$
11. (B) 6% debentures amount = 10,000 × 100

    = ₹ 10,00,000

    Number of Debentures $= \frac{8,00,000}{80}$

    = 10,000 debentures
12. (B) No. of Debentures Issued $= \frac{9,00,000}{100-10}$

    = 10,000 debentures
13. (C) Debenture suspense account will be opened only in case of debentures issued as collateral security.
14. (C) Debenture Application A/c (10,000 × 110) Dr 11,00,000

    Loss on Issue of Debentures A/c Dr 1,00,000

    To Debentures A/c (10,000 × 100) 10,00,000

    To Securities Premium Reserve A/c (10,000 × 10) 1,00,000

    To Premium on Redemption of Debentures A/c (10,000 × 110) 1,00,000
15. (C) Premium on redemption of debentures

    = ₹ 5,00,000

    Securities premium = 5,00,000 – 2,00,000

    = ₹ 3,00,000

    Rate of premium $= \frac{3,00,000}{50,00,000} \times 100 = 6\%$
16. (B) Premium on redemption of debentures

    = ₹ 16,00,000

    Securities premium used

    = 25,00,000 – 5,00,000 = ₹ 20,00,000

    ∴ Discount on issue of debentures

    = 20,00,000 – 16,00,000 = ₹ 4,00,000

    Rate of discount $= \frac{4,00,000}{80,00,000} \times 100 = 5\%$
17. (C) No. of Debentures $= \frac{1,20,000}{2} = 60,000$

    Now, Application money received = 60,000 × 12

    = ₹ 7,20,000
18. (C) non-current liabilities
19. (D) None of the above
20. (C) 9% debenture account = 2,000 × 100

    = ₹ 2,00,000
21. (C) Debentures issued = 2,00,000 × 100

    = ₹ 2,00,00,000

    Loss on Issue of Debentures = 5% Premium on Redemption + 5% Discount on Issue = 10%

    Loss on issue of debentures

    = 2,00,00,000 × 10/100

    = ₹ 20,00,000
22. (C) Discount on issue of debentures

    = 4,000 × 100 × 10/100 = ₹ 40,000

    Premium on redemption = 60,000 – 40,000

    = ₹ 20,000

23. (B) Discount on issue = 20,000 × 10 = ₹ 2,00,000

Premium on redemption = 4,00,000 – 2,00,000 = ₹ 2,00,000

24. (A) Discount on issue of debentures = 75,000 – 50,000 = ₹ 25,000

$$\text{Discount \%} = \frac{25,000}{5,00,000} \times 100 = 5\%$$

25. (A) Loss on issue of debentures = (3,000 × 5) + (3,000 × 10) = ₹ 45,000

26. (C) Debenture Application and Allotment A/c Dr

To X% Debentures A/c

27. (D) None of the above

28. (D) (ii) (iii) (i)

29. (C) A ⇒ Loss on issue of debentures

$$= 1,00,000 \times \frac{10}{100} = 10,000$$

B ⇒ Loss on issue of debentures

$$= 1,00,000 \times \frac{14}{100} = 14,000$$

C ⇒ Loss on issue of debentures

$$= 1,00,000 \times \frac{4}{100} = 4,000$$

30. (C) (ii) (iii) (i)

Assertion-Reason Questions

1. (B) Both Assertion (A) and Reason (R) are true, but Reason (R) is not the correct expalanation of Assertion (A)
2. (C) Non-current liabilities are those obligations that are due for settlement is more than one year.
3. (B) Both Assertion (A) and Reason (R) are true, but Reason (R) is not the correct expalanation of Assertion (A)
4. (A) Both Assertion (A) and Reason (R) are true and Reason (R) is the correct explanation of Assertion (A)
5. (C) Interest an debentures is a charge against profit and not appropriation of profits.

Correct/Incorrect Statements

1. (A) Both statements are correct
2. (A) Both statements are correct
3. (D) Premium on redemption of debentures account is debited at the time of redemption of debentures at premium.

   Loss on issue of debentures account is debited at the time of issue of debentures at premium.
4. (B) Debentures issued as collateral security are not entitled to interest because they does not carry any right till the time loan is being repaid.
5. (C) Statement I is incorrect and Statement II is correct

Case Based Questions

1. (i) (B) No. of Debentures $= \frac{24,00,000}{120} = 20,000$

(ii) (C) Interest $= (20,00,000 + 10,00,000) \times \frac{9}{100}$

= ₹ 2,70,000

(iii) (B) Loss on issue of debentures

$$= 20,00,000 \times \frac{10}{100} = ₹\ 2,00,000$$

2. (i) (A) No. of Debentures $= \frac{7,50,000}{125} = 6,000$

(ii) (B) Loss on issue of debenture

$$= 5,00,000 \times \frac{20}{100} = ₹\ 1,00,000$$

(iii) (C) Interest

$$= \left(5,00,000 \times \frac{10}{100}\right) + \left(6,00,000 \times \frac{10}{100}\right)$$

= ₹ 1,10,000

Subjective Questions

1. **JOURNAL**

Date	Particulars	LF	Amt (Dr)	Amt (Cr)
(i)	Plant and Machinery A/c Dr		4,50,000	
	To Ish Ltd.			4,50,000
	(Being plant and machinery purchased from Ish Ltd.)			
(ii)	Ish Ltd. A/c Dr		4,50,000	
	Discount on Issue of Debentures A/c Dr		1,00,000	
	To Bank A/c			50,000
	To 6% Debentures A/c (5,000 × 100)			5,00,000
	(Being 5,000 debentures of ₹ 100 each issued at a discount of 20% and ₹ 50,000 paid through cheque)			

Working Note

$$\text{Number of Debentures} = \frac{4,00,000}{(100-20)} = 5,000$$

2. **JOURNAL**

Date	Particulars	LF	Amt (Dr)	Amt (Dr)
	Building A/c Dr		35,00,000	
	Plant & Machinery A/c Dr		8,00,000	
	Stock A/c Dr		4,00,000	
	Trade Receivables A/c Dr		4,00,000	
	Goodwill A/c Dr		10,00,000	
	To Creditors A/c			3,00,000
	To Outstanding Expenses A/c			1,00,000
	To Ajay Enterprises			57,00,000
	(Being assets and liabilities taken over by Ajay Ltd.)			
	Ajay Enterprises Dr		7,00,000	
	To Bank A/c			7,00,000
	(Being payment made by cheque)			
	Ajay Enterprises Dr		50,00,000	
	To 9% Debentures A/c			40,00,000
	To Securities Premium A/c			10,00,000
	(Being debentures issued to vendor)			

3. **JOURNAL**

Date	Particulars	LF	Amt (Dr)	Amt (Cr)
	Sundry Assets A/c Dr		15,00,000	
	To Sundry Creditors A/c			2,00,000
	To **Rohit & Co.**			**12,00,000**
	To **Capital Reseve A/c**			**1,00,000**
	(Being business of Rohit & Co. purchased for a consideration of ₹ 12,00,000)			
	Rohit & Co. Dr		**12,00,000**	
	Discount on Issue of Debenture A/c Dr		**6,00,000**	
	To 9% Debentures A/c			**18,00,000**
	(Being paid to Rohit & Co. by issue of **12,000**, 9% debentures of 150 each at a discount of ₹ 50)			

4. **In the Books of Youth Ltd.**
JOURNAL

Date	Particulars	LF	Amt (Dr)	Amt (Cr)
	Bank A/c Dr		15,00,000	
	To Bank Loan A/c			15,00,000
	(Being the loan taken from State Bank of India)			
	Debenture Suspense A/c Dr		10,00,000	
	To 11% Debentures A/c			10,00,000
	(Being the 11% debentures deposited as collateral security)			

Balance Sheet of Youth Ltd. (An extract)

Particulars	Note No.	Amt (₹)
I. **EQUITY AND LIABILITIES**		
1. **Non-current Liabilities**		
Long-term Borrowings	1	15,00,000

Notes to Accounts

Particulars		Amt (₹)
1. **Long-term Borrowings**		
Secured Loan from State Bank of India		15,00,000
10,000, 11% Debentures of ₹ 100 each	10,00,000	
(–) Debenture Suspense	(10,00,000)	—
(Deposited as collateral security)		15,00,000

5. **JOURNAL**

Date	Particulars	LF	Amt (Dr)	Amt (Dr)
(i)	Bank A/c Dr		5,36,250	
	To Debenture Application & Allotment A/c			5,36,250
	(Being application money received)			
	Debenture Application & Allotment A/c Dr		5,36,250	
	Loss on Issue of Debentures A/c Dr		29,250	
	To 9% Debentures A/c			4,87,500
	To Securities Premium Reserve A/c			48,750
	To Premium on Redemption A/c			29,250
	(Being debentures issued at premium and repayable at premium)			

Date	Particulars		LF	Amt (Dr)	Amt (Dr)
(ii)	Bank A/c	Dr		4,87,500	
	To Debenture Application & Allotment A/c				4,87,500
	(Being application money received)				
	Debenture Application & Allotment A/c	Dr		4,87,500	
	Loss on Issue of Debentures A/c	Dr		43,875	
	To 9% Debenture A/c				4,87,500
	To Premium on Redemption A/c				43,875
	(Being debenture issued at par and repayable at premium)				

6.

JOURNAL

Date	Particulars		LF	Amt (Dr)	Amt (Cr)
(i)	Bank A/c (200× 900)	Dr		1,80,000	
	To Debenture Application and Allotment A/c				1,80,000
	(Being the application money received on 200, 9% debentures)				
	Debenture Application and Allotment A/c (200× 900)	Dr		1,80,000	
	Discount on Issue of Debentures A/c (200× 100)	Dr		20,000	
	To 9% Debentures A/c (200× 1,000)				2,00,000
	(Being the application money transferred to debentures account)				
	Securities Premium Reserve A/c	Dr		15,000	
	Statement of Profit and Loss	Dr		5,000	
	To Discount on Issue of Debentures A/c				20,000
	(Being discount on issue of debentures written-off)				
(ii)	Bank A/c (300× 950)	Dr		2,85,000	
	To Debentures Application and Allotment A/c				2,85,000
	(Being amount received on application)				
	Debenture Application and Allotment A/c	Dr		2,85,000	
	Loss on Issue of Debentures A/c (300× 50) + (300× 100)	Dr		45,000	
	To 11% Debentures A/c (300× 1,000)				3,00,000
	To Premium on Redemption of Debentures A/c (300× 100)				30,000
	(Being the application money transferred to debentures account)				
	Securities Premium Reserve A/c	Dr		35,000	
	Statement of Profit and Loss	Dr		10,000	
	To Loss on Issue of Debentures A/c				45,000
	(Being loss on issue of debentures written-off)				

7.

JOURNAL

Date	Particulars		LF	Amt (Dr)	Amt (Cr)
(i)	Bank A/c (10,000× 105)	Dr		10,50,000	
	To Debenture Application and Allotment A/c				10,50,000
	(Being 9% debenture issued @ ₹ 105 and money received on application and allotment)				

Date	Particulars		LF	Amt (Dr)	Amt (Cr)
	Debenture Application and Allotment A/c	Dr		10,50,000	
	To 9% Debentures A/c				10,00,000
	To Securities Premium A/c				50,000
	(Being application and allotment money transferred to 9% debentures account)				
(ii)	Bank A/c	Dr		10,00,000	
	To Debenture Application and Allotment A/c				10,00,000
	(Being money received on issue of 10% debentures @ ₹ 100)				
	Debenture Application and Allotment A/c	Dr		10,00,000	
	Loss on Issue of Debentures A/c	Dr		1,00,000	
	To 10% Debentures A/c (10,000× 100)				10,00,000
	To Premium on Redemption of Debentures A/c				1,00,000
	(Being issue of 10% debentures at par and redeemable at 10% premium)				
(iii)	Bank A/c	Dr		9,00,000	
	To Debenture Application and Allotment A/c				9,00,000
	(Being money received on issue of 9% debentures @ ₹ 90)				
	Debenture Application and Allotment A/c	Dr		9,00,000	
	Loss on Issue of Debentures A/c	Dr		1,50,000	
	To 9% Debentures A/c				10,00,000
	To Premium on Redemption of Debentures A/c				50,000
	(Being 9% debentures issued at 10% discount and redeemable at 5% premium)				

8. **JOURNAL**

Date	Particulars		LF	Amt (Dr)	Amt (Cr)
2023					
Apr 1	Bank A/c	Dr		9,00,000	
	To Debentures Application and Allotment A/c				9,00,000
	(Being application received for 10,000 debentures)				
Apr 1	Debentures Application and Allotment A/c	Dr		9,00,000	
	Discount on Issue of Debentures A/c	Dr		1,00,000	
	To 9% Debentures A/c				10,00,000
	(Being debenture application money adjusted)				
2024					
Mar 31	Securities Premium A/c	Dr		1,00,000	
	To Discount on Issue of Debenture A/c				1,00,000
	(Being discount on issue of debentures written-off)				

Dr **Discount on Issue of Debenture Account** Cr

Date	Particulars	Amt (₹)	Date	Particulars	Amt (₹)
2023			2024		
Apr 1	To 9% Debentures A/c	1,00,000	Mar 31	By Securities Premium A/c	1,00,000
		1,00,000			1,00,000

CHAPTER -8

Financial Statements and Their Analysis

Types & Nos. of Questions

Multiple Choice Questions - 30
Assertion-Reason Questions - 7
Correct/Incorrect Statements - 6
Case Based Questions - 2 Cases, *each with 3 Questions*
Subjective Questions - 10

Trend Analysis

On the basis of analysis of last 2 years' papers, it is found that on an average 1 Multiple Choice Question and 2 Short Answer Type Questions are asked from this chapter.

Focus Topics of the Chapter

- Meaning of Financial Statements
- Statement of Profit and Loss
- Balance Sheet
- Meaning of Financial Statement Analysis
- Comparative Statements and Common Size Statements

Multiple Choice Questions

No. of Questions : **30** Suggested Time : **45 Minutes**

Direction Each of the question given below is Multiple Choice Question (MCQ) i.e. there are four options/ choices for answer, out of which ONLY ONE is correct. You have to select the correct option.
A response box is given with each option, mark (✓) in the box of the correct option. For each correct answer you will get 1 mark, while there is no penalty for incorrect answer or missed out questions.

1. Section 129 (1) of the Companies Act, 2013, requires that the financial statements of a company shall

(A) give a true and fair view of the state of affairs of the company ☐
(B) comply with the accounting standards notified by the central government ☐
(C) be in the form as provided in Schedule III ☐
(D) All of the above ☐

2. Which of the following is available for distribution of dividend?

(A) Revenue reserve ☐
(B) Capital reserve ☐
(C) Capital redemption reserve ☐
(D) Securities premium reserve ☐

3. Short-term loans and advances are considered as

(A) current assets ☐
(B) short-term provision ☐
(C) short-term borrowings ☐
(D) other current liabilities ☐

4. As per Section 2(40) of the Companies Act, 2013, financial statements do not include

(A) balance sheet ☐
(B) statement of profit and loss ☐
(C) notes to accounts ☐
(D) ratio analysis ☐

5. Which of the following is not considered as a part of capital reserve?

(A) Profit on sale of goods and services ☐
(B) Gain on sale of non-current investment ☐
(C) Gain on sale of current investment ☐
(D) Profit on reissue of forfeited shares ☐

6. Cash credit is shown under

(A) short-term borrowings ☐
(B) long-term borrowings ☐
(C) cash and cash equivalents ☐
(D) trade payables ☐

7. Which of the following is not part of intangible asset?

(A) Trademark ☐
(B) Recipe and formula ☐
(C) Stores and spares ☐
(D) Prototype ☐

8. Debentures which are to be redeemed in current year are required to be shown under

(A) other current liability ☐
(B) long-term borrowings ☐
(C) trade payable ☐
(D) short-term borrowings ☐

9. Loan payable on demand is required to be shown as

(A) other current liability ☐
(B) long-term borrowings ☐
(C) short-term borrowings ☐
(D) None of the above ☐

10. .... is included in current assets while preparing balance sheet as per revised Schedule III but excluded from current assets while calculating current ratio.
(A) Debtors ☐
(B) Cash and cash equivalent ☐
(C) Loose tools and stores and spares ☐
(D) Prepaid expense ☐

11. Financial statements are prepared on certain basic assumptions (pre-requisites) known as ....
(A) provision of Companies Act, 2013 ☐
(B) accounting standards ☐
(C) postulates ☐
(D) basis of accounting ☐

12. Ajanta Ltd. issued 10% debentures of ₹ 8,00,000 on 1st April, 2019 which are redeemable in five equal yearly instalments starting from 1st April, 2022. How would this information be presented in the balance sheet as at 31st March, 2021?
(A) ₹ 8,00,000 as long-term borrowings ☐
(B) ₹ 8,00,000 as other non-current liability ☐
(C) ₹ 8,00,000 as current liability ☐
(D) ₹ 1,60,000 as other current liability and ₹ 6,40,000 as long-term borrowing ☐

13. A company has an operating cycle of eight months. It has accounts receivables amounting to ₹ 1,00,000 out of which ₹ 60,000 have a maturity period of 11 months.
How would this information be presented in the balance sheet?
(A) ₹ 40,000 as current assets and ₹ 60,000 as non-current assets ☐
(B) ₹ 60,000 as current assets and ₹ 40,000 as non-current assets ☐
(C) ₹ 1,00,000 as non-current assets ☐
(D) ₹ 1,00,000 as current assets ☐

14. 'Public deposits' appear in the company's balance sheet under the head/sub-head
(A) intangible assets ☐
(B) current liabilities ☐
(C) shareholders' funds ☐
(D) non-current liabilities ☐

15. Opening and closing stock of raw material is shown in the statement of profit and loss under the sub-head
(A) cost of material consumed ☐
(B) purchase of stock-in-trade ☐
(C) change in inventories ☐
(D) None of the above ☐

16. Staff welfare expenses is depicted in statement of profit and loss under sub-head ....
(A) other expenses ☐
(B) finance cost ☐
(C) employees benefit expenses ☐
(D) other incomes ☐

17. Profit on sale of fixed assets is required to be shown in
(A) revenue from operation ☐
(B) other income ☐
(C) finance cost ☐
(D) other expenses ☐

18. Employee benefit expense includes
(A) bonus ☐
(B) depreciation ☐
(C) income tax ☐
(D) interest on debt ☐

19. Which of the following is/are the tools of vertical analysis?
(i) Ratio analysis
(ii) Comparative statements
(iii) Common size statements

Codes
(A) Only (i) ☐
(B) Only (iii) ☐
(C) Both (i) and (ii) ☐
(D) Both (i) and (iii) ☐

20. Which of the following statements are correct?

(i) Horizontal analysis is made to review and analyse the financial statements of a number of years.

(ii) Vertical analysis is made to review and analyse the financial statements of one particular year only.

(iii) Vertical analysis is also termed as time series analysis.

Codes

(A) Both (i) and (ii) ☐

(B) Both (i) and (iii) ☐

(C) Both (ii) and (iii) ☐

(D) (i), (ii) and (iii) ☐

21. Which of the following is a limitation of financial statement analysis?

(A) It is just a study of reports of the company ☐

(B) It judges the ability of the firm to repay its debts ☐

(C) It identifies the reasons for change in financial position ☐

(D) It ascertains the relative importance of different components of the financial position of the firm ☐

22. The limitations of the comparative statement is/are

(A) ignores price level changes ☐

(B) variation in accounting policies ☐

(C) Both (A) and (B) ☐

(D) None of the above ☐

23. The tool of 'analysis of financial statements' which helps to assess the profitability, solvency and efficiency of an enterprise is known as *[CBSE 2024]*

(A) cash flow statement ☐

(B) comparative statement ☐

(C) common size statement ☐

(D) ratio analysis ☐

24. 'Freedom to choose method of depreciation' highlights which limitation of financial statement analysis?

(A) Historical analysis ☐

(B) Qualitative aspect ignored ☐

(C) Not free from bias ☐

(D) Ignore price level changes ☐

25. Which of the following is a tool of analysis of financial statements?

(i) Cash flow statement

(ii) Statement of profit and loss

(iii) Notes to accounts

(iv) Balance sheet *[CBSE 2023]*

Codes

(A) Only (i) ☐ (B) (i) and (ii) ☐

(C) Only (ii) ☐ (D) (i), (ii) and (iv) ☐

26. Match the items given in Column I with the correct heading/sub-heading given in Column II.

Column I	Column II
A. 9% debenture redeemable during the current year	(i) Intangible assets
B. Loose tools	(ii) Current liabilities
C. Copyright	(iii) Cash and cash equivalents
D. Cash at bank	(iv) Inventories

Codes

	A	B	C	D	
(A)	(i)	(ii)	(iii)	(iv)	☐
(B)	(iii)	(ii)	(iv)	(i)	☐
(C)	(iv)	(iii)	(ii)	(i)	☐
(D)	(ii)	(iv)	(i)	(iii)	☐

27. Match the following

Column I	Column II
A. Comparative statements	(i) Ratio analysis
B. Common size statements	(ii) Horizontal analysis
C. Liquidity ratio	(iii) Vertical analysis

Codes

	A	B	C	
(A)	(i)	(ii)	(iii)	☐
(B)	(iii)	(ii)	(i)	☐
(C)	(ii)	(i)	(iii)	☐
(D)	(ii)	(iii)	(i)	☐

28. Match the following

	Column I		Column II
A.	Interest due on calls-in-advance	(i)	Other current liability
B.	Interest due on calls-in-arrears	(ii)	Non-current liability
C.	Long-term borrowings	(iii)	Other current assets

Codes

	A	B	C	
(A)	(i)	(ii)	(iii)	☐
(B)	(i)	(iii)	(ii)	☐
(C)	(iii)	(i)	(ii)	☐
(D)	(ii)	(iii)	(i)	☐

29. Match the following

	Column I		Column II
A.	Unpaid dividend	(i)	Other current liability
B.	Provision for provident fund	(ii)	Contingent liability
C.	Proposed dividend	(iii)	Long-term provision

Codes

	A	B	C			A	B	C	
(A)	(i)	(ii)	(iii)	☐	(B)	(i)	(iii)	(ii)	☐
(C)	(ii)	(iii)	(i)	☐	(D)	(ii)	(i)	(iii)	☐

30. Match the following

	Column I		Column II
A.	Mining rights	(i)	Tangible assets
B.	Loss during the year	(ii)	Intangible assets
C.	Computer	(iii)	Reserves and surplus

Codes

	A	B	C			A	B	C	
(A)	(ii)	(iii)	(i)	☐	(B)	(i)	(ii)	(iii)	☐
(C)	(iii)	(i)	(ii)	☐	(D)	(ii)	(i)	(iii)	☐

Assertion-Reason Questions

No. of Questions : **7** Suggested Time : **10 Minutes**

Direction Each of the question given below consist of the two statements; one labelled as **Assertion** (A) and other as **Reason** (R). List of common options applicable for each question is given below

(A) Both Assertion (A) and Reason (R) are true and Reason (R) is the correct explanation of Assertion (A)

(B) Both Assertion (A) and Reason (R) are true, but Reason (R) is not the correct explanation of Assertion (A)

(C) Assertion (A) is true, but Reason (R) is false

(D) Assertion (A) is false, but Reason (R) is true

You have to select the codes as *A, B, C* or *D* as your answer to the question by marking (✓) in the response box given against each option.

1. **Assertion** (A) Contingent liabilities are those liabilities which may or may not arise because they depend on the happening of an event in future.

Reason (R) Contingent liabilities are shown in the balance sheet under the heading non-current liabilities.

(A) ☐ (B) ☐ (C) ☐ (D) ☐

2. **Assertion** (A) Financial statements are the end product of accounting process. They are collection of reports about an organisation's financial report, financial position and cash flow.

Reason (R) Financial statements provide information about the performance and the financial position of a business.

(A) ☐ (B) ☐ (C) ☐ (D) ☐

3. **Assertion** (A) Financial statement analysis ignores qualitative factors.

Reason (R) Financial statement analysis focuses on liquidity position of business only.

(A) ☐ (B) ☐ (C) ☐ (D) ☐

4. **Assertion** (A) Financial statement analysis helps an analyst to arrive at a decision.

Reason (R) Financial statement analysis helps an analyst to make decision regarding the operations of the firm.

(A) ☐ (B) ☐
(C) ☐ (D) ☐

5. **Assertion** (A) Preliminary expenses are to be written-off completely in the year in which such expenses are incurred.

Reason (R) Preliminary expenses should be written-off first from securities premium and balance from statement of profit and loss.

(A) ☐ (B) ☐ (C) ☐ (D) ☐

6. **Assertion** (A) The focus of calculation of working capital revolves around managing the operating cycle of the business.

Reason (R) It is because the concept of operating cycle is required to ascertain the liquidity of assets and urgency of payments to liabilities.

(A) ☐ (B) ☐ (C) ☐ (D) ☐

7. **Assertion** (A) The bank charges charged by the bank are included in finance cost.

Reason (R) Bank charges are an expense not incurred in connection with raising finance but for availing the services of the bank.

(A) ☐ (B) ☐ (C) ☐ (D) ☐

Correct/Incorrect Statements

No. of Questions : **6** Suggested Time : **10 Minutes**

Direction Each of the question given below consist of the two statements. List of common options applicable for each question is given below

(A) Both statements are correct
(B) Statement I is correct and Statement II is incorrect
(C) Statement I is incorrect and Statement II is correct
(D) Both statements are incorrect

You have to select the codes as *A, B, C* or *D* as your answer to the question by marking (✓) in the response box given against each option.

1. **Statement I** Loose tools are shown as inventories in balance sheet.

Statement II Reserve capital is that part of share capital that a company resolves not to sell at any time it desires.

(A) ☐ (B) ☐ (C) ☐ (D) ☐

2. **Statement I** Financial statement analysis is free from bias.

   Statement II Qualitative aspects are not ignored in the financial statement analysis.

   (A) ☐ (B) ☐ (C) ☐ (D) ☐

3. **Statement I** Proposed dividend for the current year will be relevant for the next financial year.

   Statement II Proposed dividend of the previous year will be accounted in the current year after it is declared by the shareholders in their annual general meeting.

   (A) ☐ (B) ☐ (C) ☐ (D) ☐

4. **Statement I** Finance cost includes the interest cost and bank charges.

   Statement II Revenue from operation includes money collected from sale of goods and services.

   (A) ☐ (B) ☐ (C) ☐ (D) ☐

5. **Statement I** All inventories are always treated as current assets.

   Statement II Loose tools are considered as non-current assets.

   (A) ☐ (B) ☐ (C) ☐ (D) ☐

6. **Statement I** Declaration of proposed dividend is contingent upon shareholders approval in their annual general meeting.

   Statement II After the proposed dividend is declared, it becomes liability for the company.

   (A) ☐ (B) ☐ (C) ☐ (D) ☐

Case Based Questions

No. of Questions : **2** Suggested Time : **10 Minutes**

Direction This section contains 2 cases having 3 questions of 1 mark each. You have to write the answer of each question based on the context of the related case.

Case 1.

Particulars	31st March, 2024 (₹)	31st March, 2023 (₹)
Revenue from Operations	24,00,000	18,00,000
Other Incomes (% of Revenue from Operations)	15%	25%
Expenses (% of Revenue from Operations)	60%	50%
Tax Rate	40%	40%

Questions

(i) What will be the amount of expenses for the year ended 31st March, 2023?

(A) ₹ 15,00,000 ☐ (B) ₹ 9,00,000 ☐
(C) ₹ 12,00,000 ☐ (D) ₹ 14,00,000 ☐

(ii) What will be the percentage change of other incomes?

(A) 20% ☐ (B) 15% ☐
(C) 25% ☐ (D) (–)20% ☐

(iii) What is the profit after tax for the year ended 31st March, 2024?

(A) ₹ 7,92,000 ☐
(B) ₹ 8,10,000 ☐
(C) ₹ 5,28,000 ☐
(D) ₹ 13,20,000 ☐

Case 2.

Balance Sheet
as at 31st March, 2024

Particulars	Note No.	31st March, 2024 (₹)
I. EQUITY AND LIABILITIES		
1. **Shareholders' Fund**		
(i) Share Capital		2,50,000
(ii) Reserves and Surplus		80,000
2. **Current Liabilities**		
Trade Payable		70,000
Total		4,00,000
II. ASSETS		
1. **Non-current Assets**		
(i) Property, Plant & Equipment and Intangible Assets		
(a) Property, Plant and Equipment		1,60,000
(b) Intangible Assets		20,000
2. **Current Assets**		
(i) Inventories		80,000
(ii) Trade Receivables		1,20,000
(iii) Cash and Cash Equivalents		20,000
Total		4,00,000

Questions

(i) What is the percentage of property, plant and equipment on total assets?

(A) 20% ☐ (B) 30% ☐
(C) 40% ☐ (D) 45% ☐

(ii) What is the percentage of cash and cash equivalent on total assets?

(A) 5% ☐ (B) 3% ☐
(C) 8% ☐ (D) 12% ☐

(ii) What is the percentage of shareholders' fund on total equity and liabilities?

(A) 62.5% ☐ (B) 60% ☐
(C) 82.5% ☐ (D) 80% ☐

Subjective Questions

Free Response Questions, Open-ended Questions etc.

No. of Questions : **10** Suggested Time : **70 Minutes**

1. Classify the following items under major head and sub-head (if any) in the balance sheet of a company as per Schedule III of the Companies Act, 2013.
   (i) Provision for tax
   (ii) Provision for warranties
   (iii) Income received in advance
   (iv) Capital advance

2. Classify the following items under major heads and sub-heads (if any) in the balance sheet of a company as per Schedule III, Part I of the Companies Act, 2013. *[CBSE 2023]*
   (i) Capital work-in-progress
   (ii) Calls-in-advance
   (iii) Computer software

3. JW Ltd. was a company manufacturing geysers. As a part of its long-term goal for expansion, the company decide to identify the opportunity in rural areas. Initial plan was to rolled out for Bhiwani village in Haryana. Since the village did not have regular supply of electricity, the company decided to manufacture solar geysers.

   The core team consisting of the regional manager, accountant and the marketing manager was taken from the head office and the remaining employees were selected from the village and neighbourhood areas.

   At the time of preparation of financial statements, the accountant of company fell sick and the company deputed a junior accountant temporarily from the village for two months.

The balance sheet prepared by the junior accountant showed the following items against the major heads and sub-head mentioned which were not as per Schedule III of the Company Act, 2013.

Items	Major Heads/Sub-heads
Loose tools	Trade Receivables
Cheque in hand	Current Investment
Term loan from bank	Other Long-term Liabilities
Computer software	Tangible Fixed Assets

Present the above items under the correct major heads and sub-heads as per Schedule III of the Companies Act, 2013.

4. Classify the following items under major heads and sub-heads (if any) in the balance sheet of a company as per Schedule III, Part I of the Companies Act, 2013 *[CBSE 2024]*

(i) Accrued income (ii) Capital advances

(iii) Capital work-in-progress

5. "It is the process of identifying the financial strengths and weakneses of the firm by properly establishing relationships between the various items of the balance sheet and the statement of profit and loss." Identify the process and state two objectives of the process identified. *[CBSE 2023]*

6. From the following information, prepare a comparative balance sheet of Depth Ltd.

Particulars	2023-24 (₹)	2022-23 (₹)
Equity Shares Capital	25,00,000	25,00,000
Fixed Assets (Tangible)	36,00,000	30,00,000
Reserves and Surplus	6,00,000	5,00,000
Investments (Non-current)	5,00,000	5,00,000
Long-term Loans	15,00,000	15,00,000
Current Assets	10,50,000	15,00,000
Current Liabilities	5,50,000	5,00,000

7. From the following information, prepare a comparative statement of profit and loss for the year ending 31st March, 2024.

Particulars	2023-24	2022-23
Revenue from Operations	300% of cost of material consumed	200% of cost of material consumed
Cost of Material Consumed	₹ 2,40,000	₹ 2,00,000
Other Expenses	20% of cost of material consumed	20% of cost of material consumed
Tax	50%	50%

8. Following information is extracted from the statement of profit and loss of Crypto Finance Ltd. for the year ended 31st March, 2023 and 2024. Fill in the missing figures.

Comparative Statement of Profit and Loss
for the years ended 31st March, 2023 and 2024

Particulars	31st March, 2023 (₹)	31st March, 2024 (₹)	Absolute Increase/ Decrease (₹)	Percentage Increase/ Decrease (%)
I. Revenue from Operations	10,00,000	...	2,00,000	20%
II. Other Income	...	60,000	...	20%
III. Total Revenue (I + II)	...	12,60,000	...	20%
IV. Expenses Employee Benefit Expenses	(50,000)	(60,000)	(10,000)	...
V. Profit before Tax	10,00,000	12,00,000	2,00,000	...
(−) Tax (50%)	(5,00,000)	(6,00,000)	(1,00,000)	...
VI. Profit after Tax	5,00,000	6,00,000	1,00,000	20%

9. Prepare a common size balance sheet of X Ltd. from the following information [CBSE 2024]

Balance Sheet of X Ltd.
as at 31st March, 2023

Particulars	Note No.	31st March, 2023 (₹)	31st March, 2022 (₹)
I. **EQUITY AND LIABILITIES**			
1. **Shareholders' Funds**			
(i) Equity Share Capital		30,00,000	15,00,000
(ii) Reserves and Surplus		10,00,000	5,00,000
2. **Non-current Liabilities**		20,00,000	20,00,000
3. **Current Liabilities**		20,00,000	10,00,000
Total		80,00,000	50,00,000
II. **ASSETS**			
1. **Non-current Assets**		40,00,000	30,00,000
2. **Current Assets**			
Inventories		40,00,000	20,00,000
Total		80,00,000	50,00,000

10. From the information extracted from the statement of profit and loss of Appy Ltd. for the year ended 31st March, 2023 and 31st March, 2024, prepare a common size statement of profit and loss.

Particulars	Note No.	31st March, 2024 (₹)	31st March, 2023 (₹)
Revenue from Operations		8,00,000	10,00,000
Gross Profit		60%	70%
Other Expenses		2,20,000	2,60,000
Tax Rate		50%	50%

Answers

If your answer matches with the answer given here then put (✓) in the box otherwise put (✗). In case you did not attempt the question leave the box blank.

Multiple Choice Questions

1.	D	☐	2.	A	☐
3.	A	☐	4.	D	☐
5.	A	☐	6.	A	☐
7.	C	☐	8.	D	☐
9.	C	☐	10.	C	☐
11.	C	☐	12.	D	☐
13.	D	☐	14.	D	☐
15.	C	☐	16.	C	☐
17.	B	☐	18.	A	☐
19.	D	☐	20.	A	☐
21.	A	☐	22.	C	☐
23.	D	☐	24.	C	☐
25.	A	☐	26.	D	☐
27.	D	☐	28.	B	☐
29.	B	☐	30.	A	☐

Your Score__________ *(No. of Correct Answers)*

Assertion-Reason Questions

1. C ☐	2. B ☐	3. C ☐
4. A ☐	5. B ☐	6. B ☐
7. D ☐		

Your Score__________ *(No. of Correct Answers)*

Correct/Incorrect Statements

1. B ☐	2. D ☐
3. A ☐	4. C ☐
5. B ☐	6. A ☐

Your Score__________ *(No. of Correct Answers)*

Case Based Questions

1. (i) B ☐	(ii) D ☐
(iii) A ☐	
2. (i) C ☐	(ii) A ☐
(iii) C ☐	

Your Score__________ *(No. of Correct Answers)*

Explanations

Multiple Choice Questions

1. (D) All of the above
2. (A) Revenue reserve
3. (A) current assets
4. (D) ratio analysis
5. (A) Profit on sale of goods and services
6. (A) short-term borrowings
7. (C) Stores and spares
8. (D) short-term borrowings
9. (C) short-term borrowings
10. (C) Loose tools and stores and spares
11. (C) postulates
12. (D) ₹ 1,60,000 as other current liability and ₹ 6,40,000 as long-term borrowing
13. (D) ₹ 1,00,000 as current assets
14. (D) non-current liabilities
15. (C) change in inventories
16. (C) employees benefit expenses
17. (B) other income
18. (A) bonus
19. (D) Both (i) and (iii)
20. (A) vertical analysis is also termed as static analysis.
21. (A) It is just a study of reports of the company
22. (C) Both (A) and (B)
23. (D) ratio analysis
24. (C) Not free from bias
25. (A) Only (i)
26. (D) (ii) (iv) (i) (iii)
27. (D) (ii) (iii) (i)

28. (B) (i) (iii) (ii)

29. (B) (i) (iii) (ii)

30. (A) (ii) (iii) (i)

Assertion-Reason Questions

1. (C) Contingent liabilities are disclosed in notes to accounts.
2. (B) Both Assertion (A) and Reason (R) are true, but Reason (R) is not the correct explanation of Assertion (A)
3. (C) Financial statements analysis not only focuses on liquidity position, but also put focus on solvency of the business, operations of the business and profitability of the business.
4. (A) Both Assertion (A) and Reason (R) are true and Reason (R) is the correct explanation of Assertion (A)
5. (B) Both Assertion (A) and Reason (R) are true, but Reason (R) is not the correct explanation of Assertion (A)
6. (B) Both Assertion (A) and Reason (R) are true, but Reason (R) is not the correct explanation of Assertion (A)
7. (D) The bank charges charged by the bank are not included in finance cost.

Correct/Incorrect Statements

1. (B) Statement I is correct and Statement II is incorrect
2. (D) Financial statement analysis is not free from bias. It is based on personal judgement and abilities.

   Financial statement analysis takes into consideration only monetary transactions, not qualitative.
3. (A) Both statements are correct
4. (C) Bank charges are not a part of financial cost.
5. (B) Loose tools are part of inventories.
6. (A) Both statements are correct

Case Based Questions

1. (i) (B) Amount of Expenses $= 18,00,000 \times \frac{50}{100}$

   $= ₹\ 9,00,000$

   (ii) (D) Other incomes of 2023 and 2024

   $= 4,50,000$ and $3,60,000$

   Absolute change $= 3,60,000 - 4,50,000$

   $= (90,000)$

   Percentage change $= \frac{(90,000)}{4,50,000} \times 100 = (20\%)$

   (iii) (A) Total Income = Revenue from Operations + Other Incomes

   $= 24,00,000 + 3,60,000 = ₹\ 27,60,000$

   Expenses = 60% of Revenue from Operations

   $= 60\%$ of $24,00,000 = ₹\ 14,40,000$

   Profit before Tax = Total Revenue − Expenses

   $= 27,60,000 - 14,40,000 = ₹\ 13,20,000$

   Profit after Tax = Profit before Tax − Tax

   $= 13,20,000 - 40\%$ of $13,20,000 = ₹\ 7,92,000$

2. (i) (C) Percentage of Property, Plant and Equipment on Total Assets

   $= \frac{\text{Property, Plant and Equipment}}{\text{Total Assets}} \times 100$

   $= \frac{1,60,000}{4,00,000} \times 100 = 40\%$

   (ii) (A) Percentage of Cash and Cash Equivalent on Total Assets

   $= \frac{\text{Cash and Cash Equivalent}}{\text{Total Assets}} \times 100$

   $= \frac{20,000}{4,00,000} \times 100 = 5\%$

   (iii) (C) Shareholders' Fund $= 2,50,000 + 80,000$

   $= ₹\ 3,30,000$

   Percentage of Shareholders' Fund on Total Equity and Liabilities

   $= \frac{\text{Shareholders' Fund}}{\text{Total Equity and Liabilities}} \times 100$

   $= \frac{3,30,000}{4,00,000} \times 100 = 82.5\%$

Subjective Questions

1. (i) Provision for Tax – Current Liabilities – Short-term Provisions

   (ii) Provision for Warranties – Non-current Liabilities – Long-term Provisions

   (iii) Income Received in Advance – Current Liabilities – Other Current Liabilities

   (iv) Capital Advance – Non-current Assets – Long-term Loans and Advances

2.

S.No.	Items	Major Head	Sub-head
(i)	Capital Work-in-progress	Non-current Assets	Property, Plant & Equipment and Intangible Assets
(ii)	Calls-in-advance	Current Liabilities	Other Current Liabilities
(iii)	Computer Software	Non-current Assets	Intangible Assets

3.

Items	Head	Sub-head
Loose Tools	Current Assets	Inventories
Cheque-in-hand	Current Assets	Cash and Cash Equivalent
Term Loan from Bank	Non-current Liabilities	Long-term Borrowings
Computer Software	Non-current Assets	Property, Plant & Equipment and Intangible Assets-Intangible Assets

4.

S.No.	Items	Major Head	Sub-head
(i)	Accrued Income	Current Assets	Other Current Assets
(ii)	Capital Advances	Non-current Assets	Long-term Loans and Advances
(iii)	Capital Work-in-progress	Non-current Assets	Property, Plant and Equipment

5. The process referred in the given statement is financial statement analysis.

The objectives of analysis of financial statements are as follows

(i) To judge the financial stability of an enterprise.

(ii) To measure the short-term and long-term solvency of enterprise.

(iii) To measure the operating efficiency and profitability of an enterprise.

(iv) To compare the intra-firm position, inter-firm position and pattern position within the industry.

6.

Comparative Balance Sheet of Depth Ltd.
as at 31st March, 2023 and 2024

Particulars	Note No.	31st March, 2023 (₹) A	31st March, 2024 (₹) B	Absolute Change (Increase or Decrease) (₹) C = B – A	Percentage Change (%) D = C/A × 100
I. EQUITY AND LIABILITIES					
1. **Shareholders' Fund**					
(i) Share Capital		25,00,000	25,00,000	0	0
(ii) Reserve and Surplus		5,00,000	6,00,000	1,00,000	20
2. **Long-term Liabilities**					
Long-term Borrowings		15,00,000	15,00,000	0	0
3. **Current Liabilities**		5,00,000	5,50,000	50,000	10
Total		50,00,000	51,50,000	1,50,000	3
II. ASSETS					
1. **Non-current Assets**					
(i) Fixed assets		30,00,000	36,00,000	6,00,000	20
(ii) Non-current Investment		5,00,000	5,00,000	0	0
2. **Current Assets**		15,00,000	10,50,000	(4,50,000)	(30)
Total		50,00,000	51,00,000	1,50,000	3

7. **Comparative Statement of Profit and Loss**
for the year ended 31st March, 2023 and 2024

Particulars	2022-23 (₹)	2023-24 (₹)	Absolute Change (₹)	Percentage Change (%)
I. Revenue from Operations	4,00,000	7,20,000	3,20,000	80
II. Expenses				
Cost of Material Consumed	2,00,000	2,40,000	40,000	20
Other Expenses	20,000	48,000	28,000	140
Total Expenses	2,20,000	2,88,000	68,000	30.91
III. Profit before Tax	1,80,000	4,32,000	2,52,000	140
(−) Tax @ 50% (I–II)	(90,000)	(2,16,000)	(1,26,000)	140
IV. **Profit after Tax**	90,000	2,16,000	1,26,000	140

8. **Comparative Statement of Profit and Loss**
for the year ended 31st March, 2023 and 2024

Particulars	31st March, 2023 (₹) A	31st March, 2024 (₹) B	Absolute Change (Increase/ Decrease) (₹) C = B − A	Percentage Change (Increase/ Decrease) (%) D = C / A × 100
I. Revenue from Operations	10,00,000	**12,00,000**	2,00,000	20%
II. Other Income	**50,000**	60,000	**10,000**	20%
III. Total Revenue (I + II)	**10,50,000**	12,60,000	**2,10,000**	20%
IV. Employee Benefit Expenses	(50,000)	(60,000)	(10,000)	**20%**
V. Profit before Tax (III – IV)	10,00,000	12,00,000	2,00,000	**20%**
VI. (−) Tax @ 50%	(5,00,000)	(6,00,000)	(1,00,000)	**20%**
VII. Profit after Tax (V – VI)	5,00,000	6,00,000	1,00,000	20%

Working Note

Let the other income of (2016-17) = x = A ; Given other income of (2017-18) = ₹ 60,000 = B

Given % change of other income = 20% = D

$$D = \frac{B-A}{A} \times 100 \Rightarrow 20 = \frac{60{,}000 - x}{x} \times 100$$

$$\Rightarrow \quad \frac{20}{100} \times x = 60{,}000 - x \Rightarrow \frac{x}{5} + x = 60{,}000$$

$$\Rightarrow \frac{6x}{5} = 60{,}000 \Rightarrow x(A) = 60{,}000 \times \frac{5}{6} = ₹\ 50{,}000$$

∴ Absolute change in other income = B – A = 60,000 – 50,000 = ₹ 10,000

9.

Common Size Balance Sheet
as at 31st March, 2022 and 2023

Particulars	Absolute Amounts		Percentage of Balance Sheet Total (%) (2022)	Percentage of Balance Sheet Total (%) (2023)
	2022 (₹)	2023 (₹)		
I. **EQUITY AND LIABILITIES**				
1. **Shareholders' Funds**				
(i) Equity Share Capital	15,00,000	30,00,000	30	37.5
(ii) Reserves and Surplus	5,00,000	10,00,000	10	12.5
2. **Non-current Liabilities**	20,00,000	20,00,000	40	25
3. **Current Liabilities**	10,00,000	20,00,000	20	25
Total	50,00,000	80,00,000	100	100
II. **ASSETS**				
1. **Non-current Assets**	30,00,000	40,00,000	60	50
2. **Current Assets**				
Inventories	20,00,000	40,00,000	40	50
Total	50,00,000	80,00,000	100	100

10.

Common Size Statement of Profit and Loss

Particulars	31st March, 2023 (₹)	31st March, 2024 (₹)	% on Revenue from Operations 31st March, 2023	% on Revenue from Operations 31st March, 2024
Revenue from Operations	10,00,000	8,00,000	100	100
(–) Expenses				
Cost of Revenue (WN)	3,00,000	3,20,000	40	30
Other Expenses	2,60,000	2,20,000	27.5	26
Total Expenses	5,60,000	5,40,000	67.5	56
Profit before Tax	4,40,000	2,60,000	32.5	44
(–) Tax @ 50%	(2,20,000)	(1,30,000)	(16.25)	(22)
Profit after Tax	2,20,000	1,30,000	16.25	22

Working Note

Cost of Revenue = 2022-23 = 8,00,000 × 40% = ₹ 3,20,000

= 2021-22 = 10,00,000 × 30% = ₹ 3,00,000

CHAPTER-9

Accounting Ratios

Types & Nos. of Questions

Multiple Choice Questions - 30
Assertion-Reason Questions - 8
Correct/Incorrect Statements - 8
Case Based Questions - 2 Cases, *with 3/4 Questions*
Subjective Questions - 8

Trend Analysis

On the basis of analysis of last 2 years' papers, it is found that on an average 3 Multiple Choice Questions and 2 Short Answer Type Questions are asked from this chapter.

Focus Topics of the Chapter

- Ratio Analysis
- Liquidity Ratios (Short-term Solvency)
- Solvency Ratios (Long-term Solvency)
- Activity/Performance/Turnover Ratios
- Profitability Ratios

Multiple Choice Questions

No. of Questions : **30** Suggested Time : **45 Minutes**

Direction Each of the question given below is Multiple Choice Question (MCQ) i.e. there are four options/ choices for answer, out of which ONLY ONE is correct. You have to select the correct option. A response box is given with each option, mark (✓) in the box of the correct option. For each correct answer you will get 1 mark, while there is no penalty for incorrect answer or missed out questions.

1. Quick ratio of Megamart Ltd. is 1.5 : 1. Which of the following transactions will result in decrease in this ratio? *[CBSE 2024]*

(A) Sale of goods costing ₹ 10,000 for ₹ 12,000

(B) Cash collected from trade receivables ₹ 41,000

(C) Purchase of goods for cash ₹ 38,000

(D) Creditors were paid ₹ 11,000

2. If total assets of a firm are ₹ 8,00,000, shareholders' fund are ₹ 3,00,000, non-current liability ₹ 4,00,000 and ratio between non-current assets and shareholders' fund is 2:1, then current ratio will be

(A) 3 : 1 ☐ (B) 5 : 1 ☐

(C) 2 : 1 ☐ (D) 1 : 1 ☐

3. Current ratio of Vidur Pvt. Ltd. is 3 : 2. Accountant wants to maintain it at 2 : 1. Following options are available

(i) He can repay bills payable

(ii) He can purchase goods on credit

(iii) He can take short-term loan

Codes

(A) Only (i) ☐

(B) Only (ii) ☐

(C) Both (i) and (ii) ☐

(D) Both (ii) and (iii) ☐

4. Total assets are ₹ 10,00,000, non-current assets ₹ 6,00,000, shareholders' fund ₹ 4,00,000, reserves and surplus ₹ 1,00,000, non-current liability ₹ 3,00,000. Current ratio will be

(A) 2 : 1 ☐ (B) 1 : 2 ☐

(C) 3 : 4 ☐ (D) 4 : 3 ☐

5. ...... is also known as the acid test ratio. *[CBSE 2024]*

(A) Current ratio ☐

(B) Quick ratio ☐

(C) Gross profit ratio ☐

(D) Return on investment ratio ☐

6. A transaction which involves a decrease in debt equity ratio and increase in current ratio is

(A) issue of debentures for cash ☐

(B) issue of equity shares for cash ☐

(C) redemption of preference shares for cash ☐

(D) issue of debentures against the purchase of fixed assets ☐

7. Calculate debt, if capital employed is ₹ 50,00,000, shareholders' fund ₹ 32,00,000, current liabilities ₹ 8,00,000.

(A) ₹ 10,00,000 ☐ (B) ₹ 18,00,000 ☐

(C) ₹ 32,00,000 ☐ (D) ₹ 42,00,000 ☐

8. Debt-equity ratio of Dhamaka Ltd is 3 : 1. Which of the following will result in decrease in this ratio?

(A) Issue of debentures for cash of ₹ 2,00,000 ☐

(B) Issue of debentures of ₹ 3,00,000 to vendors from whom machinery was purchased ☐

(C) Goods purchased on credit of ₹ 1,00,000 ☐

(D) Issue of equity shares of ₹ 2,00,000 ☐

9. Which of the following is not a solvency ratio? [CBSE 2023]

(A) Return on investment ☐
(B) Interest coverage ratio ☐
(C) Proprietary ratio ☐
(D) Total assets to debt ratio ☐

10. What will be the impact of issuing ₹ 5,00,000 equity share to vendor for building purchased on the debt and equity of X Ltd.?

(A) Debt will increase and equity will decrease ☐
(B) Debt will remain same and equity will increase ☐
(C) Debt will decrease and equity will increase ☐
(D) Debt will remain same and equity will decrease ☐

11. From the following information, the 'proprietor's funds' are [CBSE 2023]

Current Assets	₹ 20,00,000
Non-current Assets	₹ 40,00,000
Long-term Borrowings	₹ 25,00,000
Proprietary Ratio	25%

(A) ₹ 10,00,000 ☐ (B) ₹ 14,00,000 ☐
(C) ₹ 24,00,000 ☐ (D) ₹ 15,00,000 ☐

12. From the following calculate interest coverage ratio

Net profit after tax ₹ 12,00,000; 10% debentures ₹ 1,00,00,000; tax rate 40%

(A) 1.2 times ☐ (B) 3 times ☐
(C) 2 times ☐ (D) 5 times ☐

13. Debt equity ratio is 2 : 1, total asset to debt ratio is 3 : 2, total assets are ₹ 3,00,000. Shareholders' fund will be are

(A) ₹ 2,00,000 ☐ (B) ₹ 4,00,000 ☐
(C) ₹ 1,00,000 ☐ (D) ₹ 50,000 ☐

14. Net profit after tax is ₹ 1,20,000, interest coverage ratio 3 times, rate of tax 50%, calculate value of 10% debentures.

(A) ₹ 10,00,000 ☐ (B) ₹ 14,00,000 ☐
(C) ₹ 12,00,000 ☐ (D) ₹ 8,00,000 ☐

15. Debt equity ratio is 1 : 5. Total assets are ₹ 1,00,000 and total external liabilities are ₹ 75,000. Current liabilities will be

(A) ₹ 60,000 ☐ (B) ₹ 70,000 ☐
(C) ₹ 75,000 ☐ (D) ₹ 90,000 ☐

16. If revenue from operations is ₹ 4,00,000, average inventory is ₹ 55,000, rate of gross loss is 10%, then inventory ratio will be

(A) 8 times ☐ (B) 11 times ☐
(C) 10 times ☐ (D) 12 times ☐

17. Which of the following equation is correct? [CBSE 2023]

(A) Cost of Revenue from Operations = Revenue from Operations + Gross Profit ☐
(B) Cost of Revenue from Operations = Opening Inventory – Net Purchases + Direct Expenses – Closing Inventory ☐
(C) Cost of Revenue from Operations = Opening Inventory + Closing Inventory ☐
(D) Cost of Revenue from Operations = Revenue from Operations – Gross Profit ☐

18. If the operating ratio of Aman Ltd. is 60%, its operating profit ratio will be [CBSE 2023]

(A) 100% ☐ (B) 60% ☐
(C) 40% ☐ (D) 160% ☐

19. If total sales is ₹ 2,50,000 and credit sales is 25% of cash sales. The amount of credit sales is

(A) ₹ 50,000 ☐ (B) ₹ 2,50,000 ☐
(C) ₹ 16,000 ☐ (D) ₹ 3,00,000 ☐

20. What will be the amount of gross profit of a firm if its average inventory is ₹ 80,000, inventory turnover ratio is 6 times, and the selling price is 25% above cost?

(A) ₹ 1,20,000 ☐ (B) ₹ 1,60,000 ☐
(C) ₹ 2,00,000 ☐ (D) None of these ☐

21. The two basic measures of operational efficiency of a company are

(A) inventory turnover ratio and working capital turnover ratio ☐
(B) liquid ratio and operating ratio ☐
(C) liquid ratio and current ratio ☐
(D) gross profit margin and net profit margin ☐

22. The .... may indicate that the firm is experiencing stock outs and lost sales.

(A) average payment period ☐
(B) inventory turnover ratio ☐
(C) average collection period ☐
(D) quick ratio ☐

23. Cost of revenue from operations is ₹ 21,000 which is 70% of revenue from operations. Current assets are ₹ 3,000 more than current liabilities. Working capital turnover ratio will be

(A) 7 times ☐ (B) 8 times ☐
(C) 9 times ☐ (D) 10 times ☐

24. Net profit after tax ₹ 1,20,000, tax 40%, salary ₹ 10,000, wages ₹ 25,000, carriage outward ₹ 30,000. Gross profit will be

(A) ₹ 2,40,000 ☐ (B) ₹ 4,15,000 ☐
(C) ₹ 4,35,000 ☐ (D) ₹ 4,60,000 ☐

25. Opening inventory ₹ 10,000, closing inventory ₹ 10,000 more than opening, inventory ratio 5 times, selling price 1/3rd above cost. Gross profit ratio will be

(A) 15% ☐ (B) 25% ☐
(C) 50% ☐ (D) 60% ☐

26. Which of the following are included in traditional classification of ratios?

(i) Liquidity Ratio
(ii) Statement of Profit and Loss Ratio
(iii) Balance Sheet Ratio
(iv) Profitability Ratio
(v) Composite Ratio
(vi) Solvency Ratio

Codes

(A) (ii), (iii) and (v) ☐
(B) (i), (iv) and (vi) ☐
(C) (i), (ii) and (vi) ☐
(D) All of the above ☐

27. The following groups of ratios primarily measure risk

(A) liquidity, activity and profitability ☐
(B) liquidity, activity and inventory ☐
(C) liquidity, activity and debt ☐
(D) liquidity, activity and profitability ☐

28. Revenue from operations ₹ 6,00,000, gross profit 25% on cost. Calculate gross profit ratio will be

(A) 40% ☐ (B) 25% ☐
(C) 20% ☐ (D) 80% ☐

29. Match the following

Column I	Column II
A. Current Assets – Inventory – Prepaid Expense	(i) Net Sales
B. Total Assets – Capital Employed	(ii) Current Liability
C. Cost of Revenue from Operations + Gross Profit	(iii) Liquid Assets

Codes

	A	B	C			A	B	C	
(A)	(i)	(iii)	(ii)	☐	(B)	(ii)	(i)	(iii)	☐
(C)	(ii)	(iii)	(i)	☐	(D)	(iii)	(ii)	(i)	☐

30. Match the following if each of the ratio is 2 : 1

Column I	Column II
A. Repayment of loan on debt equity ratio	(i) Increase
B. Purchase of goods for cash on current ratio	(ii) Decrease
C. Sale of goods on quick ratio	(iii) No change

Codes

	A	B	C			A	B	C	
(A)	(i)	(iii)	(ii)	☐	(B)	(ii)	(i)	(iii)	☐
(C)	(ii)	(iii)	(i)	☐	(D)	(iii)	(ii)	(i)	☐

Assertion-Reason Questions

No. of Questions : **8** Suggested Time : **15 Minutes**

Direction Each of the question given below consist of the two statements; one labelled as **Assertion** (A) and other as **Reason** (R). List of common options applicable for each question is given below

(A) Both Assertion (A) and Reason (R) are true and Reason (R) is the correct explanation of Assertion (A)

(B) Both Assertion (A) and Reason (R) are true, but Reason (R) is not the correct explanation of Assertion (A)

(C) Assertion (A) is true, but Reason (R) is false

(D) Assertion (A) is false, but Reason (R) is true

You have to select the codes as *A, B, C* or *D* as your answer to the question by marking (✓) in the response box given against each option.

1. **Assertion (A)** Current ratio establishes relationship between current assets and current liabilities.

   Reason (R) The objective of this ratio is to measure the ability of the firm to meet its short-term obligations as and when due without relying upon the realisation of inventories.

   (A) ☐ (B) ☐ (C) ☐ (D) ☐

2. **Assertion (A)** A high debt-equity ratio is risky.

   Reason (R) It may put the firm into difficulty to pay long-term debts.

   (A) ☐ (B) ☐ (C) ☐ (D) ☐

3. **Assertion (A)** Increasing the value of closing inventory increases profit.

   Reason (R) Increasing the value of closing inventory reduces cost of goods sold.

   (A) ☐ (B) ☐ (C) ☐ (D) ☐

4. **Assertion (A)** Current ratio should be very high.

   Reason (R) A very high current ratio implies heavy investment in current assets which reflects under-utilisation of resources.

   (A) ☐ (B) ☐ (C) ☐ (D) ☐

5. **Assertion (A)** A low debt equity ratio is always preferred.

   Reason (R) A low debt equity ratio reflects more security to the long-term lenders.

   (A) ☐ (B) ☐ (C) ☐ (D) ☐

6. **Assertion (A)** Sale of goods will not affect the gross profit ratio.

   Reason (R) Sale of goods for cash will not affect the gross profit ratio, as the sales and gross profit will increase by the same percentage.

   (A) ☐ (B) ☐ (C) ☐ (D) ☐

7. **Assertion (A)** Net profit ratio is based on all inclusive concept of profit.

   Reason (R) It relates revenue from operations to net profit after operating as well as non-operating expenses and incomes.

   (A) ☐ (B) ☐ (C) ☐ (D) ☐

8. **Assertion (A)** Interest coverage ratio is a measure of security of interest payable on long-term debt.

   Reason (R) Interest coverage ratio expresses the relationship between profits available for payment of interest and the amount of interest payable.

   (A) ☐ (B) ☐ (C) ☐ (D) ☐

Correct/Incorrect Statements

No. of Questions : **8**

Suggested Time : **15 Minutes**

Direction Each of the question given below consist of the two statements. List of common options applicable for each question is given below

(A) Both statements are correct

(B) Statement I is correct and Statement II is incorrect

(C) Statement I is incorrect and Statement II is correct

(D) Both statements are incorrect

You have to select the codes as *A, B, C* or *D* as your answer to the question by marking (✓) in the response box given against each option.

1. **Statement I** Quick ratio is also known as acid test ratio.

   Statement II Quick ratio is calculated to check long-term solvency of the business.

   (A) ☐ (B) ☐ (C) ☐ (D) ☐

2. **Statement I** Debt to capital employed ratio expresses the relation between long-term debt and capital employed.

   Statement II Gross profit helps in fixing selling prices and assessing efficiency of trading activities.

   (A) ☐ (B) ☐ (C) ☐ (D) ☐

3. **Statement I** Debt means non-current liabilities.

   Statement II Debt = Total Assets – Equity – Current Liabilities.

   (A) ☐ (B) ☐ (C) ☐ (D) ☐

4. **Statement I** Operating Ratio – Operating Profit Ratio = 100%.

   Statement II Operating ratio is computed to reveal the operating margin of products sold.

   (A) ☐ (B) ☐ (C) ☐ (D) ☐

5. **Statement I** Low inventory ratio is a danger position for a firm.

   Statement II Low inventory ratio is due to outdated stock or less buying.

   (A) ☐ (B) ☐ (C) ☐ (D) ☐

6. **Statement I** High inventory turnover ratio is good for the organisation, except when goods are bought in small lots or sold quickly at low margins to realise cash.

   Statement II Current ratio is an indicator of the enterprises ability to meet its short-term obligations.

   (A) ☐ (B) ☐ (C) ☐ (D) ☐

7. **Statement I** If current assets and current liabilities both reduce by an equal amount, ratio will reduce.

   Statement II If current assets and current liabilities both increase by an equal amount, ratio will reduce.

   (A) ☐ (B) ☐ (C) ☐ (D) ☐

8. **Statement I** Net profit ratio is a fair indicator of the profitability of any concern.

   Statement II Net profit ratio also helps in inter-firm and inter-industry comparison.

   (A) ☐ (B) ☐ (C) ☐ (D) ☐

Case Based Questions

No. of Questions : **2** Suggested Time : **10 Minutes**

Direction This section contains cases having 3/4 Questions of 1 mark each. You have to write the answer of each question based on the context of the related case.

Case 1

Year Amount	2020 (in ₹)	2019 (in ₹)	2018 (in ₹)
Outstanding Expenses	50,000	40,000	25,000
Prepaid Expenses	3,00,000	2,50,000	3,50,000
Trade Payables	18,00,000	16,00,000	14,00,000
Inventory	11,00,000	10,00,000	11,00,000
Trade Receivables	12,00,000	8,00,000	10,00,000
Cash in Hand	17,00,000	12,00,000	15,00,000
Revenue from Operations	24,00,000	18,00,000	20,00,000
Gross Profit Ratio	12%	15%	18%

[CBSE QB]

Questions

(i) Current ratio for the year 2020 will be ....

(A) 2:1 ☐ (B) 1.8:1 ☐
(C) 2.32:1 ☐ (D) 2.4:1 ☐

(ii) Quick ratio for the year 2018 will be ....

(A) 1.75:1 ☐ (B) 1.8:1 ☐
(C) 0.94:1 ☐ (D) 1.25:1 ☐

(iii) Inventory turnover ratio for the year 2020 will be ....

(A) 1.62 times ☐ (B) 1.82 times ☐
(C) 1.55 times ☐ (D) 1.92 times ☐

(iv) Cost of revenue from operations for the year 2020 would be ....

(A) ₹ 21,12,000 ☐
(B) ₹ 21,13,000 ☐
(C) ₹ 21,15,000 ☐
(D) ₹ 21,17,000 ☐

Case 2 Profit after tax was ₹ 6,00,000, tax rate was 40%, 15% debentures were ₹ 20,00,000, 10% bank loan was ₹ 20,00,000, 12% preference share capital ₹ 30,00,000, equity share capital ₹ 40,00,000, reserves and surplus were ₹ 10,00,000, sales ₹ 3,75,00,000 and sales return ₹ 15,00,000.

Questions

(i) Calculate capital employed.

(A) ₹ 90,00,000 ☐
(B) ₹ 1,00,00,000 ☐
(C) ₹ 70,00,000 ☐
(D) ₹ 1,20,00,000 ☐

(ii) Calculate return on investment.

(A) 15% ☐ (B) 12.5% ☐
(C) 20% ☐ (D) 25% ☐

(iii) Calculate net assets turnover ratio.

(A) 2 times ☐ (B) 3 times ☐
(C) 4 times ☐ (D) 5 times ☐

Subjective Questions

Free Response Questions, Open-ended Questions etc.

No. of Questions : **8** Suggested Time : **65 Minutes**

1. A business has a current ratio of 3 :1 and quick ratio of 1.2 : 1. If working capital is ₹ 1,80,000, calculate total current assets and inventory. *[CBSE 2024]*

2. The quick ratio of a company is 2 : 1. State giving reason which of the following transactions would reduce, improve or not change in quick ratio?
   (i) Cash paid to trade payables.
   (ii) Sale of goods of ₹ 2,000 for ₹ 3,000.
   (iii) Payment of outstanding liability.
   (iv) Purchase of goods for cash.

3. Current ratio of firm is 1.5 : 1. Its working capital is ₹ 2,00,000, total assets of ₹ 8,00,000 and total debt of ₹ 7,00,000. Calculate debt equity ratio.

4. From the following calculate (i) debt equity ratio (ii) total assets to debt ratio and (iii) proprietary ratio.

Particulars	Amt (₹)	Particulars	Amt (₹)
Equity Share Capital	2,00,000	12% Debentures	16,00,000
10% Preference Share Capital	3,00,000	Current Liabilities	6,80,000
General Reserves	2,50,000	Tangible Assets	21,00,000
Surplus	1,50,000	Current Investments	8,80,000
Long-term Investments	2,00,000		

5. Calculate trade receivable turnover ratio if, closing debtors ₹ 40,000, net credit revenue being 25% of net cash revenue, excess of closing debtors over opening debtors ₹ 20,000, total revenue from operations ₹ 1,50,000.

6. Calculate 'operating profit ratio' from the following information *[CBSE 2024]*

Revenue from operations	₹ 10,00,000
Gross profit	25% on cost
Office and administrative expenses	₹ 18,000
Selling and distribution expenses	₹ 2,000
Loss by theft	₹ 20,000

7. The current ratio of a company is 2 : 1. State giving reasons, which of the following transactions would improve, reduce or not change the ratio. *[CBSE 2023]*
   (i) Purchased goods on credit ₹ 40,000
   (ii) Sale of furniture of ₹ 8,000 at a loss of ₹ 2,000
   (iii) Cash received from trade receivables ₹ 15,000
   (iv) Issued equity shares ₹ 6,00,000

8. 'These ratios are calculated for measuring the efficiency of operations of business based on effective utilisation of resources'.
   (i) Identify the types of ratios being discussed above.
   (ii) Explain any two ratios of the types of ratios identified in (i) above. *[CBSE 2023]*

Answers

If your answer matches with the answer given here then put (✓) in the box otherwise put (✗). In case you did not attempt the question leave the box blank.

Multiple Choice Questions

1. C ☐ 2. C ☐
3. A ☐ 4. D ☐
5. B ☐ 6. B ☐
7. B ☐ 8. D ☐
9. A ☐ 10. B ☐
11. D ☐ 12. B ☐
13. C ☐ 14. C ☐
15. B ☐ 16. A ☐
17. D ☐ 18. C ☐
19. A ☐ 20. A ☐
21. A ☐ 22. B ☐
23. D ☐ 24. A ☐
25. B ☐ 26. A ☐
27. D ☐
28. C ☐
29. D ☐
30. C ☐

Your Score__________ (*No. of Correct Answers*)

Assertion-Reason Questions

1. C ☐ 2. B ☐
3. A ☐ 4. D ☐
5. D ☐ 6. A ☐
7. A ☐ 8. A ☐

Your Score__________ (*No. of Correct Answers*)

Correct/Incorrect Statements

1. B ☐ 2. A ☐
3. A ☐ 4. D ☐
5. A ☐ 6. A ☐
7. C ☐ 8. D ☐

Your Score__________ (*No. of Correct Answers*)

Case Based Questions

1. (i) C ☐ (ii) A ☐
(iii) D ☐ (iv) A ☐
2. (i) D ☐ (ii) B ☐
(iii) B ☐

Your Score__________ (*No. of Correct Answers*)

Explanations

Multiple Choice Questions

1. (C) Current liabilities will remain unchanged but liquid assets are decreased by outflow of cash

2. (C) $\frac{\text{Non-current Assets}}{\text{Shareholders' Fund}} = \frac{2}{1}$

∴ Non-current Assets = 3,00,000 × 2 = ₹ 6,00,000

Now, Total Assets = Current Assets + Non-current Assets

8,00,000 = Current Assets + 6,00,000

Current Assets = ₹ 2,00,000

Now, Total Assets = Shareholders' Fund + Non-current Liabilities + Current Liabilities

8,00,000 = 3,00,000 + 4,00,000 + Current Liabilities

∴ Current Liabilities = ₹ 1,00,000

So, Current Ratio = $\frac{\text{Current Assets}}{\text{Current Liabilities}} = \frac{2,00,000}{1,00,000}$

= 2 : 1

3. (A) Only (i)

4. (D) Current Assets = Total Assets – Non-current Assets

= 10,00,000 – 6,00,000 = ₹ 4,00,000

Total Assets = Shareholders' Fund + Non-current Liabilities + Current Liabilities (x)

10,00,000 = 4,00,000 + 3,00,000 + x

∴ Current Liabilities (x) = ₹ 3,00,000

So, Current Ratio = $\frac{4,00,000}{3,00,000}$ = 4 : 3

5. (B) Quick ratio

6. (B) issue of equity shares for cash

7. (B) Capital Employed = Shareholders' Fund + Debt

$$50,00,000 = 32,00,000 + \text{Debt}$$

$$\text{Debt} = ₹\,18,00,000$$

8. (D) Issue of equity shares will increase the equity of the company and debt remains unchanged.

9. (A) Return on investment

10. (B) Debt will remain same and equity will increase.

11. (D) Total Assets = 20,00,000 + 40,00,000 = ₹ 60,00,000

$$\text{Proprietary Ratio} = \frac{\text{Proprietor's Funds}}{\text{Total Assets}}$$

$$\text{Proprietor's Funds} = 60,00,000 \times \frac{25}{100} = ₹\,15,00,000$$

12. (B) Interest Coverage Ratio

$$= \frac{12,00,000 + \left(\frac{12,00,000}{60} \times 40\right) + 10,00,000}{10,00,000}$$

= 3 times

13. (C) $\frac{\text{Total Assets}}{\text{Debt}} = \frac{3}{2} \Rightarrow \frac{3,00,000}{\text{Debt}} = \frac{3}{2}$

$$\text{Debt} = ₹\,2,00,000$$

Now, $\frac{\text{Debt}}{\text{Equity}} = \frac{2}{1} \Rightarrow \frac{2,00,000}{\text{Equity}} = \frac{2}{1}$

$\therefore$ Equity = ₹ 1,00,000

14. (C)

Net Profit after Tax	=	1,20,000
(+) Tax $\left(\frac{1,20,000 \times 50}{50}\right)$	=	1,20,000
Net Profit before Tax	=	2,40,000
(+) Interest	=	10% of x
Net Profit before Interest and Tax		2,40,000 + 10% of x

So, Interest Coverage Ratio

$$= \frac{\text{Net Profit before Interest and Tax}}{\text{Fixed Interest Charges}}$$

$$3 = \frac{2,40,000 + 10\% \text{ of } x}{10\% \text{ of } x}$$

$$3 \times \frac{10}{100} x = 2,40,000 + \frac{10}{100} x$$

$$\frac{3}{10} x - \frac{x}{10} = 2,40,000$$

$$\therefore \quad x = \frac{2,40,000 \times 10}{2} = ₹\,12,00,000$$

15. (B) Equity = Total Assets – Total External Liabilities

= 1,00,000 – 75,000 = ₹ 25,000

$$\text{Debt Equity Ratio} = \frac{\text{Debt}}{\text{Equity}} \Rightarrow \frac{1}{5} = \frac{\text{Debt}}{25,000}$$

$\therefore$ Debt = ₹ 5,000

So, Current Liabilities = 75,000 – 5,000 = ₹ 70,000

16. (A) Cost of Revenue from Operations
= Revenue from Operations + Gross Loss
= 4,00,000 + 40,000 = ₹ 4,40,000

Inventory Turnover Ratio

$$= \frac{\text{Cost of Revenue from Operations}}{\text{Average Inventory}}$$

$$= \frac{4,40,000}{55,000} = 8 \text{ times}$$

17. (D) Cost of Revenue from Operations = Revenue from Operations – Gross Profit

18. (C) Operating Ratio + Operating Profit Ratio = 100

Operating Profit Ratio = 100 – 60 = 40%

19. (A) Let the cash sales be x

Total Sales = Cash Sales + Credit Sales

$$2,50,000 = x + \frac{25x}{100} \Rightarrow 2,50,000 = \frac{125x}{100}$$

$$x = 2,50,000 \times \frac{100}{125} = ₹\,2,00,000$$

$$\text{Credit Sales} = 2,00,000 \times \frac{25}{100} = ₹\,50,000$$

20. (A) Cost of Goods Sold = 80,000 × 6 = ₹ 4,80,000

$$\text{Gross Profit} = 4,80,000 \times \frac{25}{100} = ₹\,1,20,000$$

21. (A) inventory turnover ratio and working capital turnover ratio

22. (B) inventory turnover ratio

23. (D) Cost of Revenue from Operations

$$= \frac{70}{100} \times \text{Revenue from Operations}$$

$$\frac{21,000 \times 100}{70} = \text{Revenue from Operations}$$

$\therefore$ Revenue from Operations = ₹ 30,000

Now, Current Assets = Current Liabilities + 3,000

Current Assets – Current Liabilities = 3,000

$\therefore$ Working Capital = ₹ 3,000

Now, Working Capital Turnover Ratio

$$= \frac{\text{Revenue from Operations}}{\text{Working Capital}} = \frac{30,000}{3,000} = 10 \text{ times}$$

24. (A) Net Profit after Tax 1,20,000

(+) Tax $\left(\frac{1,20,000 \times 40}{60}\right)$ 80,000

Net Profit before Tax 2,00,000

Now, Net Profit before Tax = Gross Profit – Indirect Expense

2,00,000 = Gross Profit – 10,000 – 30,000

∴ Gross Profit = ₹ 2,40,000

25. (B) Average Inventory

$$= \frac{\text{Opening Inventory} + \text{Closing Inventory}}{2}$$

$$= \frac{10,000 + 20,000}{2} = ₹\,15,000$$

Inventory Turnover Ratio

$$= \frac{\text{Cost of Revenue from Operations}}{\text{Average Inventory}}$$

$$5 = \frac{\text{Cost of Revenue from Operations}}{15,000}$$

∴ Cost of Revenue from Operations = ₹ 75,000

Gross Profit = $75,000 \times \frac{1}{3}$ = ₹ 25,000

Cost of Revenue from Operations + Profit = Sales

75,000 + 25,000 = Sales

1,00,000 = Revenue from Operations

Now, Gross Profit Ratio

$$= \frac{\text{Gross Profit}}{\text{Revenue from Operations}} \times 100$$

$$= \frac{25,000}{1,00,000} \times 100 = 25\%$$

26. (A) (ii), (iii) and (v)

27. (D) liquidity, activity and profitability

28. (C) Cost of Revenue from Operations

= Revenue from Operations – Gross Profit

$$x = 6,00,000 - \left(\frac{25}{100} + x\right)$$

$$x + \frac{25}{100}x = 6,00,000$$

$$x = \frac{6,00,000 \times 100}{125} = ₹\ 4,80,000$$

Gross Profit = 4,80,000 × 25/100 = ₹ 1,20,000

Now, Gross Profit Ratio

$$= \frac{\text{Gross Profit}}{\text{Revenue from Operations}} \times 100$$

$$= \frac{1,20,000}{6,00,000} \times 100$$

= 20%

29. (D) (iii) (ii) (i)

30. (C) (ii) (iii) (i)

Assertion-Reason Questions

1. (C) Assertion (A) is true, but Reason (R) is false
2. (B) Both Assertion (A) and Reason (R) are true, but Reason (R) is not the correct explanation of Assertion (A)
3. (A) Both Assertion (A) and Reason (R) are true and Reason (R) is the correct explanation of Assertion (A)
4. (D) Assertion (A) is false, but Reason (R) is true
5. (D) Assertion (A) is false, but Reason (R) is true
6. (A) Both Assertion (A) and Reason (R) are true and Reason (R) is the correct explanation of Assertion (A)
7. (A) Both Assertion (A) and Reason (R) are true and Reason (R) is the correct explanation of Assertion (A)
8. (A) Both Assertion (A) and Reason (R) are true and Reason (R) is the correct explanation of Assertion (A)

Correct/Incorrect Statements

1. (B) Quick ratio is calculated to check the short-term solvency of the business.
2. (A) Both statements are correct
3. (A) Both statements are correct
4. (D) Operating Ratio + Operating Profit Ratio = 100%

   Operating profit ratio helps in computing operating margin.
5. (A) Both statements are correct
6. (A) Both statements are correct
7. (C) If current assets and current liabilities both reduce by an equal amount, ratio will improve.
8. (D) Return on Investment (RoI) is a fair indicator of the profitability of any concern. Return on Investment (RoI) also helps in inter-firm and inter-industry comparison.

Case Based Questions

1. (i) (C) Current Ratio

$$= \frac{\text{Current Assets}}{\text{Current Liabilities}} = \frac{43,00,000}{18,50,000} = 2.32 : 1$$

Current Assets = Prepaid Expenses + Inventory + Trade Receivables + Cash in Hand

= 3,00,000 + 12,00,000 + 11,00,000 + 17,00,000

= ₹ 43,00,000

Current Liabilities = Outstanding Expenses + Trade Payables

= 50,000 + 18,00,000 = ₹ 18,50,000

(ii) (A) Quick Ratio $= \frac{\text{Liquid Assets}}{\text{Current Liabilities}}$

$$= \frac{25,00,000}{14,25,000} = 1.75 : 1$$

Liquid Assets = Trade Receivables + Cash in Hand

= 10,00,000 + 15,00,000 = ₹ 25,00,000

Current Liabilities = Outstanding Expenses + Trade Payables

= 25,000 + 14,00,000 = ₹ 14,25,000

(iii) (D) Inventory Turnover Ratio (2020)

$$= \frac{\text{Cost of Revenue from Operations}}{\text{Average Inventory}}$$

$$= \frac{21,12,000}{11,00,000} = 1.92 \text{ times}$$

Average Inventory

$$= \frac{\text{Opening Inventory} + \text{Closing Inventory}}{2}$$

$$= \frac{10,00,000 + 12,00,000}{2} = ₹\ 11,00,000$$

(iv) (A) Cost of Revenue from Operations (2020)

	Amt (₹)
Revenue from Operation	24,00,000
(–) Gross Profit $\left(24,00,000 \times \frac{12}{100}\right)$	(2,88,000)
	21,12,000

2. (i) (D) Capital Employed = Equity Share Capital + Preference Share Capital + Reserves and Surplus + Debentures + Loan

= 40,00,000 + 30,00,000 + 10,00,000 + 20,00,000 + 20,00,000

= ₹ 1,20,00,000

(ii) (B) Return on Investment

$$= \frac{\text{Net Profit before Interest and Tax}}{\text{Capital Employed}} \times 100$$

$$= \frac{6,00,000 + 4,00,000 + 3,00,000 + 2,00,000}{1,20,00,000} \times 100$$

$$= \frac{15,00,000}{1,20,00,000} \times 100 = 12.5\%$$

(iii) (B) Net Assets Turnover Ratio

$$= \frac{\text{Revenue from Operations}}{\text{Capital Employed}}$$

$$= \frac{3,60,00,000}{1,20,00,000} = 3 \text{ times}$$

Subjective Questions

1. (C) Let current liabilities be = x

Current Ratio $= \frac{\text{Current Assets (CA)}}{\text{Current Liabilities (CL)}} = \frac{3}{1} = \frac{CA}{x}$

∴ Current Assets (CA) = $3x$

Now, Working Capital = Current Assets – Current Liabilities

$1,80,000 = 3x - x$

∴ x (Current Liabilities) = ₹ 90,000

So, Current Assets = $3x = 3 \times 90,000$ = ₹ 2,70,000

Now, Quick Ratio

$$= \frac{\text{Liquid Assets (LA)}}{\text{Current Liabilities (CL)}} = \frac{1.2}{1} = \frac{LA}{90,000}$$

∴ Liquid Assets = 1,08,000

Also, Liquid Assets = Current Assets – Inventory

1,08,000 = 2,70,000 – Inventory

So, Inventory = 2,70,000 – 1,08,000 = ₹ 1,62,000

2. (i) Cash paid to trade payables will decrease current assets as well as current liabilities. So, it will increase the ratio.

(ii) Sale of goods will increase cash by ₹ 3,000 and decrease stock by ₹ 2,000. So, numeration will increase, so ratio will also increase.

(iii) Payment of outstanding liability will decrease both cash as well as current liability. So, ratio will increase.

(iv) Purchase of goods for cash will increase stock and decrease cash. So, ratio will not change.

3. Current Ratio $= \frac{1.5}{1}$

∴ Current Assets = 1.5 Current Liabilities

Now, Working Capital = Current Assets – Current Liabilities

$2{,}00{,}000 = 1.5$ Current Liabilities – Current Liabilities

$2{,}00{,}000 = 0.5$ Current Liabilities

$$\text{Current Liabilities} = \frac{2{,}00{,}000}{0.5} = ₹\ 4{,}00{,}000$$

So, Current Assets = 1.5 × 4,00,000 = ₹ 6,00,000

Now, Total Debt = Long-term Debt + Current Liabilities

7,00,000 = Long-term Debt + 4,00,000

Long-term Debt = ₹ 3,00,000

Equity = Total Assets – Total Debt

= 8,00,000 – 7,00,000 = ₹ 1,00,000

$$\text{Now, Debt Equity Ratio} = \frac{\text{Debt}}{\text{Equity}} = \frac{3{,}00{,}000}{1{,}00{,}000} = 3:1$$

4. (i) Debt = 12% Debentures = ₹ 16,00,000

Equity = Equity Share Capital + 10% Preference Share Capital + General Reserve + Surplus

= 2,00,000 + 3,00,000 + 2,50,000 + 1,50,000
= ₹ 9,00,000

Total Assets = Equity + Debt + Current Liabilities

= 9,00,000 + 16,00,000 + 6,80,000 = ₹ 31,80,000

$$\text{Debt Equity Ratio} = \frac{\text{Debt}}{\text{Equity}} = \frac{16{,}00{,}000}{9{,}00{,}000} = 16:9$$

(ii) Total Assets to Debt Ratio

$$= \frac{\text{Total Assets}}{\text{Debt}} = \frac{31{,}80{,}000}{16{,}00{,}000} = 1.98:1$$

(iii) Proprietary Ratio

$$= \frac{\text{Equity}}{\text{Total Assets}} = \frac{9{,}00{,}000}{31{,}80{,}000} \times 100 = 28.30\%$$

5. $$\frac{\text{Closing Debtor} + \text{Opening Debtor}}{2} = \text{Average Debtors}$$

$$\text{Average Debtors} = \frac{40{,}000 + 20{,}000}{2} = ₹\ 30{,}000$$

Credit Revenue from Operations = Total Revenue from Operations – Cash Revenue from Operations

$$\frac{25}{100} \times x = 1{,}50{,}000 - x \Rightarrow \frac{25}{100}x + \frac{x}{1} = 1{,}50{,}000$$

$$x = \frac{1{,}50{,}000 \times 100}{125} = 1{,}20{,}000$$

So, Net Credit Revenue from Operations

$$= 1{,}20{,}000 \times \frac{25}{100} = ₹\ 30{,}000$$

Now, Trade Receivables Turnover Ratio

$$= \frac{\text{Net Credit Revenue from Operations}}{\text{Average Recievables}}$$

$$= \frac{30{,}000}{30{,}000} = 1 \text{ time}$$

6. Operating Profit Ratio

$$= \frac{\text{Operating Profit}^*}{\text{Revenue from Operations}} \times 100$$

$$= \frac{1{,}80{,}000}{10{,}00{,}000} \times 100 = 18\%$$

*Operating Profit = Gross Profit** – Operating Expenses

= 2,00,000 – (18,000 + 2,000) = ₹ 1,80,000

**Gross Profit = 25% on Cost *or* 1/4 on Cost *or* 1/5 on Sales

= 10,00,000 × 1/5 = ₹ 2,00,000

7. (i) The current ratio will reduce when goods are purchased on credit for ₹ 40,000 because current assets and current liabilities both will increase by the same amount.

(ii) Sale of furniture of ₹ 8,000 at a loss of ₹ 2,000 will improve the current ratio because the net effect of ₹ 6,000 will increase the current assets and no change in current liabilities.

(iii) There will no change in current ratio when the cash is received from trade receivables ₹ 15,000 due to one of the current assets i.e. trade receivables decreases and other current assets i.e. cash and cash equivalents increases by the same amount and no change in current liabilities.

(iv) The issue of equity shares will improve the current ratio due to increase in current assets i.e. cash and cash equivalents by ₹ 6,00,000 and no change in current liabilities.

8. (i) Turnover or activity ratios are calculated for measuring the efficiency of operations of business based on effective utilisation of resources.

(ii) (a) **Inventory Turnover Ratio** This ratio shows the relationship between the cost of revenue from operations during a given period and the average amount of inventory carried during that period.

(b) **Working Capital Turnover Ratio** This ratio shows the relationship between working capital and revenue from operations. It shows the number of times the working capital has been rotated in generating sales.

CHAPTER - 10

Cash Flow Statement

Types & Nos. of Questions

Multiple Choice Questions	-	30
Assertion-Reason Questions	-	8
Correct/Incorrect Statements	-	8
Case Based Questions	-	2 Cases, *with 3/4 Questions*
Subjective Questions	-	5

Trend Analysis

On the basis of analysis of last 2 years' papers, it is found that on an average 3 Multiple Choice Questions and 1 Long Answer Type Question are asked from this chapter.

Focus Topics of the Chapter

- Meaning of Cash Flow Statement
- Cash Flow from Operating Activities
- Cash Flow from Investing Activities
- Cash Flow from Financing Activities
- Preparation of Cash Flow Statement

Multiple Choice Questions

No. of Questions : **30** Suggested Time : **45 Minutes**

Direction Each of the question given below is Multiple Choice Question (MCQ) i.e. there are Four Options/ Choices for answer, out of which ONLY ONE is correct. You have to select the correct option.
A response box is given with each option, mark (✓) in the box of the correct option. For each correct answer you will get 1 mark, while there is no penalty for incorrect answer or missed out questions.

1. Which of the following is not an operating activity?
   (A) Rent received ☐
   (B) Rent paid ☐
   (C) Cash sales ☐
   (D) Cash purchases ☐

2. What will be the effect of transaction 'payment of employee benefit expenses' on the cash flow statement? *[CBSE 2024]*
   (A) Outflow from operating activities ☐
   (B) Outflow from investing activities ☐
   (C) Outflow from financing activities ☐
   (D) No effect on cash flow ☐

3. What will be the effect of issue of bonus shares on cash flow statement?
   (A) No effect ☐
   (B) Inflow in financing activity ☐
   (C) Inflow in operating activity ☐
   (D) Inflow in investing activity ☐

4. 'Dividend paid' by a financial enterprise will come under which kind of activity from the following while preparing cash flow statement? *[CBSE 2023]*
   (A) Operating activity ☐
   (B) Investing activity ☐
   (C) Financing activity ☐
   (D) Both (B) and (C) ☐

5. 'Interest received on investments' will come under which type of activity from the following, while preparing cash flow statement of a non-financial enterprise? *[CBSE 2023]*
   (A) Investing activity ☐
   (B) Financing activity ☐
   (C) Operating activity ☐
   (D) Both (B) and (C) ☐

6. Which of the following will result in flow of cash? *[CBSE 2023]*
   (A) Cash withdrawn from the bank ₹ 50,000 ☐
   (B) ₹ 2,00,000, 9% debentures issued to vendors of machinery ☐
   (C) ₹ 30,000 received from debtors ☐
   (D) Cheques of ₹ 20,000 deposited in the bank ☐

7. Refund of income tax received will come under
   (A) operating activity ☐
   (B) investing activity ☐
   (C) financing activity ☐
   (D) cash and cash equivalents ☐

8. Interest received on investment by financing company will be treated as
   (A) operating activity ☐
   (B) investing activity ☐
   (C) financing activity ☐
   (D) cash and cash equivalents ☐

9. Pick the odd one out.
(A) Bank overdraft raised ☐
(B) Rent received ☐
(C) Investment in shares ☐
(D) Patents acquired ☐

10. Which of the following is not an item of investing activity?
(A) Purchase of building ☐
(B) Purchase of equipment ☐
(C) Purchase of marketable securities ☐
(D) Investment in shares ☐

11. Which of the following transactions will result in no flow of cash?
(A) Issue of shares ☐
(B) Purchase of goodwill ☐
(C) Withdrew cash from bank ☐
(D) Redemption of debentures at premium ☐

12. Which of the following should be excluded from cash flow statement?
(A) Purchase of machinery by issue of shares ☐
(B) Redemption of debentures by issue of shares ☐
(C) Loss of goods due to theft ☐
(D) Both (A) and (B) ☐

13. While calculating cash flow from operating activities, which of the following will be deducted?
(A) Decrease in inventories ☐
(B) Decrease in trade receivables ☐
(C) Decrease in trade payables ☐
(D) Increase in outstanding salary ☐

14. What will be the correct sequence of the following for calculation of cash flow from operating activity?
(i) Deduct tax paid
(ii) Calculation of net profit before tax
(iii) Add increase in current liability and decrease in current assets
(iv) Adjustment related to non-cash transactions

Codes
(A) (i), (ii), (iii), (iv) ☐
(B) (iv), (iii), (ii), (i) ☐
(C) (ii), (iv), (iii), (i) ☐
(D) (ii), (iii), (iv), (i) ☐

15. Increase in balance of statement of profit and loss is ₹ 50,000, proposed dividend ₹ 60,000, provision for tax on 31st March, 2024 ₹ 80,000, provision for tax on 31st March, 2023 ₹ 60,000, tax paid ₹ 35,600.
Net profit before tax will be
(A) ₹ 1,90,000 ☐
(B) ₹ 1,55,680 ☐
(C) ₹ 1,68,600 ☐
(D) ₹ 1,17,680 ☐

16. Calculate cash flow from operating activities.

Particulars	31st March, 2023 (₹)	31st March, 2022 (₹)
Surplus, i.e. Balance in Statement of Profit and Loss	3,80,000	2,30,000
General Reserve	50,000	20,000
Provision for Depreciation on Machine	50,000	40,000
Goodwill	45,000	60,000
Provision for Doubtful Debt	25,000	30,000

(A) ₹ 1,90,000 ☐ (B) ₹ 1,95,000 ☐
(C) ₹ 2,00,000 ☐ (D) ₹ 2,05,000 ☐

17. Following information is available

Particulars	31st March, 2023 (₹)	31st March, 2022 (₹)
Trade Receivables	15,000	10,000
Outstanding Expenses	15,000	10,000
Creditors	50,000	40,000
Inventory	2,000	3,000
Bank Overdraft	40,000	30,000

If cash flow from operating activities is ₹ 3,40,000, calculate operating profit before working capital changes
(A) ₹ 3,39,000 ☐
(B) ₹ 3,29,000 ☐
(C) ₹ 3,19,000 ☐
(D) ₹ 3,51,000 ☐

18. Following balances were appearing in the books of a firm.

Particulars	2023-24 (₹)	2022-23 (₹)
Machinery	50,000	40,000
Provision for Depreciation	8,000	10,000

During the year, a machine costing ₹ 20,000 on which depreciation charged ₹ 5,000, was sold for ₹ 8,000. Calculate the amount of depreciation to be shown in operating activities.

(A) ₹ 5,000 ☐ (B) ₹ 8,000 ☐
(C) ₹ 3,000 ☐ (D) ₹ 2,000 ☐

19. Profits after all appropriations were ₹ 2,00,000, proposed dividend of last year ₹ 7,000 and proposed dividend of current year ₹ 8,000, interim dividend paid ₹ 10,000, goodwill written-off ₹ 2,000. Net profit before tax will be

(A) ₹ 2,00,000 ☐ (B) ₹ 2,20,000 ☐
(C) ₹ 2,18,000 ☐ (D) ₹ 2,17,000 ☐

20. Insurance claim received by Albert Co. Ltd. of ₹ 5,00,000 for loss of machinery due to theft will be recorded in cash flow statement in which of the following manner?

(A) Added under operating activities as extraordinary item and subtracted from operating activities also. ☐
(B) Subtracted under operating activities as extraordinary item and added to operating activities also. ☐
(C) Added under operating activities as extraordinary item and outflow under investing activity also. ☐
(D) Subtracted under operating activities as extraordinary item and inflow under investing activities also. ☐

21. Sale of current investment will be shown under

(A) operating activity ☐
(B) financing activity ☐
(C) investing activity ☐
(D) cash and cash equivalents ☐

22. Venkat Ltd. a financial company had advanced a loan of ₹ 3,00,000, invested ₹ 6,00,000 in shares of other company and purchased machinery for ₹ 9,00,000. It received dividend of ₹ 70,000 on investment in shares.

The company sold an old machine of the book value of ₹ 79,000 at a loss of ₹ 10,000. Calculate cash flow from/used in investing activities.

(A) ₹ 15,00,000 ☐ (B) ₹ 13,61,000 ☐
(C) ₹ (15,00,000) ☐ (D) ₹ (13,61,000) ☐

23.

Particulars	Purchased (₹)	Sold (₹)
Investments	2,00,000	1,80,000
Goodwill	3,00,000	—

From the above information, 'cash flows from investing activities' will be *[CBSE 2024]*

(A) inflow ₹ 3,20,000 ☐
(B) outflow ₹ 3,20,000 ☐
(C) outflow ₹ 20,000 ☐
(D) inflow ₹ 20,000 ☐

24. From the following information find out the inflow of cash by sale of office equipments.

	31st March, 2024 (₹)	31st March, 2023 (₹)
Office Equipment	2,00,000	3,00,000

Additional Information

Depreciation for the year 2023-24 was ₹ 40,000. Purchase of office equipment purchased during the year ₹ 30,000.

Part of office equipment sold at a profit of ₹ 12,000.

(A) ₹ 1,00,000 ☐ (B) ₹ 1,02,000 ☐
(C) ₹ 90,000 ☐ (D) ₹ 1,12,000 ☐

25. Paid ₹ 4,00,000 to acquire shares in SJS Ltd. and received a dividend of ₹ 40,000 after acquisition. These transactions will result in

(A) cash used in investing activities ₹ 4,00,000 ☐
(B) cash generated from financing activities ₹ 4,40,000 ☐

(C) cash used in investing activities ₹ 3,60,000 ☐
(D) cash generated from financing activities ₹ 3,60,000 ☐

26. Following extract of a company is given.

Particulars	2023 (₹)	2022 (₹)
10% Debentures	7,00,000	5,00,000

Fresh debentures were issued on 1st October, 2023. Amount to be charged for interest on debentures will be

(A) ₹ 50,000 ☐ (B) ₹ 60,000 ☐
(C) ₹ 70,000 ☐ (D) ₹ 20,000 ☐

27. Match the following

Column I	Column II
A. Increase in goodwill	(i) Operating activity
B. Decrease in goodwill	(ii) Investing activity
C. Decrease in bank overdraft	(iii) Financing activity

Codes

	A	B	C			A	B	C	
(A)	(i)	(ii)	(iii)	☐	(B)	(ii)	(iii)	(ii)	☐
(C)	(iii)	(ii)	(i)	☐	(D)	(ii)	(i)	(iii)	☐

28. Match the following

Column I	Column II
A. Dividend received by mutual fund company on its investment in other company's shares	(i) Operating activity
B. Dividend paid by a non-financing company	(ii) Investing activity
C. Dividend received by a manufacturing company	(iii) Financing activity

Codes

	A	B	C	
(A)	(i)	(ii)	(iii)	☐
(B)	(i)	(iii)	(ii)	☐
(C)	(ii)	(iii)	(i)	☐
(D)	(iii)	(i)	(ii)	☐

29. Match the following

Column I	Column II
A. Issue of bonus shares	(i) Outflow of cash
B. Interest paid on debentures	(ii) Inflow of cash
C. Rent received	(iii) No flow of cash

Codes

	A	B	C			A	B	C	
(A)	(i)	(iii)	(ii)	☐	(B)	(ii)	(i)	(iii)	☐
(C)	(iii)	(i)	(ii)	☐	(D)	(ii)	(iii)	(i)	☐

30. While preparing cash flow statement, match the following activities.

Column I	Column II
A. Payment of cash to acquire debenture by an investing company	(i) Financing activity
B. Purchase of goodwill	(ii) Investing activity
C. Dividend paid by manufacturing company	(iii) Operating activity

Codes

	A	B	C	
(A)	(i)	(ii)	(iii)	☐
(B)	(ii)	(i)	(iii)	☐
(C)	(iii)	(i)	(ii)	☐
(D)	(iii)	(ii)	(i)	☐

Assertion-Reason Questions

No. of Questions : **8** Suggested Time : **15 Minutes**

Direction Each of the question given below consist of the two statements; one labelled as **Assertion** (A) and other as **Reason** (R). List of common options applicable for each question is given below

(A) Both Assertion (A) and Reason (R) are true and Reason (R) is the correct explanation of Assertion (A)
(B) Both Assertion (A) and Reason (R) are true, but Reason (R) is not the correct explanation of Assertion (A)
(C) Assertion (A) is false, but Reason (R) is true
(D) Assertion (A) is true, but Reason (R) is false

You have to select the codes as *A, B, C* or *D* as your answer to the question by marking (✓) in the response box given against each option.

1. **Assertion** (A) Cheques and drafts in hand are not considered while preparing cash flow statement.

   Reason (R) Cheques and drafts in hand are considered as financing activity.

   (A) ☐ (B) ☐ (C) ☐ (D) ☐

2. **Assertion** (A) Rent received is an investing activity by a manufacturing concern.

   Reason (R) It is a principle revenue producing activity for manufacturing concern.

   (A) ☐ (B) ☐ (C) ☐ (D) ☐

3. **Assertion** (A) Redemption of debentures by converting them into equity shares would result into outflow of cash.

   Reason (R) It is a non-cash transaction, but cash flow statement shows inflows and outflows of cash and cash equivalents.

   (A) ☐ (B) ☐ (C) ☐ (D) ☐

4. **Assertion** (A) Cash flow ignores two basic accounting principles *viz* 'full disclosure' and 'accrual concept'.

   Reason (R) It facilitates the management for short-term plans.

   (A) ☐ (B) ☐ (C) ☐ (D) ☐

5. **Assertion** (A) An inflow or outflow between components of cash and cash equivalent is not considered.

   Reason (R) It is called management of cash.

   (A) ☐ (B) ☐
   (C) ☐ (D) ☐

6. **Assertion** (A) Purchase of goods on credit will not affect cash and cash equivalents.

   Reason (R) Purchase of goods on credit does not involve cash.

   (A) ☐ (B) ☐
   (C) ☐ (D) ☐

7. **Assertion** (A) Depreciation is added back to net profit while calculating cash flow from operating activity.

   Reason (R) Depreciation is a non-cash expense.

   (A) ☐ (B) ☐
   (C) ☐ (D) ☐

8. **Assertion** (A) Purchase and sale of shares on behalf of customers is an operating activity.

   Reason (R) They are being purchased for their customers.

   (A) ☐ (B) ☐
   (C) ☐ (D) ☐

Correct/Incorrect Statements

No. of Questions : **8** Suggested Time : **15 Minutes**

Direction Each of the question given below consist of the two statements. List of common options applicable for each question is given below

(A) Both statements are correct
(B) Statement I is correct and Statement II is incorrect
(C) Statement I is incorrect and Statement II is correct
(D) Both statements are incorrect

You have to select the codes as *A, B, C* or *D* as your answer to the question by marking (✓) in the response box given against each option.

1. Statement I Increase in patents of a company will be an operating activity.

Statement II Decrease in goodwill is an investing activity.

(A) ☐ (B) ☐ (C) ☐ (D) ☐

2. Statement I Proposed dividend of previous year does not result in flow of cash.

Statement II Redemption of debentures decreases cash and cash equivalents.

(A) ☐ (B) ☐
(C) ☐ (D) ☐

3. Statement I Purchase of shares is always considered as an investing activity.

Statement II Dividend paid is usually considered as a financing activity.

(A) ☐ (B) ☐
(C) ☐ (D) ☐

4. Statement I Investment with more than 365 days of maturity is treated as cash equivalents.

Statement II Buy-back of shares would result in inflow of cash.

(A) ☐ (B) ☐
(C) ☐ (D) ☐

5. Statement I Increase in bank overdraft will be added in operating activity.

Statement II Decrease in bank overdraft will be subtracted from financing activity.

(A) ☐ (B) ☐ (C) ☐ (D) ☐

6. Statement I Sale of machinery is credited to machinery account.

Statement II Loss on sale of machine is credited to machinery account.

(A) ☐ (B) ☐ (C) ☐ (D) ☐

7. Statement I Sale of marketable securities will result in no flow of cash.

Statement II Debentures issued as collateral security will result in inflow of cash.

(A) ☐ (B) ☐ (C) ☐ (D) ☐

8. Statement I Financing activities relate to long-term funds or capital of an enterprise.

Statement II Separate disclosure of cash flows arising from financing activities is important because they represent the extent to which expenditures have been made for resources intended to generate future income and cash flows. *[CBSE 2024]*

(A) ☐ (B) ☐ (C) ☐ (D) ☐

Case Based Questions

No. of Questions : **2** Suggested Time : **10 Minutes**

Direction This section contains 2 cases having 3/4 questions of 1 mark each. You have to write the answer of each question based on the context of the related case.

Case 1 Krishika an alumni of IIM Ahemdabad initiated her startup Krishika Ltd. in 2018. The profits of Krishika Ltd. in the year 2019-20 after all appropriations was ₹ 31,25,000. This profit was arrived after taking into consideration the following items *[CBSE QB]*

S. No.	Particulars	Amt (₹)
(i)	Gain on sale of fixed tangible assets	12,50,000
(ii)	Goodwill written-off	7,80,000
(iii)	Transfer to general reserve	8,75,000
(iv)	Provision for taxation	4,37,500

Additional Information

Particulars	31st March, 2020 (₹)	31st March, 2019 (₹)
Prepaid expenses	7,50,000	5,00,000
Inventory	10,50,000	8,20,000
Trade payables	4,50,000	3,50,000
Trade receivables	6,20,000	5,90,000

Qustions

(i) Net profit before tax will be ....

(A) ₹ 22,50,000 ☐
(B) ₹ 35,62,500 ☐
(C) ₹ 39,67,500 ☐
(D) ₹ 44,37,500 ☐

(ii) Operating profit before working capital changes will be ....

(A) ₹ 52,17,500 ☐
(B) ₹ 64,67,500 ☐
(C) ₹ 39,67,500 ☐
(D) ₹ 39,69,500 ☐

(iii) Cash flow from operating activities before tax will be ....

(A) ₹ 35,57,500 ☐ (B) ₹ 40,67,500 ☐
(C) ₹ 37,87,500 ☐ (D) ₹ 35,67,300 ☐

(iv) Cash flow from operating activities will be ....

(A) ₹ 39,95,000 ☐
(B) ₹ 31,20,000 ☐
(C) ₹ 40,67,500 ☐
(D) ₹ 31,00,000 ☐

Case 2 A company has the balance of plant and machinery on 1st April, 2023 as ₹ 5,00,000 and on 31st March, 2024 at ₹ 8,00,000. It also had a balance of accumulated depreciation as ₹ 1,00,000 and ₹ 1,50,000 on 1st April, 2023 and 31st March, 2024 respectively. There is increase in goodwill by ₹ 20,000. A piece of machine costing ₹ 1,00,000 on which accumulated depreci ation was ₹ 25,000, was sold for ₹ 90,000.

Qustions

(i) Plant and machinery purchased during the year will be

(A) ₹ 3,85,000 ☐
(B) ₹ 4,30,000 ☐
(C) ₹ 4,15,000 ☐
(D) ₹ 4,00,000 ☐

(ii) Depreciation to be shown in operating activity will be

(A) ₹ 25,000 ☐
(B) ₹ 50,000 ☐
(C) ₹ 75,000 ☐
(D) ₹ 1,00,000 ☐

(iii) Cash flow from/used in investing activities will be

(A) cash used ₹ 4,00,000 ☐
(B) cash used ₹ 3,30,000 ☐
(C) cash used ₹ 4,20,000 ☐
(D) cash used ₹ 5,10,000 ☐

Subjective Questions

Free Response Questions, Open-ended Questions etc.

No. of Questions : **5**

Suggested Time : **40 Minutes**

1. Following is the extract from the balance sheet of Venus Ltd.

Particulars	31st March, 2024 (₹)	31st March, 2023 (₹)
EQUITY AND LIABILITIES		
Equity Share Capital	8,00,000	8,00,000
10% Preference Share Capital	6,00,000	6,00,000
Surplus, i.e. Balance in Statement of Profit and Loss	4,00,000	7,20,000
Unpaid Dividend	...	20,000

Additional Information

(i) Proposed dividend on equity shares will be ₹ 1,60,000 for 2023 and ₹ 2,00,000 for 2024 respectively.

(ii) An interim dividend of ₹ 40,000 on equity shares was paid.

Calculate net profit before tax.

2. Following the balance sheet of Bharat Gas Ltd. as at 31st March, 2023

Balance Sheet of Bharat Gas Ltd.
as at 31st March, 2023

Particulars	Note No.	31st March, 2023 (₹)	31st March, 2022 (₹)
I. **EQUITY AND LIABILITIES**			
1. **Shareholders' Funds**			
(i) Share Capital		14,00,000	10,00,000
(ii) Reserves and Surplus	1	5,00,000	4,00,000
2. **Non-current Liabilities**			
Long-term Borrowings		5,00,000	1,40,000
3. **Current Liabilities**			
(i) Trade Payables		1,00,000	60,000
(ii) Short-term Provisions	2	80,000	60,000
Total		25,80,000	16,60,000
II. **ASSETS**			
1. **Non-current Assets**			
(i) Property, Plant & Equipment and Intangible Assets			
(a) Property, Plant and Equipment	3	16,00,000	9,00,000
(b) Intangible Assets	4	1,40,000	2,00,000
2. **Current Assets**			
(i) Inventories		2,50,000	2,00,000
(ii) Trade Receivables		5,00,000	3,00,000
(iii) Cash and Cash Equivalents		90,000	60,000
Total		25,80,000	16,60,000

Notes to Accounts

Particulars	31st March, 2023 (₹)	31st March, 2022 (₹)
1. **Reserves and Surplus**		
Balance in Statement of Profit and Loss	5,00,000	4,00,000
	5,00,000	4,00,000
2. **Short-term Provisions**		
Provision for Taxation	80,000	60,000
	80,000	60,000
3. **Property, Plant and Equipment**		
Machinery	18,50,000	10,00,000
(–) Accumulated Depreciation	(2,50,000)	(1,00,000)
	16,00,000	9,00,000
4. **Intangible Assets**		
Goodwill	1,40,000	2,00,000
	1,40,000	2,00,000

Additional Information

During the year a machine costing ₹ 3,00,000 on which accumulated depreciation was ₹ 45,000 was sold for ₹ 1,35,000.

Calculate 'cash flows from operating activities'. *[CBSE 2024]*

3. Read the following hypothetical text and answer the given question on this basis

Madhav is a young entrepreneur. On 1st April, 2019, he formed a partnership firm with two of his friends, Mohan and Sohan. They started their business of exporting dry fruits. Their business was a successful business. Now they wanted to expand the business in many other countries. For meeting the financial requirements, they changed the form of business organisation and formed Madhav Ltd. The balance sheet of Madhav Ltd. as at 31st March, 2022 was as follows

Balance Sheet of Madhav Ltd.
as at 31st March, 2022

Particulars	Note No.	31st March 2022 (₹)	31st March 2021 (₹)
I. **EQUITY AND LIABILITIES**			
1. **Shareholders' Funds**			
(i) Share Capital		35,00,000	25,00,000
(ii) Reserves and Surplus (Statement of P & L)		12,50,000	10,00,000
2. **Non-current Liabilities**			
Long-term Borrowings (10% Debentures)		12,50,000	3,50,000
3. **Current Liabilities**			
(i) Short-term Borrowings (Bank overdraft)		50,000	75,000
(ii) Trade Payables		2,50,000	1,50,000
(iii) Short-term Provisions	1	1,50,000	75,000
Total		64,50,000	41,50,000
II. **ASSETS**			
1. **Non-current Assets**			
Fixed Assets			
(i) Tangible Assets	2	40,00,000	22,50,000
(ii) Intangible Assets (Goodwill)		3,50,000	5,00,000
2. **Current Assets**			
(i) Inventories		6,25,000	5,00,000
(ii) Trade Receivables		12,50,000	7,50,000
(iii) Cash and Cash Equivalents		2,25,000	1,50,000
Total		64,50,000	41,50,000

Notes to Accounts

Particulars	31st March, 2022 (₹)	31st March, 2021 (₹)
1. **Short-term Provisions**		
Provision for Tax	1,50,000	1,50,000
2. **Tangible Assets**		
Plant and Machinery	44,00,000	25,00,000
(−) Accumulated Depreciation	(4,00,000)	(2,50,000)
	40,00,000	22,50,000

Additional Information

(i) A part of the machine costing ₹ 1,25,000 accumulated depreciation thereon being ₹ 50,000 was sold for ₹ 45,000 during the year.

(ii) Interest of ₹ 1,25,000 was paid on debentures.

Calculate cash flows from 'investing activities' and 'financing activities' of Madhav Ltd. from the information provided above. [CBSE 2023]

4. From the following balance sheet of Redexx Ltd. prepare cash flow statement.

Balance Sheet of Redexx Ltd.
as at 31st March, 2024

Particulars	Note No.	31st March, 2024 (₹)	31st March, 2023 (₹)
I. **EQUITY AND LIABILITIES**			
1. **Shareholders' Fund**			
(i) Share Capital		2,50,000	2,00,000
(ii) Reserves and Surplus		1,80,000	80,000
2. **Non-current Liabilities**			
Long-term Borrowings 10% Debentures		80,000	50,000
3. **Current Liabilities**			
(i) Trade Payables		1,50,000	1,00,000
(ii) Other Current Liabilities		15,000	20,000
Total		6,75,000	4,50,000

Particulars	Note No.	31st March, 2024 (₹)	31st March, 2023 (₹)
II. ASSETS			
1. Non-current Assets			
(i) Property, Plant and Equipment & Intangible Assets			
(a) Property, Plant and Equipment		2,74,000	1,15,000
(b) Non-current Investment		65,000	50,000
2. Current Assets			
(i) Inventories		2,00,000	1,50,000
(ii) Trade Receivables		30,000	70,000
(iii) Cash and Cash Equivalents		1,06,000	65,000
Total		6,75,000	4,50,000

Additional Information

(i) Debentures were issued on 1st October, 2023.

(ii) Interim dividend paid ₹ 10,000.

5. From the following balance sheet of Star Ltd. prepare cash flow statement.

Balance Sheet of Star Ltd.
as at 31st March, 2024

Particulars	Note No.	31st March, 2024 (₹)	31st March, 2023 (₹)
I. EQUITY AND LIABILITIES			
1. Shareholders' Fund			
(i) Share Capital	1	8,00,000	5,00,000
(ii) Reserves and Surplus	2	2,50,000	1,30,000
2. Non-current Liabilities			
Long-term Borrowings	3	4,00,000	3,00,000
3. Current Liabilities			
(i) Trade Payable		1,93,000	1,38,000
(ii) Other Current Liabilities	4	7,000	12,000
Total		16,50,000	10,80,000
II. ASSETS			
1. Non-current Assets			
(i) Property, Plant & Equipment and Intangible Assets			
(a) Property, Plant and Equipment		7,00,000	4,20,000
(b) Non-current Investment		2,75,000	3,50,000
2. Current Assets			
(i) Inventories		3,00,000	1,50,000
(ii) Trade Receivables		2,00,000	60,000
(iii) Cash and Cash Equivalents		1,75,000	1,00,000
Total		16,50,000	10,80,000

Notes to Accounts

Particulars	31st March, 2024 (₹)	31st March, 2023 (₹)
1. Share Capital		
Equity Share Capital	7,00,000	3,20,000
9% Preference Share Capital	1,00,000	2,00,000
	8,00,000	5,00,000
2. Reserves and Surplus		
General Reserve	1,50,000	1,20,000
Surplus, i.e. Balance in Statement of Profit and Loss	1,00,000	10,000
	2,50,000	1,30,000
3. Long-term Borrowings		
10% Debentures	4,00,000	3,00,000
4. Other Current Liabilities		
Premium on Redemption of Preference Share	7,000	12,000

Additional Information

(i) Non-current investments were sold at a profit of 20%.

(ii) Preference shares were redeemed at a premium of 5% on 1st April, 2023.

(ii) Machine costing ₹ 2,50,000 on which depreciation charged was ₹ 80,000 was sold for ₹ 1,50,000. Depreciation charged during the year amounted to ₹ 70,000.

Answers

If your answer matches with the answer given here then put (✓) in the box otherwise put (✗). In case you did not attempt the question leave the box blank.

Multiple Choice Questions

1. A ☐	2. A ☐
3. A ☐	4. C ☐
5. A ☐	6. C ☐
7. A ☐	8. A ☐
9. A ☐	10. C ☐
11. C ☐	12. D ☐
13. C ☐	14. C ☐
15. A ☐	16. C ☐
17. B ☐	18. C ☐
19. D ☐	20. D ☐
21. D ☐	22. D ☐
23. B ☐	24. B ☐
25. C ☐	26. B ☐
27. D ☐	28. B ☐
29. C ☐	30. D ☐

Your Score__________ (*No. of Correct Answers*)

Assertion-Reason Questions

1. D ☐	2. D ☐
3. C ☐	4. B ☐
5. A ☐	6. A ☐
7. A ☐	8. D ☐

Your Score__________ (*No. of Correct Answers*)

Correct/Incorrect Statements

1. D ☐	2. C ☐
3. A ☐	4. D ☐
5. C ☐	6. A ☐
7. B ☐	8. A ☐

Your Score__________ (*No. of Correct Answers*)

Case Based Questions

1. (i) D ☐	(ii) C ☐
(iii) A ☐	(iv) B ☐
2. (i) D ☐	(ii) C ☐
(iii) B ☐	

Your Score__________ (*No. of Correct Answers*)

Explanations

Multiple Choice Questions

1. (A) Rent received
2. (A) Outflow from operating activities
3. (A) No effect
4. (C) Financing activity
5. (A) Investing activity
6. (C) ₹ 30,000 received from debtors
7. (A) operating activity
8. (A) operating activity
9. (A) Bank overdraft raised
10. (C) Purchase of marketable securities
11. (C) Withdrew cash from bank
12. (D) Both (A) and (B)
13. (C) Decrease in trade payables
14. (C) (ii), (iv), (iii), (i)
15. (A)

Particulars	Amt (₹)
Net Profit after Tax	50,000
(+) Proposed Dividend	60,000
(+) Provision for Tax made	80,000
Net Profit before Tax	1,90,000

16. (C) **Cash Flow from Operating Activities**

Particulars	Amt (₹)
Net Profit after Tax	1,50,000
(+) Transfer to General Reserve	30,000
Net Profit before Tax	1,80,000
(+) Provision for Depreciation	10,000
Goodwill Written-off	15,000
	2,05,000

Particulars	Amt (₹)
(–) Decrease in Provision for Doubtful Debts	(5,000)
Cash Flow from Operating Activities	2,00,000

17. (B)

Particulars	Amt (₹)
Cash Flow from Operating Activities	3,40,000
(+) Trade Receivables	5,000
(–) Outstanding Expenses	(5,000)
Creditors	(10,000)
Inventory	(1,000)
Operating Profit before Working Capital Changes	3,29,000

18. (C) ₹ 3,000

19. (D)

Particulars	Amt (₹)
Net Profit after Tax	2,00,000
(+) Proposed Dividend	7,000
(+) Interim Dividend	10,000
Net Profit before Tax	2,17,000

20. (D) Subtracted under operating activities as extraordinary item and inflow under investing activities also.

21. (D) cash and cash equivalents

22. (D) **Cash Flow from Investing Activities**

Particulars	Amt (₹)
Investment in Shares	(6,00,000)
Purchase of Machine	(9,00,000)
Dividend Received	70,000
Sales of Machine	69,000
Cash Used in Investing Activities	(13,61,000)

23. (B) **Calculation of Cash Flow from Investing Activities**

Investing Activities	**Amt (₹)**
Purchase of Investment	(2,00,000)
Sale of Investment	1,80,000
Purchase of Goodwill	(3,00,000)
Outflow	(3,20,000)

24. (B) Sale of office equipment = 3,00,000 + 30,000 + 12,000 – 40,000 – 2,00,000 = ₹ 1,02,000

25. (C) cash used in investing activities ₹ 3,60,000.

26. (B) Interest on Debentures

$$= 5,00,000 \times \frac{10}{100} \times \frac{6}{12} + 7,00,000 \times \frac{10}{100} \times \frac{6}{12}$$

= 25,000 + 35,000 = ₹ 60,000

27. (D) (ii) (i) (iii) **28.** (B) (i) (iii) (ii)

29. (C) (iii) (i) (ii) **30.** (D) (iii) (ii) (i)

Assertion-Reason Questions

1. (D) Assertion (A) is true, but Reason (R) is false
2. (D) Assertion (A) is true, but Reason (R) is false
3. (C) Assertion (A) is false, but Reason (R) is true
4. (B) Both Assertion (A) and Reason (R) are true, but Reason (R) is not the correct explanation of Assertion (A)
5. (A) Both Assertion (A) and Reason (R) are true and Reason (R) is the correct explanation of Assertion (A)
6. (A) Both Assertion (A) and Reason (R) are true and Reason (R) is the correct explanation of Assertion (A)
7. (A) Both Assertion (A) and Reason (R) are true and Reason (R) is the correct explanation of Assertion (A)
8. (D) Its not an operating activity but brokerage received is an operating activity.

Correct/Incorrect Statements

1. (D) Increase in patents is an investing activity. Decrease in goodwill is an operating activity.
2. (C) Statement I is incorrect and Statement II is correct
3. (A) Both statements are correct
4. (D) Investment with more than 365 days of maturity is a non-current investment. Buy-back of shares would result in outflow of cash.
5. (C) Increase in bank overdraft will be added in financing activity
6. (A) Both statements are correct
7. (B) Debentures issued as collateral security will result in no flow.
8. (A) Both statements are correct

Case Based Questions

1. (i) (D)

	Amt (₹)
Net Profit after Tax	31,25,000
(+) Transfer to Reserves	8,75,000
(+) Provision for Tax	4,37,500
Net Profit before Tax	44,37,500

(ii) (C)

	Amt (₹)
Net Profit before Tax	44,37,500
(+) Goodwill Written-off	7,80,000
(–) Gain on Sale of Fixed Tangible Asset	(12,50,000)
Operating Profit before Working Capital Changes	39,67,500

(iii) (A) **Cash Flow from Operating Activities before Tax**

Particulars		Amt (₹)
Operating Profit before Working Capital Changes		39,67,500
(+) Decrease in Current Assets and Increase in Current Liabilities		
Trade Payable		1,00,000
(–) Increase in Current Assets and Decrease in Current Liabilities		
Prepaid Expenses	(2,50,000)	
Inventory	(2,30,000)	
Trade Receivables	(30,000)	(5,10,000)
		35,57,500

(iv) (B)

	Amt (₹)
Cash Flow from Operating Activities before Tax	35,57,500
(–) Tax	(4,37,500)
Cash Flow from Operating Activities after Tax	31,20,000

2. (i) (D) Plant and Machinery Purchased

= 8,00,000 + 25,000 (Depreciation) + 90,000 (Sale) – 15,000 (Profit) – 5,00,000 = ₹ 4,00,000

(ii) (C) Depreciation Charged during the Year = 1,50,000 + 25,000 – 1,00,000 = ₹ 75,000

(iii) (B) **Cash Used in Investing Activities**

Particulars	Amt (₹)
Purchase of Machine	(4,00,000)
Purchase of Goodwill	(20,000)
Sale of Machine	90,000
Cash Flow from Investing Activities	(3,30,000)

Subjective Based Questions

1.

Particulars	Amt (₹)
Net Profit after Tax	(3,20,000)
(+) Dividend on Preference Shares	60,000
Interim Dividend	40,000
Proposed Dividend on Equity Shares	1,60,000
Net Profit before Tax	(60,000)

2. **Cash Flow from Operating Activities**

for the year ending 31st March, 2023

Particulars		Amt (₹)
Cash Flow from Operating Activity		
Net Profit before Tax (1,00,000 + 80,000)		1,80,000
Adjustment for		
(+) Accumulated Depreciation (WN2)	1,95,000	
Loss on Sale of Machinery (WN1)	1,20,000	
Goodwill Written-off	60,000	3,75,000

Particulars		Amt (₹)
Operating Profit before Working Capital Changes		5,55,000
(−) Increase in Current Assets and Decrease in Current Liabilities		
Inventories	(50,000)	
Trade Receivables	(2,00,000)	(2,50,000)
(+) Decrease in Current Assets and Increase in Current Liabilities		
Trade Payables		40,000
Cash Generated from Operations		3,45,000
(−) Payment of Tax		(60,000)
Net Cash from Operating Activities		2,85,000

Working Notes

1. Dr **Machinery Account** Cr

Particulars	Amt (₹)	Particulars	Amt (₹)
To Balance b/d	10,00,000	By Accumulated Depreciation A/c	45,000
To Cash A/c (Purchase) (Bal. fig.)	11,50,000	By Cash A/c (Sale)	1,35,000
		By Loss on Sale	1,20,000
		By Balance c/d	18,50,000
	21,50,000		21,50,000

2. Dr **Accumulated Depreciation Account** Cr

Particulars	Amt (₹)	Particulars	Amt (₹)
To Machinery A/c	45,000	By Balance b/d	1,00,000
To Balance c/d	2,50,000	By Statement of Profit and Loss (Bal. fig.)	1,95,000
	2,95,000		2,95,000

3. **Cash Flow Statement** (Investing and Financing Activities)
for the year ended 31st March, 2022

Particulars		Amt (₹)
I. **Cash Flow from Investing Activities**		
Proceeds from Sale of Plant and Machinery	45,000	
Purchase of Plant and Machinery (WN 1)	(20,25,000)	19,80,000
Net Cash Used in Investing Activities		(19,80,000)
II. **Cash Flow from Financing Activities**		
Proceeds from Issue of Shares	10,00,000	
Proceeds from Issue of Debentures	9,00,000	
Interest paid on Debentures	(1,25,000)	
Net Cash Flow from Financing Activities		17,75,000

Working Note

Dr **Plant and Machinery Account** Cr

Particulars	Amt (₹)	Particulars	Amt (₹)
To Balance b/d	25,00,000	By Bank A/c	45,000
To Bank A/c (Bal. Fig.) (Purchase of plant and machinery)	20,25,000	By Accumulated Depreciation A/c	50,000
		By Profit and Loss A/c (Loss on sale of machinery)	30,000
		By Balance c/d	44,00,000
	45,25,000		45,25,000

4. **Cash Flow Statement**

Particulars		Amt (₹)
A. **Cash Flow from Operating Activities**		
Net Profit before Tax (1,00,000 + 10,000)		1,10,000
(+) Adjustments for Non-cash Transactions		
Interest on Debentures		6,500
Operating Profit before Working Capital Changes		1,16,500
(+) Increase in Trade Payables		50,000
(+) Decrease in Trade Receivables		40,000
(–) Decrease in Other Current Liabilities		(5,000)
(–) Increase in Inventories		(50,000)
Cash Flow from Operating Activities		1,51,500
B. **Cash Flow from Investing Activities**		
Purchase of Plant	(1,59,000)	
Purchase of Investments	(15,000)	
Cash Used in Investing Activities		(1,74,000)
C. **Cash Flow from Financing Activities**		
Issue of Share Capital	50,000	
Issue of Debentures	30,000	
Interest Paid	(6,500)	
Interim Dividend Paid	(10,000)	
Cash Flow from Financing Activities		63,500
Net Increase in Cash and Cash Equivalents		41,000
(+) Opening Cash and Cash Equivalents		65,000
Closing Cash and Cash Equivalents		1,06,000

5. **Cash Flow Statement**
for the year ended 31st March, 2024

Particulars		Amt (₹)
A. **Cash Flow from Operating Activities**		
Net Profit before Tax		1,29,000
(+) Adjustments for Non-cash Transactions		
Depreciation	70,000	
Loss on Sale of Machine	20,000	
Interest on Debentures	30,000	
(–) Profit on Sale of Investment	(15,000)	1,05,000

Particulars		Amt (₹)
Operating Profit before Working Capital Changes		2,34,000
(+) Increase in Trade Payables		55,000
(–) Increase in Inventories		(1,50,000)
(–) Increase in Trade Receivables		(1,40,000)
Cash Used in Operating Activities		(1,000)
B. **Cash Flow from Investing Activities**		
Sale of Investment	90,000	
Sale of Machine	1,50,000	
Purchase of Machine	(5,20,000)	
Cash Used in Investing Activities		(2,80,000)
C. **Cash Flow from Financing Activities**		
Issue of Shares	4,00,000	
Redemption of Preference Shares	(1,05,000)	
Interest on Debentures	(30,000)	
Dividend Paid	(9,000)	
Issue of Debentures	1,00,000	
Cash Flow from Financing Activities		3,56,000
Net Increase in Cash and Cash Equivalents		75,000
(+) Opening Cash and Cash Equivalents		1,00,000
Closing Cash and Cash Equivalents		1,75,000

Working Notes

1. **Calculation of Net Profit before Tax**

		Amt (₹)
Net Profit after Tax	=	90,000
(+) Transfer to Reserve	=	30,000
(+) Dividend on Preference Shares	=	9,000
Net Profit before Tax	=	1,29,000

2. Dr **Non-current Investment Account** Cr

Particulars	Amt (₹)	Particulars	Amt (₹)
To Balance b/d	3,50,000	By Bank (Sale)	90,000
To Statement of P & L (Profit on sale)	15,000	By balance c/d	2,75,000
	3,65,000		3,65,000

3. Dr **Properties, Plant and Equipment Account** Cr

Particulars	Amt (₹)	Particulars	Amt (₹)
To Balance b/d	4,20,000	By Depreciation	70,000
To Bank (Purchase)	5,20,000	By Bank (Sale)	1,50,000
		By Statement of P & L (Loss)	20,000
		By Balance c/d	7,00,000
	9,40,000		9,40,000